SPIRIT AND SPORT

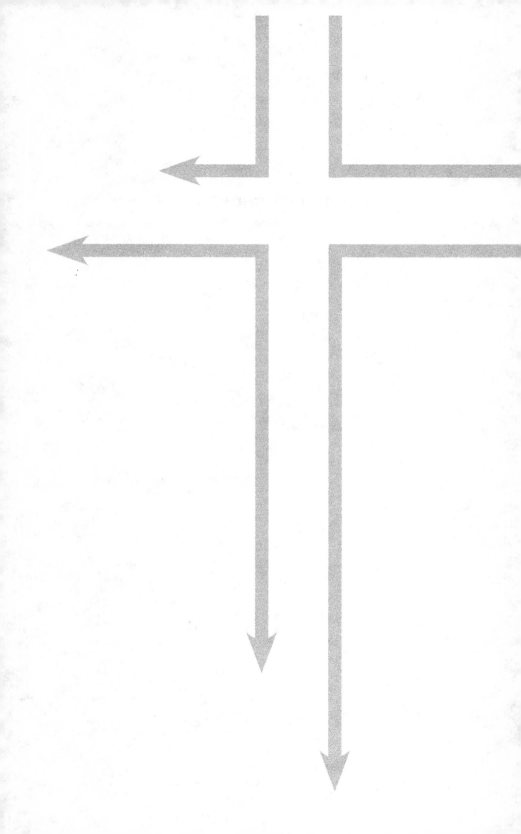

SPIRIT AND SPORT

Religion and the Fragile Athletic Body in Popular Culture

Sean Samuel O'Neil

SPORT AND POPULAR CULTURE
Brian M. Ingrassia, *Series Editor*

THE UNIVERSITY OF TENNESSEE PRESS
Knoxville

The Sport and Popular Culture series is designed to promote critical,
innovative research in the history of sport through a wide spectrum of works—
monographs, edited volumes, biographies, and reprints of classics.

LIBRARY OF CONGRESS CATALOGING-IN-PUBLICATION DATA

Names: O'Neil, Sean Samuel (Sean S.) author.

Title: Spirit and sport : religion and the fragile athletic body in popular culture / Sean Samuel O'Neil.

Description: First edition. | Knoxville : The University of Tennessee Press, 2022. | Series: Sport and popular culture | Includes bibliographical references and index. | Summary: "Sean Samuel O'Neil explores several narratives at the intersection of religion and disability across the spectrum of contemporary sports. He ties religious belief and practice to the oftentimes fragile bodies of athletes, including those with disabilities. Athletic triumph over fragility is couched in religious terms, though not always with strictly Christian connotations, and O'Neil interleaves his own limitations through an autoethnographic presentation of his battle with skin cancer and his lifelong struggle with obsessive compulsive disorder"—Provided by publisher.

Identifiers: LCCN 2022017501 (print) | LCCN 2022017502 (ebook) |
ISBN 9781621907343 (hardcover) | ISBN 9781621907350 (pdf)

Subjects: LCSH: Sports—Religious aspects. | Athletes—Religious life. | People with disabilities—Religious life. | Human body—Religious aspects. | O'Neil, Sean Samuel (Sean S.)

Classification: LCC GV706.42 .O64 2022 (print) | LCC GV706.42 (ebook) | DDC 201/.6796—dc23/eng/20220604

LC record available at https://lccn.loc.gov/2022017501
LC ebook record available at https://lccn.loc.gov/2022017502

Contents

Foreword

Human bodies are inherently frail, even if sport gives us the illusion they are not, and a level playing field almost never exists, even if sport gives us the illusion that it does.

Sean O'Neil's *Spirit and Sport: Religion and the Fragile Athletic Body in Popular Culture* offers an innovative and powerful extended musing on the intersections between disability, sport, and religion. This book is a veritable Venn diagram, the center of overlapping circles wherein football celebrity Tim Tebow kneels in the end zone before meeting with disabled children, and Bethany Hamilton, the champion "soul surfer" who lost an arm in a shark attack at age thirteen, models swimwear that some evangelicals consider too revealing. We learn that advice to "swing away," depending upon context, could mean the difference between life and death—and even the difference between a disavowal or an affirmation of faith. This volume is unique in that it challenges us to think beyond the nineteenth-century maxim of *mens sana in corpore sano*, or a "sound mind in a sound body." The unstated assumption of Muscular Christianity was that by building a strong body one could go forth and do God's work. Such were the ideas that drove Luther Halsey Gulick, James Naismith, and an entire generation of Young Men's Christian Association (YMCA) missionaries and gymnastics instructors. But what happens when our bodies do not play along? What happens when it is not merely a question of effort and willpower, but a question of the limitations of our mortal shells? What about those who were born with disabilities that make sport a greater challenge, or at some point acquired a disability that renders athletic ability diminished, reduced, or eliminated altogether?

It is often difficult for our understandings of the human body and its vast potential for heroic feats to catch up to the reality of the limitations that every human body, to some extent or another, must ultimately face. O'Neil juxtaposes the story of NFL player Steve Gleason, who became a hero of post–Hurricane Katrina New Orleans, with the story of medical examiner Bennet Omalu, who became famous for exposing the extent of Chronic Traumatic Encephelopathy (CTE) among former football players in Pittsburgh. Both Gleason and Omalu, in their own ways, invoked God and faith in their own discourses about the oftentimes violent game of American football. While Gleason turned to faith healers in a painfully unsuccessful attempt to walk again after being diagnosed with Amyotrophic Lateral Sclerosis (Lou Gehrig's Disease), Omalu summoned divine intent in his critiques of America's veritable national pastime. Essentially, said this man of faith, God never designed human bodies to absorb the high-impact, full-force blows all too common in the gridiron game. To what extent, Omalu's statement makes us wonder, did the Creator intend human bodies as machines for sport? Or is sport merely a human construct that people have spent centuries or millennia imbuing with sacred meanings? Was Gleason made to block that kick, or was that heroic moment done in defiance of the fact that his body, like all, would eventually fail? If humans are created in the image of God (*imago dei*), then what does it mean when we cannot play sports—or, at the very least, we find that we can no longer coax our bodies to play sports at the level we desire?

Some of the most powerful sections of this book employ autoethnography, a careful self-reflection that scholars in anthropology and other social sciences or humanities fields use to connect the observer's story to larger cultural or societal meanings. O'Neil periodically sheds the mantle of expert, bravely exposing himself as a human being who asks us to join him in an exploration of our bodily limitations in light of our existence on a plane where material and spiritual intersect. The author frankly discusses his own struggles with body dysmorphic disorder (BDD) and the serendipitous coincidences in his own life that helped him understand intersections between sport and spirit in relation to the frail human body. I invite you to join O'Neil as he ponders these connections, but I should also acknowledge my own limitations for writing a foreword for a book like this. I am a historian more used to telling stories about what other people did in the past and then wringing historical significance from those stories, and I admit I am a sport scholar who was never very good at sports. And although I was raised in a Protestant denomination, at some point I found it useful to move beyond what felt like the pervasive guilt that my particular church placed on many human interactions and desires. Nevertheless, I admire what O'Neil has so expertly and lovingly done in *Sport and Spirit*: encourage us to open our minds and hearts to the idea that bodies of all sorts find ways to connect to the spiritual realm, as well as the idea that sport may be one of our society's most important conduits for that process.

As I write these words it is a beautiful spring day—a Sunday, no less. March Madness will conclude soon and the lockout-delayed baseball season is (thank God, some might say) about ready to witness its first pitch. Despite unseasonal weather patterns no doubt influenced by the harsh reality of climate change, where I live the trees are starting to bud out and unfurl their leaves even in a place where many of those species should never have thrived at all. Hope springs eternal for the natural environment as it does for our bodies and minds and souls. Meanwhile, advertisements on television and the internet reveal that marketers want us to believe there are no limits to what we can achieve—at least with the right sneakers or the proper electrolyte-replenishing athletic drink or the correct moisture-wicking undershirt. Sean O'Neil, though, has done an exceptional job of taking readers to a higher and more complicated place, asking us to consider the ways that "even though we may yearn to see ourselves as having been created in a pristine image, facing our messy reality makes sacred and sporting symbols, and indeed our own flawed lives, more interesting and honest." I hope you are as moved by this book as I am.

Brian M. Ingrassia
West Texas A&M University

Preface

When I teach religion and sports in an academic setting, I remind students that each of us has a unique stance with respect to religion, and people have varying, often passionate, views about sports as well. I welcome all students as vital contributors to the class. I ask them to consider that—with all our diverse beliefs, practices, and experiences—we are embarking on a trek to discover what we can learn about religion and sports by using tools of academic inquiry. We thus bracket questions we can't answer, like whether there is a God or gods or a sacred force or forces. I discourage both proselytizing (e.g. don't try to turn a Blue Jays fan into a Yankees fan) and religion-bashing.

I also ask students to be empathetic of their colleagues since some people in the room might lean on religion in distressing moments of their lives, while others might have experienced religion as an oppressive weight from which they are still seeking relief. In short, some people suffer with religion, and others suffer from religion. When students ask me about my religion, I tell them I am an ordained Christian minister and a bishop in a church network they probably have never heard of—the Convergent Christian Communion (CCC).

Admittedly, things got complicated when I returned to class after grieving my friend's death, and unexpected, even terrifying, events transpired. Those circumstances had uncanny resemblance to the plot of a film I had assigned for that class period. Afterward, I talked with my gregarious, sweet Muslim colleague in the adjacent office. When I asked him to make sense of the strange events, I was expecting an academic answer, but he gave me a religious response: "I think it was divine intervention." When, in such cases, students accidentally or serendipitously became part of my own religious journey, I reminded them not to change their religious beliefs, or lack thereof, because of anything they heard from me. I insisted on this. I would ask them rhetorically, "Are you a white Canadian man married to a Cuban American woman named Mallory?" There never were any of those, so I would then ask the rhetorical follow-up, "Why would you change what you believe or do not believe because of someone you barely know? Your commitments were no doubt shaped by the unique sociological, political, familial, and (a)religious pathways on which you have tread and by which you are being formed." I ask the same from readers of this book.

I am willing to be as much a subject of this study as a guide. I would hope readers will receive my personal disclosures in the spirit with which they were written: a spirit of inquiry into the joy and pain of our shared plights, and an awareness of the unique symbol systems we use to navigate the most treacherous parts of our journeys.

A definition of religion from the late anthropologist Clifford Geertz serves as a theoretical backdrop to much of the material that follows in this book: "Religion is (1) a system of symbols which acts to (2) establish powerful, pervasive, and long-lasting moods and motivations in [people] by (3) formulating conceptions of a general order of existence and (4) clothing these conceptions with such an aura of factuality that (5) the moods and motivations seem uniquely realistic."[1] This definition captures the emotional states ("moods") and inclinations to act in particular ways ("motivations") at the heart of this book. People propose ideas about ultimate reality ("conceptions of a general order of existence") and make the invisible ideas concrete (they "clothe conceptions") through rituals and symbols.

A renowned scholar named Talal Asad critiqued Geertz for proposing a totalizing definition of religion that, like so many Western European projects before it, sought to encapsulate diverse and complex strands into a comprehensive whole. He argued that Geertz's definition erased meaningful differences between people groups and religious traditions, and that it was inattentive to the power dynamics that would motivate an attempt to universally define religion in the first place.[2] I do not think Geertz's definition has universal application or that it is the best definition for all cases. I do think it is the most useful one for the purposes of this book, but I have tried to maintain a light touch when it comes to theory.

In this preface, I have been writing with the same tone I would use in an academic classroom, but that is not always how I write in the body of the book itself. There, I write about "God" as if there is a God, without many caveats or qualifiers. This is not to suggest, however, that I assume my readers share my beliefs and practices. Even readers who self-identify as Christians might not recognize their own faith in the way I describe mine. It would, though, be both cumbersome and misleading for me to write this book with only detached and sober language. I am someone who has felt intoxicated with the love and Spirit of God. I have also, however, experienced such deep despair about my body that I planned to kill myself. That is a difficult confession to write, and it is a hellish feeling to experience.

When I began this project, I did not plan to use personal details. I did not anticipate that body dysmorphic disorder (BDD), a personal antagonist that I thought had weakened over the years, would revive with such overwhelming force in my life. My mental health struggles became so acute when I worked as a hospital chaplain during the pandemic that I wondered tearfully at times whether my wife would ultimately end up completing this book in my post-humous absence. Something happened, though, even before that grueling emotional stretch, that made me determined to include aspects of my personal life in this book. As is the case for so many of the meaningful events I describe in this book, the turning point was the result of a coincidence.

When I was in early stages of discussion about this project with the University of Tennessee Press, I arrived at a crossroads in my life. I was not sure I wanted to continue in academia. I went to a Christian writer's conference with the idea of possibly pitching a spiritual memoir instead. At the conference, I met with a publisher of a major press and talked about options. I left the meeting and stepped out into the hot sun. A woman sitting on a long bench in the shade welcomed me to escape the heat and join her. We talked about our respective experiences at the conference. I told her I was discerning whether I should write a spiritual memoir and abandon academic writing. I explained that I had an academic book in the works on sports, disability, and religion, but that I was uncertain about continuing that path. She wanted to know more.

I talked about how sports can function sociologically like a religion since both cultural activities involve things like myths, rituals, and symbols. I also mentioned that sports appear in some religious spaces, such as churches that use football-themed sermons; and that athletes incorporate religion into sporting spaces through rituals like crossing themselves on courts, fields, and diamonds. "And the disability angle?" she asked. "Well, I have always been interested in how Christian faith intersects with disability," I told her. I continued, "Jesus healed so many people with disabilities in the scriptures that I wonder how the Bible continues to be relevant for people with disabilities and their family members today." I explained that I want religious communities, and our society in general, to value people with disabilities, and for religious and social structures to reflect that commitment. With respect to sports, I added that I wondered what happens when an athlete who believes God gifted them to play sports is disabled by an athletic injury. "How, then, would they understand God's intervention in their life?"

My bench mate expressed such obvious interest that I began to feel renewed excitement about writing this book. "The only problem," I clarified, "is that I'm not sure I want to write in the kind of detached and sophisticated way that I would have to for an academic book. This stuff feels really personal for me," I confessed. She pulled out a picture of her daughter who has a disability. She told me how difficult it was at first to understand why God would give her a child who cannot speak and who needs so much assistance. But over the years she had become grateful for her daughter's unique expressions of love and life. "I don't know much about sports," she admitted, "but you have a chance through a popular subject to get people to think and care about things they might not normally encounter in their lives." She added with a smile, "You need to write that book." So I did.

Acknowledgments

I would like to thank all the students, colleagues, friends, family members, and mentors who made writing this book feel like a collaborative process. I would especially like to acknowledge the help of Colin Howell, a retired History professor and the founder of the Centre for the Study of Sport & Health (CSSH) at Saint Mary's University in Halifax, Nova Scotia. Colin was a consistent support from the earliest stages of this project. He was generous with his wealth of experience and insight, and he has been a kind and considerate friend throughout the journey. As a Visiting Research Fellow with the CSSH, I was grateful for an office space in which to research and write, and for the invaluable opportunities I had to share that research and receive feedback in public lectures I gave for the center.

I am also indebted to the Sport and Religion Research Alliance at the University of Tennessee Knoxville, where I am currently an Affiliated Scholar. Steven Waller has been an especially thoughtful friend and encouraging mentor. I was grateful to share my research with various graduate classes Steve teaches as a Professor in the Department of Kinesiology, Recreation, and Sport Studies.

I first began thinking and writing about the intersection of sports, disability, and religion while teaching in both the Department of Religion and the American Studies program at the University of Tennessee. I would thus like to thank all my colleagues and students who helped clarify the early shape of this project.

I also benefited greatly from the interdisciplinary insights of students and colleagues at Miami University, first as a Visiting Assistant Professor

in both the Department of Comparative Religion and American Studies
Program, and then as a VAP in the Department of Kinesiology and Health.
I experienced the same bracing collegiality with students and colleagues in
the Department of Religious Studies at Colby College in Waterville, Maine.

Many of the most emotional and meaningful teaching moments recorded
in this book occurred at Texas Christian University. I do not have space to
record all the names of students and colleagues from TCU who have forever
changed my life for the better. In short, let me just say, "Go Frogs!"

And "Go Gators" as well, of course! In particular, thank you to Anna
Peterson for her brilliant and compassionate mentorship from the earliest
stages of my PhD to the present moment.

Hazel Thomas and Kenneth Ramsey have helped me bridge academic and
ministry worlds. As my direct supervisor while I was a chaplain resident, Ken
not only facilitated opportunities to share my research in the hospital, but
he offered some of the most encouraging and meaningful feedback I have
received on this topic. My colleagues in hospital chaplaincy bear the imprint
of the grace, compassion, and insight that Hazel and Ken have modeled in
their work.

Writing a book requires endurance and hope and I lost some of both at
different stages of this long process. It seemed that whenever I was tempted
to throw in the towel, I would receive an encouraging message and Bible passage from my friend Trevor Currie. He was led by the Spirit and the Spirit
sustained this work.

Thomas Wells, Acquisitions Editor at the University of Tennessee Press, is
another inspired and inspiring figure without whom this project would not
have seen the light of day. He is the kind of editor that authors dream about:
secure and poised when giving direction on a project, but also openminded
and collaborative in navigating twists and turns in the process.

Finally, I am grateful to my wife, Mallory. She is more than I could have
thought to ask for in a partner, and much more than I deserve. She put her
heart, soul, and mind into helping me finish this book. This book and anything I do well in life is dedicated to her.

SPIRIT AND SPORT

Introduction

PLAYFUL PROCLAMATION

T his project is driven by an obsession with signs in storms, those hints that suggest even though we are not all in the same boat, neither are any of us alone in the travail. That thought helped a South African named Samkelo Radebe reframe traumatic amputations into a playful creation story. Reflecting on the complementary parts of his 4x100 relay team Radebe joked, "God probably sat down with a pencil and he was looking at everyone like, 'I'm just going to erase his hands. I don't think I like them very much. I'm going to erase [this other teammate's] legs."[1] As a black, double-arm amputee, Radebe started for a team anchored by a white, double-leg amputee. There were teammates with "opposite" amputations in the middle of the relay as well: A single-arm amputee and single-leg amputee ran second and third, respectively. In Radebe's view, the unique symmetry made it "a perfect team."[2] His creation story combines sports, disability, and religion, and, as I demonstrate in this book, intersections of that kind are ubiquitous in popular culture. I argue that, properly situated, they illuminate the value of interdependence and expose the perils of individualism. This book then not only attends to the evident joy in lighthearted stories like Radebe's, but also takes seriously the questions and themes they raise.

Exploring Interdependence

When people posit design for disability, what does that imply about the relationship between divine intervention and human suffering? For instance, when Radebe speaks about God playfully "erasing" limbs, his wide smile belies the painful parts of that creative process. Radebe had grabbed a pair of live electrical wires at the age of nine while playing with friends.[3] His subsequent hospitalization lasted nine months. His disability was thus acquired, not congenital. As a chaplain I witnessed firsthand the range of emotions and physical discomfort of adults in extended hospitalizations after traumatic amputation. It is difficult for me to imagine those searing challenges for a child and his family. I wonder if Radebe had trouble reconciling the reality of his travail with the idea of a good and loving God.

I am also intrigued by the potentially profound contribution of Radebe's simple creation story to the Jewish and Christian understanding of the "imago Dei," the concept that people are made in the image and likeness of God. Radebe's story suggests that God's "making" of people is processual; that the material out of which we are continually formed includes our quotidian experiences, both the jubilant and grueling kind. What is more, if God intentionally creates "anomalous bodies," whether at birth or over time, those bodies must reflect a dimension of God's image and likeness. This is not an entirely original concept, given the longstanding popularity of a book called *The Disabled God*, which was first published in 1994. That work has broad circulation in and deep impact on academic and theological spheres. Still, Radebe's story and many of the others I treat in this book are more accessible to an even wider audience. As I discovered in my own life, and usually by accident, these pop culture stories can also illuminate sacred texts—and vice versa.

While the imago Dei concept comes from Genesis, the first book of the Hebrew Bible,[4] a New Testament passage reinforces Radebe's celebration of the diverse disabilities of his team. The Apostle Paul compares the varied people in a community to cooperating members of a body: "If all were a single member, where would the body be? As it is, there are many members, yet one body. The eye cannot say to the hand, 'I have no need of you,' nor again the head to the feet, 'I have no need of you.'"[5] Similarly, picturing providential origins for the team's shared needs delights Radebe. "God looked at the four of us and said, 'Okay, I'll make this one perfect, just because I can.' God, man, has a great sense of humor!"[6] I know from personal experience how Radebe's gleeful athletic reflections can shed new light on Paul's more serious ecclesiastical ones. In combination, they gave me a fresh angle of perception for an embarrassing facial feature: the forehead skin that now covers a part of my nose.

Paul's metaphor of interdependence resonates deeply when I consider that at the time of my skin cancer diagnosis my nose could not say to my forehead, "I have no need of you." With Radebe's help, I picture a relay handoff and optimistic exchange. I imagine the incised, diseased skin from my nose saying

"Your turn" to the grafted, healthy part from my forehead. This also fortifies me in my longstanding battle with a cousin of obsessive-compulsive disorder (OCD) called body dysmorphic disorder (BDD). Since I still wrestle with a malady that magnifies real and perceived bodily imperfections, reminders are crucial that I cannot survive, much less thrive, by hiding my shame in isolation. I need the friends and family who have accompanied me in psychological crises. And at other moments, in other ways, they need me. Stories of interdependence thus remind me of truth I so often forget.

I found them at different stages of my own lifelong and ongoing healing journey. Some of the stories are like old faithful friends. Others of more recent acquaintance still provide a familiar promise of connection. Based on her own and others' experiences, Carrie Doehring affirms, "A memorable film or novel becomes part of our story."[7] She recounts her interactions with a young man so enthralled by Harry Potter audiobooks he listened to while delivering pizza that he "couldn't wait to hand over the pizza and get back to [his] car for the next installment."[8] Those stories not only marked his interior sense of self, but the external terrain he still revisits. "At one intersection in particular he thinks, 'That's where Harry was almost killed.'"[9] When I stand alone in a particular university classroom I experience that kind of heart-racing reminder.

One semester I assigned a film that uses sports and disability to explore providence and coincidence. In a key scene, a character passes out in an apparent medical crisis that turns out to be a paradoxically lifesaving and faith-renewing event. On the day we were supposed to discuss the film in class, while reeling from the death of my best friend in Texas, a student passed out in the classroom. That unleashed a series of dizzying coincidences, including the uncanny role of Christian scripture. Those suspenseful and enchanted moments marked the passages I read in the immediate aftermath of the aborted class period, and to which I have returned so many times since. The stunning events and biblical passages are forever entwined. This was a spontaneous and accidental case of inextricable mingling, but I conduct a more purposeful choreography of connections in this book. This is a vital task given important absences and omissions concerning sports, disability, and religion in general, and Christianity in particular.

Main Scriptural Passages for This Book

These intersections are abundant in popular culture but absent from the Bible. That sacred compendium contains references to disability and draws on metaphors of sports, but none of its writers ever combine the two. I, by contrast, not only bring stories of sports, disability, and Christianity into dialogue with scripture, but I find helpful conversation partners in two passages that might not seem obviously related to either disability or sports at first blush. In Romans chapter 8, the Apostle Paul presents his most thorough overview of the embodied and far-reaching implications of the Christian message. Paul recognizes the fragility of our bodies and compares the "groaning" of human suffering to that of non-human animals (and the rest of nature as well).[10] From Paul's perspective, this sorrowful, multi-species chorus is like the groaning of labor pains that signal new birth. Paul claims the shared lament is a reminder of a future moment when God's people will receive new imperishable bodies redesigned from the perishable material of their older forms. Since non-human animals will also be liberated from their "bondage to decay" at that point, "the creation waits with eager longing for the revealing of the children of God."[11] Relatedly, the other passage I focus on in this book explores the qualifications for being considered "children of God. "

In the Book of Acts, the author relates an encounter between a missionary named Philip and an anonymous Ethiopian eunuch. As an employee of a queen, the eunuch has some professional esteem, but as someone who either had his testicles removed or was born without them, he deals with social shame. As is the case in so many of the stories I draw from pop culture, coincidence figures prominently here. The eunuch happens to be reading scripture when Philip engages him in conversation. Convinced by Philip's subsequent teaching on that passage from the Book of Isaiah, the eunuch asks Philip a question about the boundaries of Christianity: "What prevents me from being baptized?" Aware of the mixed messages of the Hebrew Bible— scriptures that ban eunuchs from the "religious assembly of the Lord,"[12] and others that promise divine blessing and concern for such people[13]—Philip is faced with a presumably vexing dilemma. His decision to baptize the eunuch indicates reciprocal change. Philip baptizes a "racial and sexual minority,"[14] despite biblical passages prohibiting eunuchs from the assembly of the Lord, and the eunuch joins a new religious movement, despite his engagement with the more well-established tradition of Judaism. In this vein, each depends on the other to propel them to new understanding and commitments. This, then, is another example of interdependence, which is salient in much disability activism but often maligned in ableist North American culture.

Disability's Critique

Some people with disabilities are keenly aware of the challenge they present to a society that celebrates a supposedly "level playing field," where the only imagined qualifications for climbing socioeconomic ladders of success are a diligent work ethic and requisite talent. It turns out that the playing field is not often designed with disability in mind. "[W]e are subverters of an American ideal, just as the poor betray the American Dream. And to the extent that we depart from the ideal, we become ugly and repulsive to the able-bodied."[15] If so, the myth of the American dream becomes an even more imposing force against the wellbeing of disabled people when it is intertwined with the myth of individual opportunity (MIO).

The MIO is most often associated with a 19th century writer of pulp fiction named Horatio Alger. His hugely successful novels followed a pattern of a young male with little economic means demonstrating both courage and diligence, and with these attributes catching the eye of a wealthy man. The benefactor, in turn, provides the only thing the youth ever needed for social mobility: an opportunity. The boy seizes the newfound employment as a catapult to wealth. Through the years, the myth of the American dream has been superimposed on the myth of individual opportunity, adding the corollary that the United States is uniquely configured socially and politically for hard working and talented people, including immigrants, to succeed. The MIO and the American dream thus draw our attention to diligence and talent, suggesting the financially successful have received just desserts for strenuously maximizing their God-given gifts; within these frames, it looks like the poor and marginalized are reaping what they have failed to sow.

Religion mixes with the MIO. For instance, a Hall of Fame major league pitcher who grew up in a poor fishing town in Panama implies an invisible hand for the athletic marketplace: "I always felt like if I played the game the right way, if I worked hard and tried to be a good teammate and honor the game, the money would take care of itself."[16] In the socioeconomic and political sphere, such ideology disguises structural elements of inequality between people and nations. It also grants a divine imprimatur to the status quo. Failure and success can thus resound to individuals as presumed products of their character and, even more dangerously in the case of failure, as aspects of their identity.

Marie Hardin points out, "American culture glorifies tales of the rugged individualist by rejecting interdependence as weak and undesirable. Autonomy and physical fitness are valued, and physical dependence is generally viewed with disdain."[17] These celebrated traits reinforce yet another common framework, the Great Sports Myth (GSM).

The GSM refers to the widespread belief that sports are intrinsically good, and that people can either preserve that purity or sully it by their misdeeds. By assuming the purity of sports, and relegating notions of corruption to the individual plane, the GSM shields sports from social critique and hides its destructive potential. For example, the ethos of pushing limits, reflected in the Olympic motto of "Faster, Higher, Stronger" can encourage athletes to unquestioningly "over-conform" to such ideals. That, in turn, can lead to injury for athletes and callousness among their fans. Kate Bowler argues that these attitudes have thoroughly infiltrated Christianity as well. She asks provocatively, "What would it mean for Christians to give up that little piece of the American Dream that says, 'You are limitless'?"[18] For one thing, disability might emerge as a more noticeable and meaningful category of life experience and interpretation.

Disability Hiding in Plain View

Centering disability could enrich and extend discussions in the academic study of religion and sports. Consider, for instance, a wide-ranging and compelling work, with insights indispensable to the field of religion and sports in general and to this book in particular. Jeffrey Scholes and Raphael Sassower begin *Religion and Sports in American Culture* by outlining the kinds of sports stories that tend to capture attention. They use the typical cases of "important events," "amazing athletic feats," and "acts of indiscretion" as a foil to introduce an athlete who met none of these criteria. Tim Tebow never played in a Super Bowl, was not particularly skilled at his professional position, and stayed self-consciously clear from any hints of impropriety. Scholes and Sassower point out that the widespread intrigue surrounding the quarterback in the middle of the 2011 NFL season and a playoff game in 2012 centered on "the possible relationship between his strong faith and the logic-defying wins that he helped engineer for the Denver Broncos that year."[19] In this book, I extend that discussion by highlighting how Tebow and various media members forthrightly linked that athletic Christian story to disability.

Similarly, when the scholars mention the late global superstar Muhammad Ali, they point exclusively to adulation for the Muslim athlete as champion pugilist. I add a comparative examination of Ali's boxing career and his later status as a disabled icon with Parkinson's disease.

I also provide the most compelling account of "athletes and fans" appealing to the supernatural in basketball: an improbable basketball story about a high school team manager who for one evening appeared like a basketball luminary.

For the final home game of the Greece Athena High School basketball team, Coach Bill Johnson wanted to bless his team manager, Jason McElwain, an autistic teenager known affectionately around the school as "J-Mac."[20] J-Mac had displayed such indefatigable enthusiasm in his support role that it seemed fitting to give him a dream opportunity as a varsity player. Johnson decided J-Mac would suit up for the "Senior Night" game, and students made placards with pictures of J-Mac's face in preparation. Greece Athena held a secure lead with less than five minutes to play when J-Mac entered the game. His first shot was wildly off the mark. As Johnson tells it, he put his head in his hands and prayed, "Dear God, please, just get him a basket." When J-Mac subsequently connected on a three-point shot, fans exploded with cheers. Astounding observers, J-Mac made five more, each basket escalating the riotous celebration in the stands. In the waning seconds, he sunk his final shot from well beyond the three-point line, unleashing pandemonium. Fans rushed the court and hoisted him above the crowd, into the sea of placards bearing his image. He finished with 20 points and, in less than five minutes of action, was the high scorer of the game. When the grainy video of the spectacle came to the attention of producers at ESPN, they included it in their evening highlight reel. The story and video went viral; soon J-Mac was appearing alongside his coach on *The Today Show* and other well-known media venues.

Many observers offered religious explanations, even people who did not consider themselves especially religious, like Jeff Van Gundy, a good-natured curmudgeon. The former NBA coach and current television commentator intersperses complaints with his observations. With respect to J-Mac's accomplishment, however, Van Gundy spoke in uncritically glowing terms while gesturing toward transcendent power: "It makes you believe more strongly in the human spirit and that there's a greater being out there than human. I don't want to sound like a real religious person, because I'm not, but there was definitely something there that night."[21] George Pataki, then-governor of New York State, offered a similarly tentative testimony: "The outcome was tremendous; it was just terrific. It makes you wonder if the hand of God wasn't helping with the direction of that ball just a little bit."[22] Coach Johnson, a committed Catholic, gave the most adamant supernatural eyewitness account: "For anyone who was there, what unfolded in the Greece Athena gym defied any logical explanation. That's why I'm certain that a real miracle occurred right before my eyes. And I'm not the only one who believed that the good Lord was presiding over the festivities that night."[23] One of J-Mac's teammates, Rickey Wallace, thought the secular space of the court was sanctified, "It was just a blessing, something so sacred. That gym was trying to say something."[24] The idea that disadvantaged children and youth with disabilities have a God-given power to reveal truth has an ancient history far removed from J-Mac's geographic and chronological period. That history provides important context for what follows in this book.

The History of the Enchanted Child

There were places and times in which a belief in things like fairies may have arisen "in answer to some of the more puzzling mysteries—the questions of the 'untimely death of young people, . . . of both wasting diseases and strokes, paralysis and of the birth of . . . otherwise [perceived] deficient children."[25] It is no wonder that people marveled at such mysteries, appealing to an invisible realm for explanations that ranged from curse to gift. The extreme negative of what scholars now call the "symbolic paradigm" assumed illness and impairment augured misfortune, a sentiment recorded on Assyrian clay tablets from at least 2000 BCE: "When a woman gives birth to an infant . . . whose nostrils are absent, the country will be in affliction, and the house will be destroyed . . . [an infant] that have not fingers [signals] the town will have no births."[26] Susan Schoon Eberly points out, "This belief in the supernatural nature of the child born with a congenital defect continued through the Middle Ages and into the Reformation, when Martin Luther himself co-authored, in 1523, a publication which interpreted the political significance 'assigned from God' of a seriously deformed foetus found floating in the Tiber."[27]

There were also positive ancient associations with disability, since children born with evident deformities "were sometimes deified, as in the case of the Egyptian Ptah, achondroplastic dwarf, or the cyclopic Greek Polyphemous."[28] Accordingly, some names for developmental disabilities may have had a religious etymology: "For example, *cretins*, persons born without defect who develop [intellectual disability]and who may become physically deformed due to thyroid deficiency disease (hypothyroidism), may have been given the name cretin—from Chretien, Christian—in reference to the belief that they were 'God's children.'"[29]

The idea that God's presence is especially tangible and active around children with disabilities and chronic illness is embedded in popular culture. Perhaps no work has made a deeper imprint in this respect than Charles Dickens's *A Christmas Carol*.

In the 1843 novella, Dickens uses childhood illness and disability as an emotional fulcrum. The ghosts of Christmas Present, Past, and Future reveal to the miserly Ebenezer Scrooge the dire effects of his penny-pinching. One of Scrooge's workers, Bob Cratchit, is barely subsisting on his meager wages, and his indigence will prove fatal for his son Tiny Tim unless Scrooge opens his heart and pocketbook. Tiny Tim has an unnamed illness that has left him "crippled" with a cane and an "iron frame" supporting his limbs. He has an unwaveringly positive disposition, though, and over a humble Christmas dinner, declares, "God bless us, every one!" This fits a pattern Davidson et al. noticed in 19th century British children's literature: "Disabled children's patience and sweetness in suffering or in accepting their disability make a powerful impact on others at times, bringing out the best in them."[30] When the Ghost of Christmas Future shows Scrooge that Tiny Tim will die from his untreated illness, the ghastly revelation is too much for him to bear; upon waking, Scrooge lavishes bonuses on Cratchit and others. He also becomes a second father to Tiny Tim. Dickens closes the tale of moral transformation, paternalism, and benevolence by repeating Tiny Tim's exaltation: "God bless us, every one."

Longmore argues that U.S. telethons in the 1950s—like the MDA pageant, the UCP spectacle, and the Easter Seals rite—relied on patterns established in the long-running television production of *A Christmas Carol*. He explained the analogous roles.

> The hosts and audiences were huge Cratchit clans, with disabled children—and adults—playing Tiny Tim. [The various] hosts, male and female, conflated the roles of the Christmas Ghosts and Bob and Mrs. Cratchit. They were moral preceptors to potential donors, instructing them in their duty to look after Tiny Tim's siblings. At the same time, the hosts and the givers were the Cratchits gathered around the sweet pathetic children. Viewers at risk of becoming Scrooges peered through their TV screens and learned that they could join the family by opening their hearts to the afflicted Tims. By looking after the 'most weak,' they could buy a place at the telethon hearth.[31]

Those patterns are reflected in the title of a book about J-Mac, *A Coach and a Miracle: Life Lessons from a Man Who Believed in an Autistic Boy*. Indeed, it seems like J-Mac's success helped move the telethon hearth to the stadiums, propelling a new wave of ritual activity in the popular culture of sports. Increasingly, teams at various levels began to ritualize the inclusion of a person with a disability into an otherwise able-bodied contest. If the person with a disability succeeded in some feature of the contest, footage of the surprising exploits could land on the highlight reels of popular sports networks.

Belief in the divine orchestration of these events evinces what some scholars call a "re-enchantment" of the world, a retrieval of wonder occluded by the Enlightenment. The widespread intellectual push in the 18th century to

unearth discovery of truth via tools of academic inquiry also included attempts to expose the falsehood in religious dogma. On what many people
would perceive as a positive note, sociologist Max Weber suggested that
modernity was evacuating the world of superstitions that delay progress.
But rational calculations and scientific achievements, he implicitly warned,
could also divest the world of the magic and wonder that fill life with meaning.[32] If the responses to J-Mac's (and others') success represent a desire for
re-enchantment, Enlightenment-based challenges to the religious explanations still arise. Temple Grandin is Professor of Animal Science at Colorado
State University whose own remarkable life as an autistic person received
cinematic treatment in an HBO movie starring Claire Danes. While others
thought God had intervened as compensation for McElwain's disadvantages,
Grandin suggested autism may have provided some unique advantages for
the moment: "Here's what I think happened with him. People don't realize
that autistic people are always taking in huge amounts of information while
watching games. He was taking in the movements out on the basketball
courts and probably had hundreds and hundreds and hundreds of basketball
games in his mind and rehearsed them there—'This corner of the court, this
worked before.' He probably had it memorized, what he was going to do."[33]

One might assume that since the medical paradigm demystified disability,
locating impairment in the realm of biology rather than spirituality, rational
explanations like Grandin's would carry the day. They do not.

An ESPN retrospective a decade after J-Mac's performance juxtaposed
religious gratitude with medical limitation.[34] The short film shows a clip
of J-Mac receiving an ESPY for "Best Moment" and giving an acceptance
speech he punctuates with an emphatic, "Thank you, God." Narrator Tom
Rinaldi subsequently claims, "Ten years later Jason continues to do what doctors never thought would be possible." Here religious belief is subtly pitted
against science, implying medicine cannot adequately chart the life course
of an autistic person who is empowered by God.

Centering Disability Between Sports and Christianity

In addition to reviving contests of interpretive authority between enchanted
and enlightened sources, disability could be to the study, practice, and fan-
dom of religion and sports what C.S. Lewis argues "incarnation" and "Resurrection" are to the Christian faith. For Lewis, incarnation, the idea that God
descended to earth taking on flesh in the person of Jesus, and Resurrection,
that this same God-man rose from the dead to create new life for all creation,

belong inseparably linked at the center of the faith. He uses the analogy of an incomplete artistic masterpiece to imagine a Christian faith missing these two ideas. "Supposing you had before you a manuscript of some great work. . . . There then comes to you a person, saying, 'Here is a new bit of the manuscript that I found; it is the central passage of that symphony, or the central chapter of that novel."[35] Thus reunited and re-centered, incarnation and Resurrection "bring out new meaning from the whole of the rest of the work, [and make] you notice things in the rest of the work which you had not noticed before . . . "[36] I argue that this is also what would happen if disability were brought to the center of Christianity and sports, from which it would reveal new layers of older stories, and illuminate fresh paths for future study.

Consider, for instance, the stories of Tim Tebow and Bennet Omalu. As a player and then later a broadcaster, Tebow has used his popularity from the sport to raise the esteem of people with intellectual and physical disabilities. He recognizes that they are often ignored and denigrated, and his foundation organizes "Night to Shine" proms around the world to celebrate and spotlight their value. As a neuropathologist, Omalu challenged the popularity of football, but, like Tebow, he also wanted to valorize people with disabilities. In Omalu's case, however, he focused on players who were ignored or denigrated in their erratic, anguished final days of life—behavior and torment he linked to neurological impairment acquired in the NFL. "I would like to thank my Lord and Savior, Jesus Christ," Tebow would say after playing in football games. "In the name of Christ, Stop!" Bennet Omalu wrote about a sport he insisted God "never intended" people to play.[37]

Their varying relationships to disability also illuminate the topic of the Holy Spirit in the Gospel of John. In the third chapter of that Gospel, the writer depicts a man named Nicodemus as a learned seeker, open to an extended talk with a controversial rabbi. Even if Jesus is the dangerous rabble-rouser many of Nicodemus's scholarly peers think he is, Nicodemus is not only willing to hear Jesus out, but he also believes Jesus is on to something vital. He is convinced that "no one can do these signs that [Jesus does] apart from the presence of God."

In response to that compliment, Jesus lifts the conversation to a symbolic plane: "Very truly, I tell you, no one can see the kingdom of God without being born from above." Nicodemus remains in the literal: "How can anyone be born after having grown old? Can one enter a second time into the mother's womb and be born?" The conversation continues in this vein, with Jesus offering amorphous spiritual lessons and Nicodemus seeking concrete instruction. Jesus has no mercy. Nicodemus's head is spinning, but Jesus adds more dizzying gusts: "The wind blows where it chooses, and you hear the sound of it, but you do not know where it comes from or where it goes. So it is with everyone who is born of the Spirit." Eventually Jesus gets to the heart of his message: "For God so loved the world that he gave his only Son, so that everyone who believes in him may not perish but may have eternal life." John 3:16 is etched in sports because Tim Tebow stenciled that verse in his eye black.

Tebow testified to having received Jesus's offer to be "born again," and in a deceptive read-option system designed for running quarterbacks, he also moved like the unpredictable wind in Jesus's lesson to Nicodemus. He had spectacular but expected success on the college level when he wore John 3:16 under his eyes. When statistical coincidences evoked the same verse in an unforeseen professional feat three years later (to the day), some considered what Nicodemus said about Jesus might also relate to Tebow: "No one can do these signs that you do apart from the presence of God." Tebow, for his part, continued to proclaim football a God-given "platform" from which he declared the message of John 3:16 in word and deed.

While Tebow is most associated with John 3:16, other portions of the conversation between Jesus and Nicodemus relate to the uniqueness of Omalu's mission. By the time we get to those segments, Nicodemus has changed stances from interlocutor to listener, and Jesus has switched themes from love to judgment:. "And this is the judgment, that the light has come into the world, and people loved darkness rather than light because their deeds were evil." When Omalu first discovered a tangle of tau proteins in the brain of a deceased NFL football player, he worried that people would love football so much they would ignore the light he could shed on its dangers: "Deep in my spirit, I had a feeling that if I . . . dug deeper . . . whatever I might discover was going to put me in direct conflict with the passion for football that consumed Pittsburgh and most of America." Jesus explains to Nicodemus that "those who do what is true come to the light, so that it may be clearly seen. . . ." The meaning of the full version of Omalu's last name, Onyemalukwube, sounds like a loose paraphrase of that verse: "'If you know, come forth and speak.'" While Tebow wrote John 3:16 on his face, Omalu's mission was marked in his name. In addition to the meaningful last one name, his first is French for "a blessing" and his middle name can be translated to "Life is the greatest gift of all." The combination strikes Omalu as destiny, "My parents bestowed this name upon me, but I believe it was God who chose it."[38]

Not only is disability central to pivotal moments in religion and sports, but it can also expose both life-suppressing and life-giving patterns in stories—whether they are of secular, sacred, or mixed origin. To clarify this point, I provide the following contrasting examples of life-suppressing and lifegiving stories.

A grandson of royalty told himself a strikingly different story about his disability than the South African Radebe imagined for his relay team, although running is central in both narratives. The Hebrew Bible recounts the frenzied moments after a nurse learns of the assassination of a king named Saul and his son Jonathan. The nurse scoops up the king's five-year-old grandson, Mephibosheth, and bursts into a sprint from danger. In her hurry, the boy falls, causing permanent injury. Mephibosheth would never walk, let alone run. Mephibosheth's late father, Jonathan, was best friends with a man named David. David becomes king and eventually learns about the now adult Mephibosheth. King David sends a search team to locate Mephibosheth and accompany him to the palace. There he pronounces royal privileges upon his late friend's son. But when Mephibosheth learns about his turn in fortune, his immediate reply reveals his internalization of a life-suppressing and self-loathing story. In a lively paraphrase of the key verse, Eugene Peterson captures Mephibosheth's downcast demeanor: "Shuffling and stammering, not looking him in the eye, Mephibosheth said, 'Who am I that you pay attention to a stray dog like me?'"[39] A popular Christian speaker and writer thinks Mephibosheth is broadly representative. "How many times do we do the same thing? Our self-image is so contrary to the way God sees us that we miss out on God's best. God sees us as champions. We see ourselves as dead dogs."[40] As a contrast to Mephibosheth's recitation of a story of self-defeat in front of a royal audience, Radebe acted like a champion when he stepped into his brightest spotlight on his biggest stage.

When his name was announced to the packed throngs at Wembley Stadium, Radebe smiled, and triumphantly waved his stunted arms in the air. Like a beefy boxer kissing his biceps to entertain his audience and cower his opponent, Radebe kissed both arms at their points of amputation. He yelled triumphantly to the camera and walked backward with a strut, raising his arms again to roaring applause. Reflecting on the event, Radebe said it was a "day made in heaven." "The heavens declare the glory of God," writes the author of Psalm 19, and there is ironic parallel between this confident, joyous scene of a runner without hands and that same Psalm's descriptions of "the work of God's hands."[41] Footage of Radebe's eager enthusiasm before his race could provide vivid accompaniment for the psalmist's athletic simile about nature: "In the heavens God has pitched a tent for the sun. It is . . . like a champion rejoicing to run his course." Peterson evokes a stadium with his rendering of that verse: "God makes a huge dome for the sun—a superdome. . . . The daybreaking sun [is like] an athlete racing to the tape."[42] Radebe burst out of the blocks propelling his teammates in speedy exchanges that culminated with a first-place finish at the tape—a gold medal for South Africa and a new World Record for the jubilant cohort. Radebe thus not only told stories of divine design, but from a biblical perspective, he embodied them.

Still, our life experiences seldom match only the despair of Mephibosheth or the triumph of Radebe. As I have already hinted, Radebe's journey included not only laughter but tears. For the nine months of his hospitalization after his accidental electrocution as a child, his mother visited him with a beaming smile. She adopted the bright posture for his sake. On the way to and from the hospital she would cry. It is fitting, then, that a promotional video for the same Paralympics in which Radebe's team would command so much attention combines triumph with trauma. The stories of car crashes, pregnancy problems, and war wounds in the video symbolize the unexpected pain of life. Unlike Radebe's radiant demeanor, the video begins in darkness.

Promoting the Paralympics with Myth and Ritual

The staggered flickering of lights unveils the first venue, a pool. From the pool to the track, the camera follows in motion as disabled athletes wait with steely concentration. Electric guitar chords build to a thunderous proclamation from Flavor Flav, the "hype man" for the hip-hop group Public Enemy: "Well now, kick the bass for these brothers and let 'em know, what goes on!" A frenetic montage of disabled sporting images ensues as Chuck D, Public Enemy's lead rapper, drives the soundtrack into high gear with a baritone barrage of rhymes. Suddenly, the music gives way to exploding bombs. Striving athletes are replaced with toppling soldiers. Another abrupt jump cut moves the viewer to a hospital where a pregnant woman wears a strained expression while holding her stomach. A doctor reassures her bewildered partner after presumably offering news of a compromised pregnancy, "I know this must be a shock." Just as suddenly, the scene shifts to a car careening against a rail, flipping and crashing with jarring blasts of metal and glass. After the devastation, the music returns with full reverb and we are offered a rear view of a man with double leg amputations drenched in sweat hoisting himself repeatedly on a pull-up-bar. A close-up then frames another man's determined, serious stare into the camera before a wider shot shows him in a wheelchair glancing dismissively at the wreckage that was his vehicle. Dropped back into athletic competition, the viewer is now immersed with a single-leg amputee swimmer as she dives and drives forward through the water.

Even though Scholes and Sassower do not address disability in their book, the authors clear a theoretical path to expose bifurcating pitfalls in the study of cases like this. They warn against conceiving of religion and sports as antagonists from separate spheres of society—sacred and secular. Instead, the authors persuasively and helpfully suggest we consider religion and sports as mutually influencing, meaning-making activities in culture: "They are different spiders but when one moves on the web, the other is affected by the movement of the thread."[43] In that respect, religion and sports have a complex and dynamic relationship. They play sometimes overlapping but not always identical roles—whether in current conditions or historical circumstances.

In contrast to the explicitly theistic language of scripture, there are no obvious allusions to God in the Paralympic promotional video, but the fact that every tragedy in its diegetic world is a turning point, rather than a death knell, suggests someone or something is holding it all together. The athletic images that emerge from the rubble testify to a deep well of endurance. Catastrophe does not have the lost word. That belongs to Chuck D with his insistent refrain for the fallen: "Get Up!"

The brief video obviously creates an extremely compressed time lapse of the individual journeys from hardship to athletic prowess, but all the determined stares and straining muscles remind viewers that those journeys have been arduous and hard-fought. Like other "hero myths," the stories symbolized in the video are "powerful because they supply answers to questions about *who* we should be."[44] As a model *of* difficulties we face in the world, the video provides a recognizable replica. The triumphant litany of images provides a model for how we should respond to hardship. To that extent, these stories function like myths. In everyday life, "myth" connotes something false. In the academic context of the study of religion, however, a myth refers to a foundational sacred narrative that shapes people's understanding of and response to the world. In that sense, a myth's truth does not depend on historical veracity. The promotional video's depiction of a car crash is not actual footage of any Paralympian's prior accident, but it depicts the circumstances in which some athletes first became disabled. If the stories function as myths, the sporting performances in the video look like rituals—the meaningfully patterned actions that bring myths to life.

Although Radebe's playful story of providence is much sunnier than this gritty video, they function similarly. By imagining God orchestrating the events that brought his South African relay team together, Radebe provides hopeful reframing of a traumatic injury that might otherwise look only like the unintended byproduct of youthful misadventure. Thus reframed, the accident has a possible explanation and an evident purpose. Meaning of that kind propels people through hardship, helping them trust that even though human understanding is partial, there is an invisible caretaker benevolently working things out for visible good. This kind of mythmaking amounts to what anthropologist Clifford Geertz called religious "effort": "The effort is not to deny the undeniable—that there are unexplained events, that life hurts, or that rain falls upon the just—but to deny that there are inexplicable events, that life is unendurable, and that justice is a mirage."[45] It is that last point, however, that is especially troubling in the case of Radebe's team. Radebe was a celebrated light, but he was certainly not the star attraction. It was his teammate Oscar Pistorius who drew so much attention to those 2012 Olympic and Paralympic games in the first place. Six months after winning gold with Radebe, he left some people feeling like "justice is a mirage."

Pistorius's renowned athletic career included a singular achievement: he was the first amputee to compete in both the Paralympics and the Olympics. Less than a year after that unprecedented accomplishment, he fatally shot his girlfriend Reeva Steenkamp while she was defenseless behind bathroom doors. Pistorius claimed he mistook Steenkamp for an intruder. His attorneys tried to turn people away from the indomitable superhero image Pistorius acquired through his prodigious athletic success. Instead of looking up to Pistorius, as viewers were encouraged to do through commercial advertisements shot from a low angle, his attorneys wanted people to peer down at a dwarfish, vulnerable man who—stripped of his prosthetics and given the realistic threat of an intruder—feels hair-trigger terror. The documentaries, books, and articles I deal with on Pistorius contextualize disability within "intersectional" factors of power and inequality, including South Africa's history of racial apartheid with attendant violent repression and dissent; the nation's continued struggles with violence through widespread and often deadly home invasions; the racial and racist perceptions of that violence; and a national reckoning with systemic violence against women in particular, especially in the context of domestic partnerships. "'Intersectionality,' or the study of how these dimensions of inequality co-construct one another, is a leading paradigm in women's studies, American studies, ethnic studies, and allied fields, and is increasingly becoming an indispensable tool for social scientists and humanists across the disciplines who do research and activism on historical and contemporary social issues."[46]

Religion is a potentially tricky case for intersectional study, since people and social classes with the most evident positions of power and status have used religion to shore up the status quo and, by extension, their own prestige.

Pistorius was raised by a devout Christian mother who died when he was fifteen. The intensity of his own faith seems to have waxed and waned at different points in his career, but it was conspicuous at his trial. He read books on prayer, which journalists noticed, and he testified in court to religion's crucial role in helping him endure hardship. A cynical interpretation of these displays of faith might suggest Pistorius is a privileged and reckless white man trying to position himself as a virtuous supplicant deserving mercy. Nonetheless, the social prejudices and structural disadvantages of disability complicate Pistorius's privileged status. Like Pistorius's own image, disability has undergone various interpretative permutations.

Disability Paradigms

"While the problems of disabled people have been explained historically in terms of divine punishment, karma, or moral failing [all grouped on the 'symbolic model'] and post-Enlightenment in terms of biological deficit [a characteristic of the 'medical model']" there are obstacles neither paradigm highlights.[47] In the 1960s, disabled activists and their allies (particularly in the United Kingdom and parts of the Commonwealth) rejected these paradigms in favor of a "social model" of disability.[48] They clarified that a person who uses a wheelchair, for example, does not have an inherent problem, or disadvantage until they encounter a built environment designed only for those who walk. Since the problem in this case is a social one, the solutions could include some combination of the following three approaches: designing the built environment for various kinds of mobility, modifying existing structures that do not accommodate such difference, and exposing widespread beliefs that create and reinforce this physical marginalization in the first place. In the medical model, "'impairment' describes a particular physical, emotional, or cognitive trait that results in the inability of the mind or body to function as expected."[49] In the social model, disability is reframed as "socially created discrimination against people with impairments."[50]

Jeremy Schipper provides a succinct definition for a similar paradigm called the "cultural model of disability"—"the social experience of persons with certain impairments."[51] This approach demands keen attention to a person's social world, "their identifiable sphere of everyday actions and relationships."[52] The cultural model dislodges able-bodied as the default category of life. It asserts that bodies differ across cultures and time periods and so do their meanings. Hence people like Schipper, who use the cultural model to examine ancient texts, find impairments that were disabling in the cultural and historical setting of their study, but which might not be considered a disability in another culture or time. I do not understand the cultural model as making a decisive break from the social model. I am thus grateful for the comprehensive nature of Critical Disability Studies (CDS), which refuses a prima facie priority for any single model. CDS acknowledges the possibility of overlap between all the models of disability, and that differences between them are sometimes a matter of emphasis rather than kind. CDS calls for the rigorous contextualization and self-reflexivity emblematic of intersectionality. To demonstrate why it is so important to embed personal accounts of disability in broader social, cultural, and political contexts, I will provide a preview of one of the later cases in this book.

A Preview of Political and Cultural Dimensions of Disability

Steve Gleason was an NFL player who became famous for blocking a punt in the first game in the Superdome after the devastation of Hurricane Katrina. Five years later, he was diagnosed with Amyotrophic Lateral Sclerosis (ALS). The documentary *Gleason* uses a spiritual and athletic framework to chart a path forward for Steve and his wife, Michel. "Yeah, I want to beat ALS. I want to win that part of the game. But for me the biggest part of the game is beating all the other shit that you and I have talked about . . . karma from our parents, or relationships with family, or relationships with friends, or your own spirituality, and just peace in your heart. But I just think there is a bigger battle there about being able to say, 'Okay, I have this diagnosis and it's not going to crush my life, even if it does crush my body.'"[53]

Gleason helps situate these personal familiar struggles within broader political battles. Audio from a newscast fills in the details: "Tonight the federal government is saying no to some devices that give people with disabilities a voice, literally." Another newscaster explains, "Recent changes to Medicare and Medicaid have limited patient's access to speech-generation devices." Gleason's father-in-law explains the impact those changes had on their foundation.

> Team Gleason became one of the only entities that was giving these speech devices, so the people that couldn't afford it through Medicare anymore still wanted to communicate and we wanted them to be able to communicate, so we just started fulfilling all of our requests, which meant it was two and three

and four hundred thousand dollars a month. We were able to fulfill every request that people asked of us, so much so that it's depleted our money . . . so we're now actually going out and beating on doors and asking people for money again.[54]

The film later celebrates the passing of the Steve Gleason Act, which "amends title XVIII (Medicare) of the Social Security Act to make permanent the elimination of a specified payment cap under the Medicare program with respect to speech generating devices." Still, that a person who received acclaim for his hyper-efficient body would need to rely on such technological assistance makes Gleason's story seem especially tragic to some. If we define culture as "socially-established structures of meaning,"[55] or even simpler, "shared meaning,"[56] it is easier to spot our collective misunderstandings of disability.

Consider for example, the description of Gleason's technological support in an ESPN article revisiting the role of sports ten years after Hurricane Katrina: "Since he can no longer use the muscles in his mouth, he speaks through a computerized voice, his humanity blunted by a droning, syllable-centric machine. Nothing works but his eyes."[57] For an otherwise compassionate and complex piece, this is oddly demeaning. It is also unintentionally deceptive. In *Gleason*, Mike asks Steve whether he can still use his taste buds. Steve explains ALS does not affect that part of the body. Neither does it alter cognitive function. Hence the claim that "nothing works but his eyes" is misleading. The description of technological adaptations blunting Gleason's "humanity" is another misperception, a failure to recognize the diverse forms of embodiment that enrich disabled lives. Nancy Eiesland explains, "My own body composed as it is of metal and plastic, as well as bone and flesh, is my starting point for talking about 'bones and braces bodies' as a norm of embodiment."[58] Gleason goes even further, "Technology has cured me." Although he has lost the ability to speak through his vocal cords, Gleason's computer-assisted voice is no less human, or humane. He established the Steve Gleason Foundation to provide needed technology and adventurous opportunities for people living with ALS. Technological embodiment is thus a central feature of Gleason's ALS advocacy and propels his flourishing life.

The assumption that ALS and the technological reliance it requires is a fate worse than death provokes the least funny attempts at humor. As three radio personalities in Atlanta found out on June 17, 2013, the consequences for such misguided assumptions can be swift: "790 The Zone hosts Nick Cellini, Steak Shapiro and Chris Dimino were fired Monday after a segment

Monday morning in which two of the on-air personalities took a call from a third host who pretended to be Gleason by using a voice that sounded automated—mimicking another ALS patient, world-renowned physicist Stephen Hawking."[59] The nadir of their performance involved a knock-knock joke in which the person playing the part of Gleason asked to be smothered to death. For his part, Gleason accepted what he called "genuine apology" from the radio people involved. The mocking radio bit produced a public outcry, and in a Facebook post Gleason highlighted the need for more conversation and action: "In the past 36 hours lots of people have been talking. Let's talk about this ... There are zero treatments for ALS. If you take any action as a result of this event, I prefer it to be action to end ALS."[60] The radio DJs jokingly imagined a sorrowful man speaking in stilted pleas for death. Their insensitivity ironically opened space for the articulate, and very funny, Gleason to call for long, nuanced conversations about life.

Often, the only means for disabled people to overcome perceptions of an inherently tragic and sad life are indefatigable displays of positivity—changing tragedy into inspiration. Gleason, though, refused both scripts in the documentary, rejecting a dichotomy of either shiny optimism or morose travail. He offers, instead, hopeful realism:

> I feel like in many ways I'm fulfilling my purpose. I feel excited every day to get up and make a difference and an impact on people's life. I feel like I've put together a good team of people to help take care of me. I've put together a good team of people to look for solutions. People will say it is such a sad, tragic story. It is sad, and so they're right. But it's not all said. And I think there is more in my future than in my past. I believe my future is bigger than my past. So that's uplifting. That's inspiring.

Mashups, Intertextuality, and Intersectional Approaches of Study

Gleason is a white man, and as such, outside of his disability, he is a member of the dominant social group in the U.S. Disability is just one aspect of an individual's identity and lived experience, and so a person's disability must be understood in relationship to other aspects of identity, such as race, gender identity, and sexual orientation. To incorporate religion into such an intersectional analysis requires rigorous contextualization. In this book, I attend to the specific spaces and networks through which power is exercised and religion lived. Moreover, although I give Christianity, as the numerically dominant religious tradition in North America (and my own), the greatest attention, I also examine a couple of case studies relevant to Islam and Native

American spirituality, minority worldviews that have faced more frequent prejudice in the North American context. For instance, Muhammad Ali is representative of those athletes who acquired disability later in life, which led sportswriters to transfer metaphors of "battle" from the rigors of the ring to the challenges of the commonplace. Through his evident physical struggles with Parkinson's, Ali was transformed from a man once considered an indefatigable boxing champion and controversial social activist to a quiet proponent of peace and a relatable underdog.

Besides being intersectional, this book is also interdisciplinary. Insights from the study of religion and film, for example, are particularly helpful for understanding the intersection of sports, disability, and Christianity. S. Brent Plate considers film a similar "symbol-creating apparatus of culture" to religion, and I join other scholars of religion and popular culture in making the same claim about sports.[61] Since the cultural products I analyze in this study are so often mediated through visual means, it is important to consider Plate's observation about "re-creation": He proposes that both religion and film seek to reflect and "actively reimagine" the world.[62] And this re-creation process involves mixing and matching components from different mediums. Plate's description of the "mashup" process bears striking resemblance to the Paralympic promotional video with Public Enemy.

Plate explains, "The activity of world creation is a process of taking things apart and putting them back together, of reassembling the raw materials available, of dissection and analysis, and of mending fragments."[63] Peeling away the self-conscious mingling of various component elements of the commercial requires a journey through time and space. Shifts in chronology are abundant. Public Enemy's "Harder than You Think" was released in 2007, but it was employed as the soundtrack for the Paralympic promotional video I detailed from 2012. Both the 2007 version and the portion used in the Paralympic video contain a sample of another Public Enemy track they had released in 1987 called "Public Enemy No.1." And the introductory guitar riffs are pulled from an even older song, "Jazahel," which Shirley Bassey first performed in the 1970s. The geographic movements are even more vertiginous: an African-American hip-hop group sampling the music of a British singer of Nigerian and English descent for a commercial promoting Paralympic competition in London, which in turn helps elevate the American group's position on the British musical charts.

What is more, all these shifts in context alter the meanings of the same string of words. On the 1987 track, when Flavor Flav bellows, "Kick the bass for these brothers and let 'em know what goes on," he is boasting about the rise of Public Enemy, then a young hip-hop group ascending various music charts. In its sampled form on the 2007 release of "Harder than You Think," that earlier line functioned to confirm the continuing relevance of an aging group with now much younger rivals. And in the Paralympic promotional video, the phrase signals that the viewer is about to witness disability sports from an angle of vision they probably never experienced or imagined. There is, then, a seemingly indeterminate play of meanings between the multiple texts that make up this commercial.

This work will thus examine the intertextual webs of signification through which people make meaning of stories in popular culture. Marcel Danesi defines intertextuality "as the connection one text bears to other texts by allusion, inference, implication, or suggestion."[64] And as Mallory Nye explains, cultural studies has helped "*widen* our sense of 'text' beyond the specifically written, to include cultural products that can be 'read' as texts—such as television, music, art, and architecture."[65] In examining the recent boom of pop cultural narratives related to sports, disability, and religion, I treat a wide range of media, such as film, fictional novels, disability life writing, video features on ESPN—including those that cover the same athletes who have written such memoirs—and news pieces in various sporting publications, both online and in print. That such research requires an expansive reach across disciplines and programs of study makes it a compelling case to demonstrate the value and possibility of pop culture studies. "[S]ince its inception in the 1950s, pop culture studies have been characterized by *interdisciplinarity*—the adoption and integration of findings and ideas from various disciplines."[66] For this book I rely on a relatively new modification of an older discipline.

Autoethnography or How to Write About a Story You Are in

Classical ethnography involves participant observation of communities and thick descriptions of their social lives. That kind of writing can capture nuances not always visible in quantitative methods like surveying and sampling. In 1821, Thomas Carlyle proposed that discerning the often perplexing "signs of our time" requires a calm assessment of our own positions as well. This would offer mutually illuminating perspective between the world and ourselves. "Perhaps on a more serious inspection, something of its perplexity will disappear, some of its distinctive characters and deeper tendencies more clearly reveal themselves: whereby our own relationship to it and our own true aim and endeavors in it, may also become clearer."[67] Autoethnography takes the personal role of the researcher a step further, adding big-hearted feeling to cool-headed thought. Arthur Bochner and Carolyn Ellis explain that people trained in academic research who are willing to reflect humanely and write engagingly are "in an ideal position to bring to light the meanings of emotionally draining, difficult, and demanding epiphanies on which human lives turn, including our own as researchers."[68] This includes sports. If in sports we learn to push past boundaries, in life we often experience the push-back of limits. Far from discounting sports from a study of suffering, this makes it an intriguing field of inquiry into how we cultivate hope and manage disappointment. I have thus examined my own stories of sports, disability, and Christianity alongside others in this study. Since I have struggled with mental health, this book covers not just physical disabilities like paraplegia, or only intellectual disabilities like Down Syndrome, but also what are called "affective disabilities" or "affective disorders"—these include OCD, and in my case, depression, anxiety, and BDD. This self-reflexivity also shapes the book's organization.

Plan of the Book

In chapter 1, I employ an autoethnographic analysis of interconnected stories. M. Night Shyamalan's film *Signs* borrows plot details and themes from John Irving's earlier novel *A Prayer for Owen Meany*. These stories became intertwined in my own life through a prominent theme in both—coincidence. Indeed, Irving's novel and Shyamalan's film have struck resonant chords and coincidental echoes at times of suffering in my life. With respect to Irving's work, I argue that since the main characters attend to the suffering and interdependence of "all creation," traditional able-bodied approaches to competitive sports are found wanting. I then demonstrate how *Meany* served as thematic source material for *Signs*, examining how impairments are imagined as hidden strengths in both the film and novel.

Chapter 2 revisits themes of enchantment and coincidence to examine the stigma surrounding anxiety and depression among professional athletes. In an autoethnographic portion, I extend those insights to my own suffering and hope. While this chapter's themes remain relevant to Romans, I focus primarily on the story of Philip and the Ethiopian eunuch. The details of that story have striking parallels to a conversation between a professional football player who attempted suicide, and another player whose brother died by suicide. I hope that this chapter demonstrates the benefits of bringing sacred text and contemporary sport into reciprocally illuminating perspective.

In chapter 3, I focus on the theme of pilgrimage in both religion and sports. I connect my own stories of pilgrimage to various athletes, including perhaps the most well-known icon of religion and sports in American history, Tim Tebow. I examine the ways that Tebow has connected his athletic and Christian story to the lives of people with disabilities and chronic illness. I also explore how these relationships inform Tebow's athletic ethos, an approach to sports in keeping with *A Prayer for Owen Meany*.

Chapter 4 is an intersectional chapter that examines the social costs of black athletic success with reference to both Jordan Peele's comedy-horror *Get Out* and Tyler Nilson and Michael Schwartz's comedy-drama *The Peanut Butter Falcon*. In addition, I juxtapose Tebow's story with someone who shares his belief in divine communication through apparent coincidence, but who rejects the idea that God designed football as a platform for charity and salvation. Through his research onthe brains of deceased football players (and other athletes from contact sports), and the Hollywood film about his related conflict with the National Football League (NFL), Nigerian-born Bennet Omalu attacked a U.S. religion of sports with reference to race-based inequality.

In chapter 5, I extend a conversation begun in chapter 4 about inspiration and interdependence. I not only address the role of interdependence in the documentary *Gleason*, but I put the theme of teamwork in conversation with three other stories: the real-life story of Oscar Pistorius and the fictional true-to-life themes of *Logan* and *The Wrestler*. I consider them all in light of Gleason's preference for the motif of "exploration" instead of healing. I consider the social advantages of approaching suffering and hope through that integrated, interdependent perspective.

Chapter 6 extends interdependence to the natural world. Here I compare the interplay of Christianity, traumatic injury, gender, and nature in the case of Bethany Hamilton, a surfer who lost her arm in a shark attack, and Brady Jandreau, a Lakota cowboy who sustained a traumatic brain injury while competing in bronco riding. This chapter magnifies the complexities of interdependence in a world in which humans and non-human animals hurt each other at times, but also help each other flourish.

The concluding chapter assesses a stubborn reality. If people frequently shove disability into feel-good, reassuring frameworks of perpetual inspiration, the squeeze is more than awkward—it is misleading. Those representations are longstanding and widespread, but they look like cheap imitations next to the real thing. "You can do anything you put your mind to" becomes a less persuasive mantra given the complex challenges of impairment in a society structured to the benefit of nondisabled people. "Everything happens for a reason" still might enchant, but its destructive echoes register more clearly with disability in the picture. Lurking under cloying portrayals, real disabled lives present a defiant "No!" to unfounded beliefs in unbounded triumph. Likewise, disability meets sunny platitudes of Christian clarity with messier experiences of divine inscrutability. Instead of calling for the wholesale abandonment of either positivity or providence, I consider the healing power of lament I experienced as a chaplain during the pandemic of COVID-19. I conclude with the final enchanting moments of the story with which I begin chapter 1.

Chapter 1

A SIGN FOR OWEN ME(ANY):
AN AUTOETHNOGRAPHY OF GRIEF AND GRACE

My assumption is that the story of any one of us is in some measure the story
of us all. For the reader, I suppose, it is like looking through someone else's
photograph album. What holds you, if nothing else, is the possibility that
somewhere among all those shots of people you never knew and places you
never saw, you may come across something or someone you recognize.

—FREDERICK BUECHNER—

When I landed a job after my master's degree to teach college Spanish, Latin American Religion, and Latin American history, a friend
who was a graduate student in the Department of English had
the perfect parting gift: *A Prayer for Owen Meany*. He was well-acquainted
with my endless speculations about signs of a divine plan, and he thought
a book with a character who thinks about little else would be of interest.
Atheist author John Irving wrote *Meany* to answer what—or "who," as it
turns out—could make him believe in God. The response was the fictional
Owen. "Owen is unusually small and, though fiercely articulate, speaks with
a 'wrecked' voice that is impossible to imagine, and is represented on the
page with capitalized letters."[1] Owen has an unwavering devotion to God
and a momentous connection to sports. In response to a little league coach's
admonition for him to "swing away," Owen hits a foul ball that strikes and
kills his best friend's mother. Throughout the novel Owen grapples with the
cosmic implications of that horrifying event. Despite the dark subject matter, my friend wrote a lighthearted note on the inside cover, "This book is a
sign." I not only shared Owen's fascination with providence, but I had a lot
in common with the narrator as well.

The opening lines of *Meany* demonstrate Owen's profound influence on his
best friend John. "I am doomed to remember a boy with a wrecked voice—not

because of his voice, or because he was the smallest person I ever knew, or even because he was the instrument of my mother's death, but because he is the reason I believe in God; I am a Christian because of Owen Meany."[2] John joins the Anglican church, which was the same Canterbury Trail I was on at the time my friend gave me the book. John eventually moves to Canada to teach English, but the United States remains very much in his orbit. He rails about covert and corrupt U.S. involvement in Nicaragua. Besides studying the intricacies of that historical conflict during my graduate degree, I was a Canadian in the U.S. protesting American involvement in a second Iraq War. As many points of familiarity as there were between the novel and myself, it was a movie, replete with intertextual nods to *Meany*, that intertwined most thoroughly in my life.

In *Signs*, director M. Night Shyamalan drew on the fateful phrase from the novel—"swing away"—but turned it in a lifesaving rather than death-dealing direction. I, though, am dealing with death as I walk to class, with "swing away" engraved on a necklace I have been wearing for several years now. I am not sure how I will get through this class session, let alone the rest of the semester. My best friend in Fort Worth, Texas, died by suicide just last week. The students have watched the move *Signs* the night before. In addition to discussing the film, I plan to continue our lessons on American religious history with an introduction to Pentecostal and Charismatic forms of Christianity—both movements that include a belief that sometimes the Holy Spirit's power can topple a person to the ground. This segment of the lecture will include a personal dimension: I plan to discuss my mother's mental illness and the comfort she found in Pentecostalism.

Only ten minutes into class, I break down trying to read a slide about how our pain changes us. I cannot regain my composure. I would not have chosen this material had I thought my grief would manifest so dramatically. A mature student in the class, a brave serviceman, realizes I am having trouble continuing. He spontaneously reads the entire slide in a resounding voice. His support gives me a second wind. I gather myself and continue the lecture. I arrive at the portion about perceived manifestations of the Holy Spirit's power in American religious history, including people falling over. I begin the story of my mother's dramatic spiritual experience—what she and others believed was a sudden and overwhelming encounter with the Holy Spirit. In one part of the story, my mother screams in confusion, drawing a panicked huddle of fellow congregants. As I recount this in class, a student begins to faint. She comes to and reassures me she is fine. I start teaching again. She faints and collapses to the floor. A neighboring student hovers over her with a look of terror and voice of panic. She is not the only one in shock.

I am in a stunned daze trying to process what is happening. Murmurs grow into frantic student appeals for me to call security. The students help me move chairs to clear a path for the EMTs. I dismiss the class. I learn that the classmate who immediately attended to her neighbor is also her roommate. When the EMTs arrive, the student who fainted is still a little disoriented. Eventually she can answer a series of questions about her medical history, and she explains to them what she recalls about the fainting. I notice one of the first responders looking back at the image still projected from my laptop on to the board. It is a stylized scene of a biblical passage in Acts, in which early followers of Jesus lean back under the bright presence of the Holy Spirit. It looks like a couple of them are falling over. The first responder jokes that I should be careful what I teach. The levity is a huge relief.

They take the student and her roommate to the hospital. I am left alone with a campus police officer who arrived with the EMT. A series of uncanny coincidences follow on the heels of this already surreal class session. Nearly a year later, my wife and I have dinner with the student and her roommate. We talk about the real-life signs we perceived that day. I remind the students of something they already know: that scary, confusing, enchanted class session saved my semester and forever marked my faith.

In both *Meany* and *Signs*, author and auteur imagine a world in which obvious tragedies and apparent crises also carry meaning and hope. In that context, our weaknesses, impairments, and apparent disadvantages are designed to draw us together with other people, who in turn contribute a response to the most imposing of opponents—death and grief. Combined and in conversation, these stories demonstrate all three of my supporting points for centering disability in the study of religion and sports. First, they reinforce my descriptive claim for the ubiquity of disability in stories of sports and religion. Second, they implicitly but incisively critique popular frameworks related to all three subjects of the intersection. Third, both *Meany* and *Signs* focus on the hopeful interdependence exemplified in Romans 8. I have needed that for a long time.

A Personal Journey to Meaningful Signs

As a child, my liberal Roman Catholic father would pray to St. Anthony when he lost things. My mother would speak in tongues. In this mixed(up) Christian context, hope was sometimes hard to find. My family's stories are an important backdrop to understanding the diverse Christian and athletic contexts of both *Meany* and *Signs*. They also exemplify the primary sign of enchantment in both the novel and the film—coincidence.

Before my mother was a fervent Christian, she was a spectacular athlete. She succeeded at any sport she tried, but she excelled in tennis. Representing the province of New Brunswick at the Canada Games, she won a bronze in mixed doubles. When she played women's doubles in an international competition, she and her partner defeated a tough U.S. squad. In Nova Scotia, where I grew up, she amassed a heap of trophies in major singles competitions. She matched her natural athletic gifts with dogged determination. As a field hockey player in university, she was once knocked out cold during a ferocious competition. She also, however, had significant battles off the field.

Her depression, anxiety, and OCD became so acute as a young woman that she was hospitalized in psychiatric care on two occasions. She sought remedy in religion, but first had to settle a perplexing question. When my mother asked her mother whether God exists, my grandmother was blunt: "No one knows." That made my mother wonder about people who staked their professional lives on Christian claims, "What about the priests? They seem to know." My grandmother thought clergy were really in the same agnostic boat as her. "They just get paid to say there's a God," she explained. My mother was raised Anglican but unbeknownst to her, the church she attended was inquiring about a new movement called Charismatic Renewal, which borrowed an emphasis from Pentecostalism on personal and often emotional experiences of God. My mother knew nothing about Pentecostalism or its more recent offspring, but the Charismatic movement was beginning to make moderate inroads at her local Anglican church. There was nothing subtle about her Charismatic encounter in a church basement.

There, during a Bible study, she was a quiet participant in "popcorn prayer." People went around the room making short petitions. When my mother's turn arrived, she offered a simple request, "Lord, I want to go forward and not back." Upon that utterance, she sensed a wind shoot across the room and nearly knock her over. She screamed. Fellow parishioners rushed to her side in a panic. Her teeth chattered but she barely made a sound. She told the anxious inquirers surrounding her that she was not sure what had happened. When she left the Bible study, she turned on her car and heard an unfamiliar radio voice reading a passage from Acts, a New Testament book that recounts a slew of dramatic encounters with the Holy Spirit. The passage on the radio referred to a primordial encounter between Jesus's early followers and the Holy Spirit: "And they were all filled with the Holy Spirit and spoke in other tongues." According to the reading, this took place in an "upper room," but for my mother the passage clarified her experience in the church basement. She eventually left the Anglican church and became a full-fledged Pentecostal. My Catholic father had not signed up for this.

I was exposed to both Christian contexts growing up, but I had trouble reconciling them. It was clear that neither of my parents thought the other was a real Christian. I was always intrigued by questions of ultimate meaning, and I tried to find my own path, making a meaningful commitment of faith in a Wesleyan church during my adolescence. Sports, though, were a more consistent presence in my life than church. I was a tiny point guard in my freshman year of high school, standing just 5-foot-3 and weighing in at less than 130 lbs. I looked even scrawnier and shorter next to our tallest player, a versatile 6-foot-10 center of Nigerian descent who eventually played for the Canadian National Team and caught the eye of the NBA's Indiana Pacers as a second-round draft pick. Despite my shortcomings, I was good. And I got better as the years went on. Behind closed doors, though, I was troubled. I inherited my mother's significant athletic ability but also her difficult brain chemistry.

My difficulties began with what lies beneath, the crooked unseen—namely, my teeth. Not *just* my teeth, but that is a good starting point for the rest of my body. Your front teeth may have descended in pleasing partnership. Mine were in all-out war. Even in their armistice, they turned in a mutually antagonist gaze. In junior high I had such a debilitating fixation about this that I would just move my lower lip when I talked. It became so instinctual that people would usually not notice, or at least not comment. In the rare instances someone asked about the odd mannerism, I was mortified. The noticing and asking were bad, but exposing my dental shame was out of the question.

If you think I'm exaggerating how bad they looked, you may be right, because here is another important disclosure: I do not always see my body accurately, even when I am sure I am looking at the unmediated truth. I only know that retrospectively. When braces at least partly fixed my teeth complex, I moved on to my hair. In my senior year of high school, I was sure I caught the early signs of follicles in revolt, planning rapid and dramatic recession. That meant constant, wearying vigilance at the borders of my hairline. Not even external conversation could drag me from the internal mental patrol. It was torturous and isolating. It endured for years. Symptoms like this comprise what psychologists call body dysmorphic disorder (BDD). BDD is a relative of obsessive-compulsive disorder (OCD), and like OCD it ranges in intensity. It can include hallucinations, but someone struggling with BDD may also distort the meaning and importance of a real imperfection, not just a perceived one. In either case, it often leads to suicidal ideation. At my worst moments, I felt irretrievably lost. Through it all, there was an overshadowing darkness that seemed to always threaten storm.

The storm hit in full force in my third year of university. Reeling from a break-up, I was intermittently drunk and perpetually confused. I was descending to a psychological rock bottom of sorts. My faith—what was left of it—was also plummeting. Philosophy classes where belief in Jesus was compared to Elvis hysteria made Christianity seem like a deluded religion for the hapless. I did not want to be one of the delighted benighted. Finally, in an education class called "Famous Teachers," the increasingly fragile tokens of my faith fell abruptly and nearly shattered. Our professor was adamant that scholarship had exposed the great gulf between the Jesus of history and the Christ of faith. In his view, Scripture was riddled with historical inaccuracies that buried the historical Jesus in evangelistic propaganda. To drive home his point, he declared the Jesus of history was most likely conceived when Mary was raped by a Roman soldier. Ironically, it was this surging dose of iconoclasm that awakened my moribund faith.

It drove me to an intellectual, spiritual, and emotional quest for the truth. The entire notion of truth was now more vivid, closer at hand, and personable. Before the Famous Teachers class, I had assumed the remedy for my spiritual malaise would be a deeper internalization of a concept: that Jesus died for my sins. With this incessant gaze on the Jesus of history, however, I was translated from the conceptual realm of faith to the incarnational plane of "God with us." That is the meaning of "Immanuel," which is an Old Testament name that the writer of the New Testament Gospel of Matthew applies to Jesus. Granted, I was hardly convinced that the Christian claim to God-in-the-flesh was still tenable (especially given my professor's insistence to the contrary), but I now wanted it to be true more than ever, and the possibility of its truth was newly thrilling.

I prayed starkly, "God, if you are real and you reveal yourself to me, I will surrender and follow you." I meant it. Shortly afterward, I heard about a professor of religion at another university who self-identified as a Christian. I met with him, hoping he could dispel my doubts. He patiently answered my questions, but I realized during the visit that what I really wanted was something to read—a work upon which I could meditate, one that would offer a convincing intellectual response to my education professor's insistent and incessant challenges to scripture. The Christian professor recommended "A Response to Biblical Criticism," by C.S. Lewis. Since he used that article in his classes, he rustled through his cabinet to give me a copy. He could not find any. After thanking him for his time, I drove home.

When I arrived, my mother was writing a letter. Wanting to check her spelling, she asked me to grab her dictionary from downstairs. Near the dictionary, I noticed a book on the shelf that I had obtained in junior high while attending the Wesleyan church, but which had only collected dust. It now had a mystical shine. I thought to myself, 'I wonder.' I opened the book and searched through the Table of Contents. I felt a surge of excitement to see "Response to Biblical Criticism," by C.S. Lewis. I read the article, but it was the coincidence of the timing, not the persuasiveness of the content, that gave it so much personal meaning. It seemed like a hint that God was with me—as if God were a playful parent leaving a surprise gift for a beloved child. I finally found some rest for my unquiet mind. Coincidence played a role in my mother's pivot from Anglican to Pentecostal Christianity, and it led me to the same jubilant confines. Eventually though, I went on a reverse track, bringing Pentecostal enthusiasm with me on a journey back to my mother's original Christian upbringing. I found myself enamored with the contemplative nature of Anglican ritual.

Meany and Horrifying Enchantment

The Episcopal Church is the American counterpart to the Anglican church in Canada, and the official national expression in the U.S. of the global Anglican Communion. It is also the kind of church that Owen attends along with his best friend John at the beginning of the novel. Both were relative newcomers. John switched churches when his mother married his stepfather. They had been Congregationalists before the move and John is mildly discomforted and annoyed by the new, much more extensive ritual system of the Episcopal church. The move from a Roman Catholic to Episcopalian parish meant less ritual, not more, for Owen. Unlike John, Owen felt some relief in his new confines. He was a mystic, wanting immediate personal connection with God. He complained that Catholic rituals "interfered with his ability to pray—to talk to God DIRECTLY, as Owen puts it."[3] No church organizations matched Owen's intensity. John admits that "it wasn't until we found ourselves attending the same Sunday school, and the same church, that I was forced to accept that my best friend's religious faith was more certain (if not always more dogmatic) than anything I heard in either the Congregational or the Episcopal Church."[4] There are no Pentecostal or Charismatic churches mentioned in the novel, but Owen has a similar expectation to what I have witnessed in such circles: namely, that God is active in our lives, meeting us not only in sacred structures but also in the muddy mundane. Owen's belief in this divine immanence is not restricted to soft, feel-good interventions. In Owen's view, God's intervention can be as forceful and devastating as a baseball bat, which he learns as a little leaguer.

Without the stature to hammer one for the fences, Owen normally crouches to further constrict an already tight strike zone. Since pitchers have trouble throwing within that small space, Owen is dependable for drawing walks. When he changes course, he unleashes the unthinkable. On what Owen later calls a "fateful" occasion, he responds to a rare command from a tired coach who wants to get a long, boring game over with. "Swing away," the coach yells to Owen.[5] When Owen does that, he connects with the ball sending it careening foul and striking hard against a passing woman. Tabitha Wheelwright, usually called Tabby, drops on impact. Tabby is John's mother. She is also a fierce advocate and ally for Owen. He adores her. Her death leaves Owen guilt-plagued and grief-stricken.

Disability Metaphor

Irving uses disability metaphor throughout the novel to dramatize grief. When, for instance, John narrates the history of their (fictional) New England town of Gravesend, he draws attention to the sad symbolism of a *sagamore* (chief) named Watahantowet. He was responsible for the contested transfer of the land from Native American to Euro-American hands. The novel is critical of both overt and covert Anglo colonization. John explains that "instead of his signature, [Watahantowet] made his mark upon the deed in the form of his totem—an armless man."[6] When Owen's foul ball kills John's mother, he carries out an act evocative of that totem. Owen gives John his prized possession: a rigorously organized collection of baseball cards. There is a reciprocal intent to this gift. As Frederick Buechner puts it, "To trade is to give what it is that we have in return for what it is that we need, and what we have is essentially what we are, and what we need is essentially each other."[7] In the novel, it is John's stepfather, Dan Needham, who interprets Owen's gift to John in this fashion. As Dan sees it, Owen entrusts John with his treasure in an act of loving repentance, and he hopes John will return it in act of forgiving grace. John has never met his biological father, but loves and respects Dan. When Dan first began courting Tabby, he gave John a stuffed armadillo that ended up supplying endless fun and imagination for Owen, John, and other playmates. After explaining the meaning of Owen's gift of the baseball card collection, Dan surmises that John is supposed to give his greatest possession to Owen. John chooses the armadillo.

Just as John returned the baseball cards to Owen, Owen returns the armadillo to John, but with a physical change. Owen removes the claws, what John calls "the most useful and impressive parts of its curious body."[8] The declawing transforms the armadillo into a symbol of penitence and lack. John complains, "There was virtually no position I could find for the armadillo that did not make the creature resemble a supplicant—not to mention, a wretched amputee."[9] Dan, though, helps John see the poignancy of the exchange: "Dan Needham informed me that this was precisely what Owen *felt* he had done to me, and to himself: that we were both maimed and mutilated by what had happened to us."[10] Amputation thus makes visible an ineffable emotion. In this way, it facilitates in tangible form a holy triad of repentance, forgiveness, and reconciliation. All of this is a costly grace. John explains that "Watahan-towet may have been the last resident of Gravesend, New Hampshire, who really understood what everything *cost*. Here, take my land! There go my arms!"[11] Owen's figurative amputation is even more complicated since he sees himself as both God's victim and accomplice: "Here is what Owen Meany (and the armadillo) said. 'GOD HAS TAKEN YOUR MOTHER. MY HANDS WERE THE INSTRUMENT. GOD HAS TAKEN MY HANDS. I AM GOD'S INSTRUMENT.'"[12] Owen thus not only has an enchanted view of the world, but a horrifyingly enchanted one. Later Meany gets to play a character who embodies that sentiment, "The Ghost of Christmas Yet to Come."

In *Meany*, Irving makes ironic use of *A Christmas Carol* to undermine the links between disability, sentimental religiosity, and innocence that Tiny Tim's character normally evokes. Dan Needham, the man in charge of the local theater production, initially wants to cast Owen Meany as that diminutive, sweet character. Owen is older and thus a more capable actor than the children Dan had selected for the role in years past, but Owen's small stature and childlike voice help him look and sound the part. Owen, though, is neither innocent nor helpless. He is a gadfly and a firebrand. He is also sensitive to how he is perceived and knows from playing the part of an angel in a nativity play that he will be unlikely to evoke the desired sentiment for Tiny Tim: "WHEN I SAY, 'BE NOT AFRAID; FOR BEHOLD, I BRING YOU GOOD NEWS,' ALL THE BABIES CRY AND EVERYONE ELSE LAUGHS. WHAT DO YOU THINK THEY'LL DO IF I SAY, 'GOD BLESS US, EVERY ONE!'?"[13] Owen convinces Dan to cast him in a non-speaking role instead. To many people's surprise, Owen makes a thoroughly convincing ghost. He mesmerizes and terrifies the audience in that role, a combination that leads to rave reviews in the local paper. Even though Owen requested a non-speaking part for the play, he has no qualms about his voice.

Owen is convinced his usual "cracked voice" will prove essential in the long run. He believes there is a reason for his anomalous body and voice even if he cannot discern the particularities of their divine purpose. Another religious character posits more sinister origins: "I think his voice comes from the devil."[14] This assessment comes from Germaine, who is a maid to John's affluent grandmother. The grandmother dismisses the symbolic paradigm, from both the gift and curse poles of that explanatory spectrum. She insists there is a natural and visible explanation for Owen's uniqueness that has to do with the Meany family's granite business: "'Nonsense to it coming from God—or from the Devil! It comes from *granite*, that's what it comes from. He breathed in all that *dirt* when he was a baby! It made his voice queer and it stunted his growth!'"[15] Later, a singing instructor brings the medical paradigm into conflict with Owen's belief in the positive end of the symbolic paradigm.

"'Amazing!' said Mr. McSwiney. 'You've got a permanently fixed larynx,' he told Owen. 'I've rarely seen such a thing,' he said. 'Your voice box is never in repose—your Adam's apple sits up there in the position of a *permanent scream*. I could try giving you some exercises, but you might want to see a throat doctor; you might have to have surgery.'"[16] Owen is furious with the suggestion he needs to be fixed or rehabilitated. He is adamant that far from being a problem, his voice will be the means of some divinely purposed solution. "'I DON'T WANT TO HAVE SURGERY, I DON'T NEED ANY EXERCISES.' . . . IF GOD GAVE ME THIS VOICE, HE HAD A REASON.'"[17] In the concluding scenes that reason is made abundantly clear. Sport also plays a crucial role in the climax, but for much of the novel John and Owen have ambivalent feelings about athletic competition.

A Tension Between Sports and Play in *Meany*

A childless neighbor named Mr. Fish enjoys football and "cajoles" Owen and John to practice with him.[18] Neither John nor Owen share Mr. Fish's appreciation for the "aesthetics" of the sport. Jack Halberstam's reminders that children are generally "mired in difference" and "not in control of their bodies"[19] are especially apt for John and Owen's situation. John explains, "I could not master the spiral pass, and Owen's hand was so small that he refused to throw the ball at all—he only kicked it."[20] Irving introduces a tension between the learned competitive drive of an adult and the instinctive playfulness of young people. John acknowledges that "Mr. Fish was ever optimistic that Owen and I would, miraculously—one day—grow up and play pass-and-catch as it was meant to be played."[21] Ethicist Randolph Feezell expresses sympathy for the kind of viewpoint Mr. Fish exemplifies: "Surely part of the nature and attractiveness of sport does involve the intense and often satisfying experiences involved in competing, striving for victory, and becoming better."[22] He argues, however, that "such a view of sport is partial;

it leaves out too much of the joy." It is not just limited perspective but hyper-competitive descriptions that worry Feezell as "it robs sports of its magic and its imaginative appeal, and it impoverishes the rich vocabulary that can be used to reveal sport's possibilities."[23] Halberstam also warns about the dangers of communicating instruction exclusively in "serious" and "rigorous" terms, since such words convey "a form of training and learning that confirms what is already known according to approved methods of knowing, but they do not allow for visionary insights or flights of fancy."[24] Owen and John refuse these constraints.

They concoct a game with the football that accommodates diverse embodiment not only between people, but across species as well. Whether Owen kicks the ball or carries it, Mr. Fish's Labrador retriever, Sagamore, gives tireless pursuit. John and Owen enjoy watching the dog's funny contortions as it tries to corral the ball and pick it up with its mouth. This is a form of play that philosopher Kenneth Schmitz calls frolic, which among other things "is an immediate and unreflective expression of a kind of animal joy, a kicking off of the normal patterns of behavior, purposeless and without constraint."[25] "Animal joy" is a felicitous expression since John and Owen call their playful invention, "*dog*ball." Ultimately, though, even this inclusive playfulness meets a sad end. When Sagamore chases the ball into the street after one of Owen's powerful kicks, the dog is killed by an oncoming truck. In the novel, even when competitive sport is redeemed through childhood play, catastrophe still lurks.

Feezell worries about descriptions of sport that "sound too much like winning a war,"[26] and *Meany* deals with two major wars involving complicated U.S. presence in Vietnam and Nicaragua. Irving makes the connection clear: "This is a novel about the damage Americans do to themselves; sports are a part of that damage. If world news were covered as extensively, and in such detail, as the ceaseless March Madness over college basketball, wouldn't Americans be better informed about the world, and our place in it, than we are? . . . It's not literally, of course, that sports are killing us; but what we pay intense attention to, and what we ignore is surely doing us some harm."[27] While Irving rejects the idea that sports have intrinsic worth, he nonetheless imagines one of them in the service of an extreme, extrinsic good.

Once they reach prep school, Owen insists that he and John continually practice a basketball move with no evident purpose. John passes the ball to Owen, who leaps into John's arms while still holding it, and John catapults him into the air so that Owen can dunk the ball. John explains that the tandem shot became a "well-rehearsed stunt with us," one that John rues is "probably not even legal" in a game and which Owen insists is "NOT FOR A GAME."[28] Philosopher Richard Taylor's comments on meaningful activity are helpful in considering Owen's view of what John experiences as endless tedium: "Activity, and even long-drawn-out repetitive activity, has a meaning if it has some culmination, some more or less lasting end that can be considered to have been the direction and purpose of the activity."[29] Owen is motivated by the idea of an extrinsic purpose for the shot, the idea that the monotonous practice will have momentous payoff.

The Good End for Sports and Disability in *Meany*

After graduation, Owen becomes a body escort for the U.S. military during the Vietnam War. He travels with the bodies of fallen soldiers and makes official notifications to the families. On one occasion in Phoenix, John accompanies him. After they visit a bereaving family, they return to the airport where they see nuns walking with various Vietnamese children. They are refugee orphans from the war whom the sisters are connecting with adoptive parents in the United States. The nuns ask Owen to usher the children to the bathroom. Earlier in the novel, Owen dreamt he would die surrounded by Vietnamese children, but he does not hesitate when the nuns ask for his help. While they are in the bathroom, a disturbed teenager filled with xenophobic rage kicks in the door, breathing bloody murder against the children. Owen is prepared precisely for this moment.

The initially panicked children respond attentively to his simple Vietnamese instructions, "DOONG SA, DON'T BE AFRAID." John narrates, "It was not only because he spoke their language; it was his *voice* that compelled the children to listen to him—it was a voice like *their* voices."[30] In an interview, Irving confirmed that this moment in the novel reveals the divine purpose behind Owen's anomalous characteristics: "Owen has to have a voice the Vietnamese children will pay attention to, which is why he also has to be small." When the crazed teenager throws a grenade into the bathroom, Owen enacts the athletic maneuver he practiced tirelessly on the basketball court with John. John tosses the grenade to Owen who jumps into John's arms before catapulting into the air. He dunks the grenade through an open window and pins it against the ledge. Owen saves the children, but his arms are blown off in the process, calling to mind the amputated armadillo and the armless Watahantowet. John's earlier description of the armadillo as a "wretched amputee" is reframed now with Owen as a redemptive amputee. Owen quickly dies from his injuries. Irving explains, "I thought: What possibly good reason

can there be for insanely practicing sinking a basketball when you're Owen
Meany's size? Well, how about saving the lives of children? In my view, there's
no other good reason for it!"[31] Hence Irving's decision to have basketball play
a major role in Owen's tragic heroics does not absolve sports of its potential
to divide and distract. M. Night Shyamalan's 2002 film *Signs* has a similarly
ambiguous, though ultimately redemptive, depiction of sports.

Signs of Life in the Shadow of Death

Mel Gibson stars as Graham Hess, a brooding former (probably Episcopalian) priest, who is jaded by the death of his wife Colleen. She was killed by
a car while on an evening walk six months earlier. He appears strained and
harried from the moment we see him. Graham has a boy named Morgan
and a girl named Bo. We do not know their ages; they seem to be around
nine or ten and four or five, respectively. Graham's younger brother Merrill
looks like he is in his twenties; he is a failed athlete who works at a gas station. Merrill lives in another room of the farmhouse. As a baseball player,
Merrill displayed both prodigious power and spectacular shortcomings.
When he was not hitting home runs in the minor leagues, he was striking
out. The absent middle ground meant no big-league clubs wanted to take a
chance on him. His hound-dog expression evinces the damage this failure
had on his self-esteem and general sense of well-being. The baseball bat with
which he struck a record-setting home run hangs on the living room wall in
the farmhouse. The accompanying plaque records the feet and inches of that
blast and fixes the great gulf between a past filled with promise and hope
and a present marked by failure and regret. It is an epitaph to a dead dream.
This is one of two striking memorials that mark radical discontinuity. The
other is a family photo on Graham's bedside in which Colleen, ignoring the
camera, gazes lovingly at her husband. He is dressed in his clergy shirt and
collar. That symbolic piece of cloth is now an obsolete vestige, as useless as
Merrill's decorative bat on the wall.

The children still seem dazed in their grief. We are introduced to the young
Bo by a scream, emanating from the tall stalks of corn in a field where her
brother has just made an eerie discovery. The piercing sound startles Graham
and jolts Merrill out of a sound sleep. They race toward the field, converg-
ing near Bo. When Graham asks what is happening, Bo responds with her
own question, "Are you in my dream too?" In the distance, Morgan screams
for Graham. Merrill picks up Bo and they all race to find Morgan. They approach him from behind, but Morgan does not turn around. He keeps his

gaze fixed straight ahead, explaining bluntly and without expression, "The dogs are barking. They woke us up." Graham crouches next to him, touches his son's chin, and gently turns his face toward his own. He asks worriedly, "Are you hurt?" "I think God did it," Morgan replies like a mystic in a trance. "Did what?" Graham probes with palpable concern. Morgan turns his father's chin in the direction where he was staring. Graham walks slowly out into flattened corn stalks, followed by the rest of the family. An aerial view and haunting score reveal that the huge crop circle they are standing in is only a small part of the intricate design in the field. This is a genre-breaking film about God and aliens.

If there is something strange afoot in the physical landscape of Bucks County, Pennsylvania, it matches an interior family life slightly out of sorts. Whenever Bo sips water, she is convinced it is contaminated by particles, which can include "dust," "hair," and "amoebas." These are the kinds of fastidious concerns typically associated with OCD. The symptoms may have been exacerbated by grief, but we learn from Morgan that Bo had the phobia before her mother's death. He tries to explain his sister's idiosyncrasies to a stranger, "It's like a tick people have, but it's not a tick." Her compulsions work on a symbolic level in the film as well, demonstrating a kind of epistemology of saturated grief. For it is the unconscious input from your senses that tells you that the most innocent of activities, like drinking water—or driving a car, or taking an evening stroll—is just a step toward unwitting poisonous ruin. In sports when a particular region produces an outsized crop of formidable athletes, people say positively, "There must be something in the water." But trauma intensifies Bo's sense that the water in her world produces unbearable pain. And when you are young and your mom dies without warning or goodbyes, or, in my case, you are a grown-up and your uncle is struck down thousands of miles away, you know, even if everyone else pretends the world is screwed on straight, that there is something in the water.

A Tale of Two Robins

Before I was born, my cousin Robin Anne died of leukemia at three years of age. Before she died, she asked for every family member to say goodbye. As a line of people said their last words, she handed her pacifier to her father, my uncle Bill, and said, "I don't need this anymore." Such poise and understanding for a child in death's grip is hard to believe. It makes her sound like an actor from the 1950s passing with a graceful swoon onto a pillow. I do not know if it is factually accurate. I am not even sure I am remembering the details exactly as they were told to me. After all, her perceptive awareness seems too grown up. I am tempted to believe she said it, though. I want to believe she had a precocious epiphany that made her incongruously resolute and brave, that she glimpsed a shore of grace beyond her drowning horizon.

My uncle Bill medicated his grief and spun out of control. His remarkable business acumen was no match for his addiction, and two marriages failed along with his career. Bill recovered as most recovering alcoholics do, in fits and starts. Then, years later, he crashed on a floor of a hotel room in Mexico. He was so drunk and sick that he could not stand up. This is where things get unbelievable again. He claimed Robin Anne, his late daughter, was just in time. Bill felt a force pull him to his feet with titanic strength, and that was it. He got up from it all. He left that hotel room with the implacable momentum of an angel-child's push. He took the well-worn twelve steps path, ever thereafter speaking of Alcoholics Anonymous with a reverence that rivaled anyone's religious devotion. He launched successful transnational business endeavors between Canada and Mexico, including educational exchanges. He fell in love and remarried for a third time—the first marriage in which he would remain completely sober.

He named the second of his sons from this marriage Robin Carleton. When Robin Carleton turned three, the same age at which Robin Anne died from leukemia, he was diagnosed with his late sister's disease. Mercifully, the tragic pattern did not continue. Robin Carleton went into remission, and Bill held every milestone thereafter with the vice grip of a father who refused to have another child snatched away. As an older father, Bill now wanted to make sure he lived a long life, so he began a disciplined exercise regime, walking two hours a day. One day in a crosswalk only blocks from his house, he was struck by a car. He was taken away quickly by ambulance before his wife knew what happened. She identified his bloodied cap at the scene.

At the time, I was teaching Cultural Studies of Sport at Miami University in Oxford, Ohio, and commuting every few weekends back to Texas to be with my wife, dog, and cat. It was a short-term arrangement for what we hoped would be long-term gain. I was on a weekend visit to Texas when Bill was struck. My mother called from the hospital in Canada but had only sparse details. Neither she nor Bill's wife knew the severity of his injuries. When she called again later to tell me Bill was on life support, I hung up the phone, sat down on the living room chair, and wailed. My wife Mallory walked toward me, but my dog Rocky beat her to it. He nestled and leaned back against my trembling frame, planting himself like a furry anchor. I clutched and sobbed. Bill died a couple of days later.

A Prescient Message

I watched *Signs* for company. I did not know anyone else with a loved one who was killed by a car while walking. I also watched it because of its defiant, almost stubborn, insistence that as chaotic as things might seem, life has purpose. As they watch footage of unidentified aircrafts lighting the skies of Mazatlán, Mexico, Merrill worries about the end of the world. He wants his brother to offer some comfort, to play the part of a reassuring priest. "Couldn't you pretend to be like you used to be?" he pleads. Graham summarizes two approaches to unexplained events, both of which he knows personally. There are those who believe in random chance, and a competing camp that assigns meaning to what the first group calls happenstance. Graham turns the question back to Merrill: "Are you the kind that sees signs, that sees miracles? Or do you believe that people just get lucky? Or look at the question this way: Is it possible that there are no coincidences?"[32] Graham recounts his final moments with Colleen after her accident. She spouted a garbled mess indicative of a physiological system in shutdown. Her confusing last instructions included telling Graham "to see" and Merrill to "swing away." Graham editorializes, "Because the nerve endings in her brain were firing as she died and some random memory of us at one of your baseball games just popped into her head."[33] Graham lost his faith in that moment and never returned to the second group. He spits out a bitter declaration, "There is no one watching out for us, Merrill. We are all on our own." It will take an overwhelming string of coincidences to strain his incredulity.

The family comes under alien attack while hiding in the basement. Graham's son Morgan has an asthma attack during the melee. When it seems as if the aliens have retreated, the family tentatively make their way up the stairs. Graham carries a still-wheezing Morgan in his arms and reclines him on the sofa. He tells Merrill to prepare a needle for a potential epinephrine shot. Bo notices people dancing on the television and imitates their jubilant motions. Merrill and Graham realize to their great relief that the tide has turned. We hear audio from the television in the other room explaining that somewhere in the Middle East people found "a primitive means" to defeat the alien attackers. The world's terrible ordeal with the alien attack must be over, which confirms the family's travail has also come to a merciful end. Graham retrieves the television and wheels it into the living room so they can all watch the festivities. When he returns, the television reflection reveals Morgan stretched out helplessly in alien clutches, with an ominous claw hovering over his face.

Graham turns around and they stand frozen with fear at isolated points around the room. We watch the mental sequences that race through Graham's mind. A flashback returns us to Colleen's accident where we hear for the first time the entirety of her tearful dying message, including the message for Graham to "see" and Merrill to "swing away." We then witness a condensed replay of Graham's explanation to Merrill about the two kinds of visions of the world: "So you have to ask yourself what kind of person are you? Are you the kind that sees signs, see miracles or do you believe that people just get lucky? Is it possible there are no coincidences?" We are back in the house again, and suddenly Colleen's jumbled last lines have their long-awaited syntax. Graham searches the room for a sign. The camera pans with him. He notices the bat and Merrill standing next to it. Maintaining stony stillness, he delivers Colleen's message: "Swing away, Merrill. Merrill, swing away." When Merrill grabs the bat, the alien sprays a white mist into Morgan's nostrils. Bo unleashes a piercing scream. The alien turns in her direction. Merrill charges forward and drives the bat into its back. The alien drops Morgan with a thud. As in *Meany*, sports serve an extrinsic, life-saving good. Graham scoops Morgan off the ground while Merrill takes more swings, finally knocking the alien backward against a table. One of Bo's nearly full glasses of water falls over and splashes on the alien's shoulder. It turns out this is the "primitive means" of defense earlier referenced on the news. Bo's quirky, tick-like aversion to water is no mere compulsion, but also a weapon for alien-singeing warfare. In this light, Colleen's dying request to Graham is a pre-scient message.

Signs at the Gym and on the Road

I take a longer break from writing today than I was expecting, play basketball probably a little longer than I should. I am about to exit the gym when a man walks in with a Montreal Canadiens t-shirt. Since I am in Fort Worth, Texas, I do not remember ever seeing anyone here wearing Canadian team attire, except for me. On several occasions at this gym, I have worn a Montreal Alouettes t-shirt of the Canadian Football League, so the sight of another Montreal shirt stops me in my tracks. "Are you Canadian?" I ask. He is, and he beams when he hears I am from Nova Scotia. He has heard of Saint Mary's University, where my cousin Tom played and coached hockey. He asks my age. I tell him but clarify my birthday is tomorrow. He says his birthday is the day after mine. These are a few coincidental elements of this ten-minute encounter, but what I find more interesting and much more emotional is what happens next—what might never have happened had I not stopped to talk to a man in a Canadiens t-shirt who entered when I was about to exit.

This entire week my emotions have been bubbling, rattling my lid of composure. From writing this chapter, I am so freshly reacquainted with the grief of Bill's death that my eyes pool at unexpected moments. I can stop them at a glistening stage, without it all spilling over, but I feel raw. Except for the weeks immediately after the accident, I have never thought so much about Bill and that crosswalk. That is what makes the bumper sticker on the black car in front of me, as I drive home from the gym, so strange and holy: "Stop For 'Em, Not on 'Em." I am stunned by the coincidence. While I am quite sure I have never seen anyone besides me wearing a Canadian team t-shirt in my gym, I am more certain I have not seen a crosswalk awareness bumper sticker before. I want to yell out gratitude to the driver for announcing this fragility and caution to the thousands of pounds of steel all around him. There is, of course, no way to relay the message, especially since we are now separated by two other cars. We are also in different lanes. Suddenly, the driver changes lanes in front of me and pulls into a supermarket on the right, what Graham might call "a happy turn of chance." I make the same turn. I walk toward a man in his late forties. His silver chain and cross reflect brightly against his black t-shirt. I get out an introductory question about the bumper sticker, and I am soon a mess. It is his girlfriend's car, he explains, as my lips quiver. Her brother was hit in a crosswalk, and he is now a paraplegic. I choke on words trying to explain about Bill. He nervously but warmly expresses condolences. We have known each other approximately two minutes.

Early in *Signs*, when Merrill is mocked for his prolific strikeouts, he reflects sadly, "It just felt wrong not to swing." Swinging away involves risk in both sports and life. It is about taking a chance despite the possibilities of failure. With respect to pain, it means finding strength in vulnerability, even though that softness potentially exposes us to more hurt. It is turning to others with and for help even when we are inclined to hunker down and hide in safety. It is the kind of interdependent action that declares "playing it safe is another way of not really playing it at all."[34] And that risk pays off in the film. Romans 8:28 could have been the movies' tag line: "We know that all things work together for good for those who love God, who are called according to his purpose."[35] Or as Peterson puts it, "That's why we can be so sure that every detail in our lives of love for God is worked into something good."[36] In *Signs*, every detail works for good because of all the apparent bad. The alien had sprayed a lethal chemical substance into Morgan's lungs, but it did not take effect. Morgan did not inhale it, because he could not breathe. He was in the throes of an asthma attack. Hence Morgan's physical impairment, which brought him to death's door, was his saving grace. Graham says in epiphany, "That's why he has asthma." Graham newly embraces his status as a child of God. By the end of the film, Graham has rejoined the priesthood. Romans is not the only helpful biblical guide for experiencing *Signs*. Peterson's paraphrase of the eleventh chapter of Hebrews sounds uncannily like the film's conclusion: they "turned disadvantage to advantage, won battles, routed alien armies."[37] It is the kind of teamwork I have in mind when my wife and I begin talking about starting an LGBTQ+-affirming, Christ-centered, and Spirit-filled church. We know we cannot do it alone.

We meet with Lauren and Greg, married friends of ours, about our vision for such a community. Not only do they accept our invitation to join us in the venture, but they reveal something I did not know about their college-aged son: he is gay. Lauren is so excited about our plans for what we were calling The Ark: A Church for All People and a Mission with All Creation that she sends her son an email. He is not religious, but he is overjoyed at the news, heralding it enthusiastically to friends in his dorm. It is not long, though, before we hear of a dispiriting turn in Lauren and Greg's marriage. Lauren needs time to regroup, she tells us, but she still plans to eventually work with us in the church plant. She spends extended time with her son while he is on winter break from college.

On Chinese New Year, 2019, we host a celebration to introduce friends and families to the vision of the church plant. On that night we also honor my late cousin-in-law Ho's memory, a Canadian of Chinese descent who recently died. With a nod to traditions of Chinese New Year, I invite people to wear something new. Lauren arrives in a sparkling black top, but there is something unidentifiably amiss in her hug of greeting. I am thus relieved by later signs she is enjoying herself. At one point, she smiles and asks whether she can call me "Pastor" now that we are embarking on this new mission. In front of everyone, she jokes that she needs a long talk. When she does not show up for our Bible study the following week, I call, but my call goes straight to voicemail. No one knows it at this point, but she has taken her life.

Learning through Losing, from Film to Life

In church on the Sunday after her death, the Anglican priest's message is about faith and work. He asked, "What would happen if God showed up at your work?" He answered his own question, "It would change everything." I had already changed plans for the coming work week. When I found out about Lauren's death, I notified students I would miss a couple of days of classes. I also realized I was not going to be able to entirely hide my pain, so I decided I might as well link it to something instructive and germane to our class. I told students that in my absence they should watch *Signs* and read Buechner's "Adolescence and the Stewardship of Pain." When that day comes, I wake up early to pray. I check the "Verse of the Day" on the Bible app my wife downloaded onto my cell phone. I am still such a novice with it that I cannot find the verse, but instead see only the "streak" of days I have consulted the app. Shaking on the way to class, I pray for the Holy Spirit's help. I began this chapter with the story of what happened during that class session, when one of my students passed out. I will now fill in the other serendipitous details.

In the aftermath of the fainting event that ensued, I stand alone in the classroom with the campus police officer who arrived with the EMT. Officer Christian (her real name) has the same reassuring manner as the female police officer in *Signs* who accidentally calls Graham "Father" because she cannot forget his faith, even though he wants to. After hearing about my week, Officer Christian looks at me compassionately and intently before posing a question of faith, "What if God did this?" ("I think God did it," Morgan says at the beginning of *Signs*.) Unlike Morgan in the film, Officer Christian adds a possible explanation, "so that you would know you are not alone." I walk upstairs to my office and plop heavily into my chair. I feel a strange buzzing sensation as I try to make sense of the morning's chaos. It suddenly occurs to me to check again for the verse of the day. On a morning I felt faint with grief, wondering how I would endure the semester, and after a student fainted and fell, I am finally able to access today's verse: "Have you not known? Have you not heard? The Lord is the everlasting God, the Creator of the ends of the earth. He does not faint or grow weary."[38] I look up the rest of the passage from Isaiah and read the lines that follow. "He gives power to the faint, and strengthens the powerless. Even youths will faint and be weary, and the young will fall exhausted; but those who wait for the Lord shall renew their strength, they shall mount up with wings like eagles, they shall run and not be weary, they shall walk and not faint."[39] My strength is renewed.

In the next class period, we debrief about what happened, and I explain the details of my grief. We also discuss the film we were supposed to talk about during the previous class session. I point to the pivotal moment in *Signs* when an apparent medical emergency restores Graham's faith and leads him back to ministry. In that scene, Graham realizes his son's medical condition has purpose. His asthma attack closed his lungs and blocked the alien's venom in the process, thus saving his life. I ask the students, "Do you remember the son's name?" A student answers correctly but quizzically, as if it were a trick question, "Morgan?" Another student gasps with recognition. I turn to face the woman who fainted in the previous class session and say, "Hi Morgan." (Her real name.) Tears stream down her face. When she and her roommate walk by me at the dismissal, I turn and say, "We are connected for life." They both laugh and say, "Yep."

Connections between *Meany* and *Signs* and Morgan and Sean all suggest the world is enchanted. For me, it was like a fog of personal despair and confusion lifted to reveal a bright, interconnected community. But the film and novel also remind us of distortions. With respect to disability, diverse bodies can provide unique gifts that contribute to collective joy, as John and Owen experience with "dogball." Too often, though, sports, and the world in general, are tilted in the favor of the nondisabled. From this imbalanced perspective, disability slides into inspiration. Because of his short stature and childlike voice, Owen is initially expected to play a cheerfully innocent Tiny Tim. The automatic fusion of disability and inspiration flattens varied, three-dimensional lives. Neither do sports always help us recognize complexity. As Irving argues, sports can distract people from social concerns. When their importance is exaggerated, sports can also lead to feelings of failure and shame, emotions Merrill embodies for much of *Signs*. In terms of Christianity, *Signs* demonstrates the resilience of faith. Implicitly, however, it also exposes the weakness of worldviews that ignore the pervasiveness of suffering. *Meany* makes the same point and takes issue with various extremes of head and heart in Christianity: arid rationalism that leaves no room for enchantment and, conversely, dogmatism that trumps intellect. In the next chapter I consider the ways that athletes are attending to both mental and physical health at a contested intersection of, sports, disability, and faith. Coincidence remains a central feature in those stories.

Chapter 2

EUNUCHS AND SUICIDAL ATHLETES: CO-CREATING MEANING IN TIMES OF DESPAIR

irst, a scene from the Bible: Philip, a Greek-speaking, Jewish evangelist for Jesus, runs to catch up to an Ethiopian eunuch to discuss shame and salvation. Second, a parallel scene from the NFL: Hayden, a white tight end, runs to catch up to a black quarterback to discuss stigma and suicide. In the first story, it is "an angel" and "the Spirit" who orchestrate the breathless endeavor. The second hurrying scenario is likewise a product of "divine intervention," at least according to the tight end's mother.[1] Like the biblical story, a third story includes cross-cultural dynamics. A formerly suicidal Australian without limbs travels to South America where he has spellbinding effect on a popular television host, who (unbeknownst to either of them) is about to die. The drama continues with people I encounter in stories and real-life who help me co-create meaning during periods of existential dread and intense self-loathing. They save my life in the process. These ancient and recent stories reveal how once hidden topics like depression and anxiety not only come to light at the globalized intersection of religion and sports, but they also loosen the bootstraps narrative—that popular idea that all we need to get ahead is talent, diligence, and a resolute will. Increasingly people are recognizing we could all use some help. Although I will move toward a more focused application of that point, I begin with a story of broad resonance and widespread inspiration.

Over the years, and in different settings, I have asked college students which Bible story is most often evoked in athletics. Their answer is always David and Goliath. They are correct. David is a classic underdog. David wants to fight Goliath, but King Saul doubts his chances: "You are not able to go against this Philistine to fight with him, for you are but a youth, and he has been a man of war from his youth."[2] In *Hoosiers* (1986), a team chaplain rouses the spirits of an overmatched and undersized team from rural Indiana by quoting the story of that plucky Hebrew boy who out-duels a giant with a small arsenal of rocks. As players listen with nervous, rapt attention, the preacher reads the climactic lines, "And David put his hand in the bag and took out a stone and slung it. And it struck the Philistine on the head and he fell to the ground. Amen." It is difficult to imagine a dramatic sporting scenario when someone would quote the following Bible passage: "No one whose testicles are crushed or whose penis is cut off shall be admitted to the assembly of the Lord."[3] Amen? Well, that is the Hebrew Bible's backdrop to the New Testament story with which I began this chapter.

Phillip, the Eunuch, and Intersectional Liberation

The passage in Deuteronomy has to do with eunuchs, people who were either sexually mutilated or had congenital defects to that effect. Their biblical exclusion from the assembly of the Lord creates the suspense of a chance encounter described in the Book of Acts. In that New Testament story, the Holy Spirit directs an early Greek-influenced, Jewish Christian named Phillip to approach an Ethiopian eunuch who, by coincidence, is reading a passage from Isaiah at that moment. It is a passage about painful humiliation, about someone who (like the eunuch) will not reproduce or carry on his generational line.

> Like a sheep he was led to the slaughter,
>   and like a lamb silent before its shearer,
>   so he does not open his mouth.
> In his humiliation justice was denied him.
>   Who can describe his generation?
>   For his life is taken away from the earth.[4]

There is reason to believe the figure from Isaiah, who the eunuch is reading about when he meets Philip, has a skin condition, which in the cultural context of the time, would have been disabling. Acts only mentions two verses from Isaiah 53, but Jeremy Schipper argues that the broader context of what scholars call the "Suffering Servant" (Isaiah 52:13–53:12) has important implications for disability studies.

Schipper highlights a seminal study in the nineteenth century, which included a convincing case that the figure from Isaiah 52 and 53 has an impairment. Later scholars tended to interpret the disability language as a metaphor and assumed that the person described in the poem, whether fictional or historical, was able-bodied. Schipper thinks that is a misleading product of habit. Too often when scholars find someone in a text who is not clearly distinguished in categories and language they recognize as belonging to disability, they tend to conclude the person in question must be, by default, able-bodied. Schipper contends that close attention to linguistic and literary context, without such default assumptions, will help recover the figure of Isaiah 53 as a disabled person. In short, he argues that "the servant's so-called suffering in Isaiah 53 helps to poetically describe his disability as a social and political experience as opposed to simply an individual tragedy or data for a medical diagnosis."[5] Like the figure of Isaiah 53, the eunuch would have also faced social shame and stigma about his body. Understanding why requires a foray through physiognomy, an ancient practice of interpreting personality traits from physical characteristics.

Physiognomy in Comparative Perspective

Physiognomy involved three main kinds of questions: Does the person have admirable or deplorable physical characteristics? What kind of non-human animal do they resemble? And what is their race or nationality? According to that criteria, "The Ethiopian eunuch would have been viewed by Luke's auditors as sexually ambiguous, socially ostracized, and morally evil (greedy and cowardly)."[6] About the anomalous anatomy of eunuchs, the first-century Jewish historian Josephus conjectured that it was "by reason of the effeminacy of their soul that they changed the sex of their body also."[7] He called for people to "shun eunuchs who have deprived themselves of their virility."[8] Besides derisive references to anatomy, negative expectations related to race and nationality are also germane to the Ethiopian eunuch. Parsons observes that people writing from a physiognomic perspective assumed Ethiopians were "cowardly."[9] Finally, the zoological subset of physiognomy interpreted human personality traits based on people's resemblances to non-human animals. Parsons explains. "It is not surprising that the eunuch . . . should be drawn to this figure in Isaiah who, like the eunuch, is described as being in a state of humiliation 'like a sheep . . . led to the slaughter' or 'a lamb silent before its shearer' and to whom, like the eunuch, 'justice was denied' (Acts 8:32–33). He, too, is like a lamb before its 'cutter,' reduced to silence in humiliation."[10] The eunuch might have found resonances in his reading, but the passage remained at least somewhat opaque. When Philip asks the eunuch if he understands what he is reading, the eunuch admits, "How can I unless someone explains it to me?" Philip is up for the task.

He is so persuasive in connecting the suffering servant of Isaiah to the later life of Jesus that the eunuch not only embraces that interpretation but also anticipates the next step of his conversion. "What prevents me from being baptized?" he asks. Philip baptizes him as a follower of Jesus, and the eunuch is overjoyed. This is a subversive story of culture-crossing and mutually beneficial coincidence.

It was not entirely a coincidence that Atlanta Falcon tight end Hayden Hurst got to speak with Dallas Cowboys quarterback Dak Prescott, but neither was it a foregone conclusion. When Philip ran up to talk to the Ethiopian eunuch, he was following directions from "an angel of the Lord" and "the Spirit." In Hurst's case, it was his mother who told him to watch out for an opportunity to speak to Dak Prescott. Hayden knew that Dak had been through hell, and he had a hopeful message for him. In 2013, Dak's mother died of colon cancer. In 2020, her primary caretaker during her illness and Dak's brother, Jace, died by suicide. In an interview with Graham Bensinger, Dak spoke about receiving that crushing news after his own bout with anxiety and depression: "All throughout this quarantine, and this offseason, I started experiencing emotions I've never felt before, anxiety for the main one. And then, honestly, for a couple of days, before my brother passed, I would say I started experiencing depression. I didn't know necessarily what I was going through, to say the least. I hadn't been sleeping at all."[11] When he finally got some shuteye, he slept so soundly that he missed a barrage of texts and phone calls. His father had to come to his room to break the devastating news about Jace.

Anti-American Weakness?

Skip Bayless, host of Fox Sports Undisputed had trouble concealing his contempt for Dak's revelations. There was something particularly unseemly, he argued, about the quarterback of "America's team" disclosing personal weakness. On September 10, 2020, World Suicide Prevention Day, Bayless shared his displeasure:

> I'm going to ask our audience to feel free to go ahead and condemn me if you choose as cold-blooded and insensitive on this issue. I have deep compassion for clinical depression, but when it comes to the quarterback of an NFL team . . . it's the ultimate leadership position in sports. . . . Because of all that I don't have sympathy for him going public with, "I got depressed. I suffered depression early in COVID to the point that I couldn't even go workout." Look, he's the quarterback of America's team, and you know and I know that the sport

that you play it is dog-eat-dog. It is no compassion. No quarter given on the football field. If you reveal publicly any little weakness, it can effect your team's ability to believe in you in the toughest spots and it can definitely encourage others on the other side to come after you. You throw an interception, you are going to hear, "Are you depressed, number four?" You get sacked, "How did that feel? Are you down about it?" You just can't go public with it in my humble opinion.[12]

Bayless is known for polemical commentary, but usually his controversial statements are much less cruel and destructive. During a more trivial period, Bayless was a tireless defender of Tim Tebow when others doubted his place in the NFL. Bayless sparred endlessly on the subject with his then-ESPN cohost Steven A. Smith—to the consternation of some, the relief of others, and, judging from ratings, the entertainment of many. Bayless may be the most well-known advocate for Tebow's career, but another Tebow fan was disgusted with Bayless's comments about Dak. Hayden Hurst explains, "My whole life was about sports. I grew up in Jacksonville during Tim Tebow mania." While Tebow went from football to baseball, Hayden ran a reverse course. Before his transition to football, he faced a private baseball "hell" that would later connect him to Prescott. He clarifies, "As a man of God, I don't use that word lightly."[13]

When Hayden was 18, the Pittsburgh Pirates selected him in the 17th round of the MLB draft. They offered him a contract for a half a million dollars to play in the minor leagues as he developed. He packed on muscle and appeared to be headed in the right direction when he suddenly failed to steer from the mound. He could not command his pitches. They would fly away from him in uncertain trajectories. The physio-psychological condition known as the "yips" made Hayden the target of the kind of social opprobrium people with skin conditions faced in the biblical period. Historically, lepers were barred from religious assemblies; similarly, fellow pitchers wanted Hayden excluded from their gatherings on the field. "Get this kid away from me. That s*** is contagious," warned one terrified colleague. Like a biblical figure desperate for healing water, Haden soaked in every bit of technical advice he could find to recover his form. "And then I'd get into a game, and, man ... I'll never forget the sound when I hit a kid in the head with a pitch. Knocked him out. I stood there, 60 feet, six inches away, watching him lying there, still as a rock. The sound of the ball smacking against his helmet echoed in my head, while I screamed into my mind. 'You f***ing monster. Look what you did. What's wrong with you'?"[14]

Hayden sought booze, rather than counseling, for his self-loathing. He carried the habit to the University of South Carolina, where he made the football team as a preferred walk-on. The new sport did not silence the old voices. On an evening in January 2016, he downed a mix of pills and alcohol and cut his wrists. He woke up in the hospital. Hayden decided to take his shame where it tends to melt for all of us—into the light. He explains,

> There's a lot to absorb in the wake of a moment like that. After my experience, I knew one thing for sure, though: I had to give myself over to my family and my support group. I had to open up and be real for once. No more secrets, no more isolated emotions. Waking up in those handcuffs—that was my real second chance. That was my real opportunity to rid myself of the demons that had found their way into my mind in Florida.[15]

With a therapist on campus, Hayden found a trusted place to finally lay down his burdens: "I can't explain really how helpful it was just to be able to talk to someone and not feel any fear of repercussions from what I might say. I thank God for those people, and for the University of South Carolina." It was enchanted enlightenment. After making it to the NFL, he established the Hayden Hurst Family Foundation with his mother to raise "awareness of mental health issues in adolescents and teens, and to fund mental health services." Cathy Hurst was apoplectic when she heard about Bayless's comments about Dak's anxiety and depression. Dak had those feelings during the same period in which his brother took his life, just as Cathy's son had tried to do years before.[16]

In the Acts account, "the Spirit" tells Philip to run and talk to the Eunuch. Similarly, Cathy told Hayden to seize the moment if he got one. "I said to Hayden, 'You're playing the Dallas Cowboys. Wouldn't it be awesome if you got an opportunity to talk to Dak?'"[17] Luke, the author, of Acts, includes providence only implicitly in describing the coincidence of the eunuch reading a passage from scripture. By contrast, Matthew Tabeek offered an explicitly spiritual interpretation of a coincidence in Hayden and Dak's encounter. "What the Hursts didn't know at the time was that Hayden would end up being randomly selected for the team's 'Mic'd Up' video series in Week 2 when the Falcons traveled to Texas to play the Cowboys.

It turned out to be a blessing."[18]

When Hayden chased after Dak at the end of the game, he was able to share his gratitude for Dak's public vulnerability. He said, "Hey, I've got a lot of respect for what you did and came out and talked about." After Dak replied with an enthusiastic "Yeah," Hayden added, "Me and my mom have a foundation about suicide prevention. Respect the hell outta you for talking about it, man." Prescott offered a suggestion, "We can collab one day."[19]

Since he was mic'd up for the game, the clip went viral, reaching millions. Thankfully, this was a much larger audience than Bayless had for his earlier comments criticizing Prescott for his vulnerability.

In his long career of defending Tebow's football abilities, Bayless mentioned he shared Tebow's faith. He acknowledged that so that he could clarify and control the narrative. It was not Tebow's Christianity Bayless was supporting in his role of sport analyst, he insisted, but Tebow's prodigious, if atypical, football skills. Dak is also a Christian. It is difficult to understand how Bayless could say the things he said if he reads the same scriptures Dak does, since finding "strength in weakness" is a blessed if difficult experience in those pages.

Race is an obvious difference between Tebow and Dak, and black quarterbacks have long had disproportionate pressures and faced manifold prejudices. But I think there is something even more telling about Bayless's reference to being a quarterback for "America's team"—an implicit reference to the American Dream which deserves further analysis.

From the perspective of the American Dream, and the myth of individual opportunity that undergirds it, depression and anxiety should be attacked with individual resolve not communal care. People should "suck it up" (a familiar expression in sports, but an unhelpful one for processing feelings) and "man up" (another toxic turn of phrase). Bowler asks Christians to consider stopping for a moment and unburdening themselves: "What would it mean for Christians to give up that little piece of the American Dream that says, 'You are limitless?'"[20] She speculates wryly that this kind of surrender might also entail jettisoning the phrase "just do it," at least how it is sometimes dramatized.

Nike's No Limits

According to a stirring Nike advertising campaign, there are no limits to the number of sports we can dominate, first place finishes we can achieve, or death-defying stunts we can accomplish. In one ad from the campaign, a narrator makes a surprising declaration over footage of a sweat-drenched Asian teenager running with labored stride and pained expression: "This guy, he'll run a marathon." "Who will?" the runner responds incredulously. "You, man," the narrator insists. That exchange ends with the teen asking in disbelief, "Me?" The advertisement is lighthearted from the very beginning, self-aware about hyperbole. This mix of narrative commentary and back-and-forth interaction continues with two teenaged girls—a white golfer and an ethnically ambiguous tennis player. A father then hoists his white, blonde-haired toddler through the air as the boy dunks into a toy net. The narrator continues his bold predictions, "All of these athletes are terrible now, but they'll all do big things one day." He offers what initially sounds like definitive resolution: "When everyone pushes their limits, they reach their maximum potential, and they live happily ever after." But that is a set up for boundless athletic displays. In this advertising world, there are no caps on maximum potential. The "Just Do It" slogan appears across the screen in front of another ethnically ambiguous teenager on the gymnastic rings. He protests the narrator's conclusion, yelling, "Hey, I'm not done." He swings into the "Just Do It" sign shattering it into pieces. Annoyed, the narrator responds, "Oh come on, that was my tagline. Hey, story's over. What are you doing? Whoa!"

The scene switches to a black teenager about to face a professional wrestler. The narrator warns, "He is going to kill you. And your mother's going to kill me." "I'm going to kill you," the mother confirms with hands clasped in a prayer posture. But prayer seems unnecessary in a world in which a white 20-something woman runs up a hill and jumps off a cliff, and a biracial basketball player jumps from a van driven by a crash-test dummy. He soars through the air for a slam dunk. Even though Nike seems to be lampooning its "Just Do It" message, that is not how Brian Strong, the Nike Global Corporate Communications Director, explains the takeaway point: "The end is really just the beginning for someone who's looking to go beyond their limits, and that's what that shattering logo represents."[21] In this advertising world, limits can be disposed with the right perspective. "'Unlimited You' celebrates athletes that break through their perceived limitations and then run past them as if they were never there. The film reflects the full campaign, which is about pushing our potential further than we expected by embracing an unlimited mindset."[22] In real life this culturally and racially diverse array of athletes do not compete on a level playing field of boundless opportunities. The Nike campaign reinforces another deception: that our bodies can be pushed to the brink and come out unscathed. They cannot. Dak is evidence of that. He had a season-ending Achilles tear in the fifth game of the same season that he opened with his discussion of depression and anxiety.

The injured, ill, or otherwise traumatized athletic body is a frank failure in a culture that pursues victory over limits. We are frequently shielded from finitude by an immense screen of popular culture on which scripts of boundless abilities predominate. Whether they are fictional or purport to document truth, these narratives frequently traffic in the same pernicious lie: Others may fall, they assure you, but you (you!) will endure, just like this protagonist with the indomitable spirit. The religious overlay to such misplaced confidence tempts with an idolatrous promise that someone or something greater will shield us from travail, or at least restore us to glory with the same swift arc of recovery of a two-hour film. In reality, our bodies are finite, making the most strenuous attempts to master them only provisional. Our best technological enhancements are likewise temporary. If we live long enough, even those among us who are not born with differences deemed "disabilities" will eventually experience various degrees of physical and cognitive impairment. And when trauma accelerates these changes, it does so without a tidy timetable. Grief, like the God of the Hebrew and Christian scriptures, is "no respecter of persons."[23] We all lose. We all die.

From No Limits to No Limbs

If he could glimpse the future as he begins to drown his limbless body in a bathtub, ten-year-old Nick Vujicic would see himself heading a soccer ball to a television host who would die hours later. That would not be a comforting vision. But if Nick could also have a premonition of what he will be asked to do after the tragedy, he might be filled with profound meaning. He has no such vision at this young age, but an imagined future story does arrest fatal self-destruction. As he explains, "I kept thinking of the grief and guilt that would burden my parents for the rest of their lives if I took my own life. I could not do that to them."[24] By twenty-eight, when he appears on the highest-rated show on Chile's state-run television station, TVN, Nick has left the suicidal thoughts and self-drowning plans far behind. He now cherishes his abundant life.

He admits that, like anyone else, he still faces obstacles and feels discouraged at times, but he found an unshakeable joy, a pervasive sense that truth and purpose drive his life. In fact, far from wanting to end it all, he is "greedy" for more. That word, which the interpreter translates somewhat misleadingly as "avaro" (or "miserly"), catches the co-hosts of Buenos Dias a Todos ("Good Morning, Everyone") off guard. Nick clarifies that "ninety years on this earth is not long enough for me; I want to live forever in heaven."[25] That touches Felipe Camiroaga. Indeed, Carolina de Moras notices the red pool of tears in her cohost's eyes. They are all meeting for the first time, but Nick realizes something unusual is transpiring. "The interview was supposed to last twenty minutes, which is long for a guest spot, especially when a translator is needed. Yet my visit with Felipe and Carolina went on for forty minutes, which is almost unheard of on such a show."[26] It is not just the duration but the content that amazes Nick. "Even better, from my perspective, was the fact that my hosts allowed me to speak at length about what my faith means to me and how I put that faith into action by traveling around the world as an evangelist and inspirational speaker."[27] Felipe also asks Nick to put his athleticism on display. Nick was born without limbs, but he has a foot (which he calls a "flipper") that facilitates many activities, including kicking a soccer ball. Felipe brings out a ball for them to "chip" back and forth. He also tosses it a couple of times for Nick to head. When he accidentally throws it too high for his diminutive guest, Felipe runs toward Nick and kisses the top of his head. If that seems patronizing to anyone now, later retrospectives will give it a poignant aura.

That afternoon, reports emerge of a plane crash. Felipe is among the missing passengers. While there is growing fear that no one survived, TVN calls Nick and asks him to lead an on-air prayer service. After the broadcast, he also speaks to 300 employees at the station. One of them momentarily stuns Nick with incongruous joy. It is the director who allowed Felipe and Carolina's interview with Nick to roll past the usual time constraints. He is devastated like everyone else that Felipe may have perished, but he is also relieved that Nick might have led him closer to God before an untimely death. The media have long covered Felipe's prolific love life, but the director has an inside scoop about his spiritual inklings. The director is a Christian and has been talking about his faith with Felipe for some time, but it was only after his interview with Nick that Felipe said he understood the director's desire to become a preacher to "minister to needy people in Chile."[28] Carolina would later confirm that Nick had a profound impact on Felipe during the interview. She said that he reflected with her afterward about the contentment he felt, a renewed appreciation for everyone in his life. He wanted to make the most of each day, he told his cohost gleefully. When official reports confirmed the dreaded news that there were no survivors of the crash, Nick offered condolences and hope to yet another audience in Chile. Later he would write in awe about the thought "that I could be a tool in His hands used to benefit others."[29] In the aftermath of the tragedy, TVN replayed Felipe's interview with Nick several times. They showed the soccer exchange that included Felipe kissing Nick's head. Nick found a way not only to come to terms with his anomalous body but to see it as a gift for connection with others. I, on the other hand, have trouble finding that bridge.

Nick was asked to speak to grieving colleagues decades after his suicide attempt in the bathtub. I had been drowning for months when I received a similar request.

I am the only chaplain in the hospital when I get a call that a beloved nurse named Beth Mathis had a catastrophic health crisis. The procedure for organ donation will take place in a different hospital, but in ours, where she worked, I am asked to prepare to speak to grieving colleagues in the Emergency Department, where she was a charge nurse. The organizers of the impromptu memorial would like me to provide some comforting words about her death and pray in honor of her life. "She has a young daughter," they tell me. 'She has a young daughter,' I repeat to myself in horror over the few hours that pass before my speech. I try to remain present in the other difficult and meaningful encounters in the hospital throughout the afternoon, but the impending memorial remains on my mind.

I knew from an early stage of hospital chaplaincy that my body could manifest grief even before I was conscious of my sorrow. I was surprised that I got through my first week of death-bed conversations and traumatic emergencies without crying. The valve opened, though, on my first day off, when I woke up on a Saturday morning with cloudy vision. I had been crying in my sleep. I thought I was adapting and adjusting as the weeks and months went on, but my BDD began to flare with distracting regularity. During solo shifts, and between emergency calls, I carried out tormenting rituals in my hospital office. I desperately sought an angle and lighting for a selfie that would prove I was not the ugly, loathsome person my BDD was continually screaming I was. I was trying to comfort myself, but I was exacerbating the pain. Every picture in every room magnified my facial scars and confirmed my worthlessness. The accusing thoughts were literally taking my breath away. I paused in stairwells and grabbed railings while I would bend over to regroup. I prayed, of course, but I also conjured nightmarish scenarios. I took mental measurements as I walked past buildings at the end of a shift, sizing them up for a fatal fall. Those kinds of thoughts were merely episodic until I attended the funeral of my youngest patient.

When I first met Brianna Sanchez, she had just been diagnosed with cancer. She had first come to the hospital with nagging hip pain. After her diagnosis, she called for a chaplain and I arrived to meet the beautiful 25-year-old Hispanic woman with a beaming smile. At one point she walked to the bathroom to comb her long train of striking, black hair. In the meantime, I talked with her mother and one of her brothers, who welcomed me like family. When Brianna returned to her bed, she told me about a joyful phenomenon during her otherwise worrisome health crisis. She was waking up laughing after dreaming about playing kickball with angels. I had a quick decision to make at this point because lately my own life had been enchanted with angels.

When a congregant first told me that she had been seeing 11:11 at coincidental and meaningful moments, I internally dismissed the idea as astrological woo woo. But when the same thing started happening to me and others in our community, I considered new possibilities. I read online that 11:11 can signal the presence of angels. Despite the longstanding belief in an intervening Spirit in Charismatic Christianity, I had never heard much about the activity of angels. If anything, we were warned that people who talk a lot about angels tend to be New-Age-types who deviate from both scripture and orthodox Christianity. But the 11:11 experiences made the stories of angels in the Bible come to life. I was more attentive, for instance, to the role of the "angel of the Lord," and not just the Spirit, in the story of Philip and the eunuch.

By the time I met Brianna, I was thinking so much about angels I was wearing an image of one on a t-shirt under my dress shirt. It had been a sartorial invitation for angels to accompany me in my hospital work that day. Hence when Brianna told me about dreaming of playing kickball with angels, I wondered to myself whether 11:11 had any meaning for the family. Once they revealed their Charismatic evangelical faith, I was sure it would not. I assumed they would have heard the same warnings about New-Age numerological nonsense that I had in Charismatic circles.

I did not mention anything about 11:11 that day, but on another occasion, during an extended conversation with Brianna's mother and stepfather, I decided to broach the topic. I offered numerous caveats. I acknowledged my previous aversion to the topic of both angels and anything related to numerology. I also assured them that I believed coincidences can be meaningless, even if sometimes they are significant. After that nervous introduction, I talked about the fact I had worn an angel shirt the day I met Brianna, and how I wondered whether God had prepared me for that visit. I suggested perhaps God was making Brianna playfully aware of an angelic presence in her life, especially during this difficult time. I then explained that when Brianna had mentioned angels, I was tempted to share with them about the slew of 11:11 appearances in our congregation, and to ask if those numbers were meaningful for the family. Brianna's parents looked at each other and smiled. They explained that they were married at 11:11 a.m. on 11/11/2011.

Months later, my wife Mallory accompanied me to Brianna's funeral. It is not the kind of thing a hospital chaplain is supposed to do. We are expected to maintain strict boundaries between our chaplain work in the hospital and our personal lives outside of it. Drawing firm lines is meant to ensure the best care of the patient and their family, and to preserve the energy and mental health of the chaplain. But the spiritual connections between

Brianna, her family, and me made relational borders porous. Brianna's mother would update me, at my request, even when Brianna was at home between treatments in the hospital. And I prayed more for Brianna during that six-month stretch than I did for anyone else in my life—patient, family member, or friend. There was certainly relief at the end of her suffering, and there was much hope in the thought of her playing kickball with angels, but her death was also devastating. I spiraled further.

The day after the funeral, I was supposed to undergo an intense mid-year review with a panel of chaplain educators and leaders. Our supervisor acknowledged the notorious reputation for this stage of the residency: that it can be destabilizing and unnerving. But he also took great pains to enumerate its merits. He encouraged us to emotionally engage with the process, no matter how difficult we might find it. I knew, though, that after Brianna's funeral, I was not ready for further emotional strain. In typically gracious and accommodating fashion, my supervisor rescheduled my review for two weeks later. It ended up being just as grueling as I imagined, given that I felt I had to hide my suicidal state while also being honest about other dimensions of interior and relational life as a chaplain. It was a vertiginous emotional dance, and I felt dizzy at the end of it.

Mallory called immediately afterward with terrible news. Four days earlier, we had rejoiced that she was pregnant with our first child. Now she was calling to tell me she had just miscarried. We cried together on the phone. I texted my closest colleague, Trent, who was sitting in another room of the office. I asked him to join me in the room where I had taken the phone call in private. He knocked gently and entered. I told him about the miscarriage and began sobbing. I collapsed into his arms.

My suicidal ideation accelerated to the point that I started making plans to end my life. I had seen patients survive self-inflected gun shots, so I decided I would go to a gun range and learn to shoot with enough precision to ensure a single, fatal shot. The lights had gone out. I had lost hope. In scripture, a psalmist expresses confusion about despair: "Why, my soul, are you downcast? Why so disturbed within me?" (Psalm 42:5). I was likewise perplexed, especially since I was married to the woman of my dreams; the most compassionate, funny, and loving person I have ever known.

I knew on some level my thinking did not make sense, that I was not as worthless as I felt. Still, the self-loathing thoughts resounded with such force that the internal argument for suicide seemed unassailable. In a desperate grab for hope, I acknowledged my despair to Mallory. I could only mutter about some of the feelings, at first, but in loving, attentive conversation she drew out all my worst thoughts and vivid plans. We were at a desperate point, I agreed, and I needed immediate and abrupt change. She wanted me to see a psychiatrist to be prescribed medication, but I adamantly refused, insisting medication had never worked for me. She recommended I consider quitting the residency. I promised I would think and pray about that option. She laid hands on me and prayed a tender and powerful prayer for God's help.

Later, I told my chaplain cohort that my struggles with BDD were becoming overwhelming. I was having persistent suicidal thoughts. "I need help and prayer," I admitted tearfully. They took turns offering moving and compassionate prayers for my plight. My supervisor took me aside privately to make sure I was receiving professional help. I assured him I was and thanked him for his concern. I had just begun scratching the surface of my problems with a therapist at that point, and I was worried that my lack of progress meant nothing was going to fix my broken mind. After the group prayers, though, I felt some relief. Feelings of embarrassment quickly followed.

We made our way back to our respective offices and I asked Trent, "Am I going to regret that? Am I going to wish I wasn't as honest and emotional as I was just now?" He helped reframe my vulnerability as a brave act. I then pivoted in my chair, turned to my computer, and stumbled upon an ESPN article about a baseball player who had survived a suicide attempt. One line resonated as divine confirmation of Trent's message about courage. The player, Drew Robinson, was quoted about how he reframed his understanding of weakness after surviving his suicide attempt. He had since decided that reaching out for help is a strength: "Think about it. Not everyone can do it. So if not everyone can do it, but some people can, that's just like having a strength. So why can't it be a strength? Why can't it be something people are proud of? *Hey, I reached out to someone today, I told him how I felt, and I felt really good.* Why can't that be a strength?"[30] I told Trent what I had just read, and I suddenly felt like I was in that Acts story about Philip and the eunuch. I was the eunuch, feeling shame about my tormented mind, which was linked to shame about my scarred, anomalous body. In the Acts story, the eunuch is reading a passage in the Hebrew Bible that seems to relate to his own physical and social shame, and in that precise moment Philip arrives as an illuminating conversation partner. Trent was my Philip, helping me make personal connections with the article, confirming that there was indeed cause for wonder in the moment. He affirmed enthusiastically, "Yes, of course, that is God's timing that you would find that article now. God loves you." And he nodded as I enumerated all the parallels I found.

Even as a Major League Baseball player, Robinson wrestled with an unshakable sense of self-loathing. Like me, he had hated himself for as long as he could remember. No matter how many therapy sessions he attended, or self-help books he read, he could not muster hope. Like me, he planned to go to a gun range so he could learn to shoot himself. Unlike me, he put that plan in practice and then shot himself on April 17.

Twenty hours later he was confused by his reality: he had not died. He was also shocked by a foreign sensation: He wanted to live. When police responded to his 911 call, they asked him why he had done it. "I hate myself," he explained bluntly. Later I admitted to my wife that I had always found it difficult to imagine I would die of natural causes. The desire to kill myself seemed like something I was keeping at bay for most of my life, but a compulsion to which I would eventually and inevitably succumb. After many physical surgeries, continuing therapy, a strict regimen of anti-depressants, and a consistent commitment to meditation Robinson found a new calling to reach people like me. He explains, "This was a huge sign. A huge, painful sign that I'm supposed to help people get through something that they don't think is winnable."[31] Ironically, Robinson gained the new spiritual vision after losing his right eye when he shot himself.

Improbably, he began playing baseball again. I could not understand how he could do this. My friend lost an eye during a golf accident. Even though my friend had also been an avid tennis player before the accident, afterward he could not even maintain a light rally because of his altered depth perception. I wondered how someone like Robinson could connect on professional fastballs with only one eye. Playing for the Sacramento River Cats, the AAA affiliate of the San Francisco Giants, he did indeed strike out frequently. He also, however, hit some homeruns and made diving catches. I eagerly scoured social media for his latest highlight. Robinson's story added new meaning to my mantra of "Swing Away." As excited as I was about his achievements, I was more interested in his mental health roadmap. His story made me especially determined about the part of his path that I had once so quickly abandoned. I now realized it was essential for me to take medication. To make that commitment I had to face deeply internalized stigma.

In the next chapter, I discuss that journey as a "pilgrimage." The stories I consider of both internal and external pilgrimages in religion and sports build on the foundation laid in this chapter. Like the stories I recounted here, the pilgrimages of a cross-country runner with MS, the therapeutic pilgrimage of a pitcher who had faced childhood abuse, and fan pilgrimages to witness Tim Tebow in action all demonstrate how "[r]elational trust opens up a space for cocreating meanings that make emotional and spiritual sense within the narrative context of personal and communal life."[32] For athletes who deal with anxiety, depression, or any other kind of affective disorder, expectations of perpetual strength and unflappable confidence can keep them isolated in shame. People who not only draw you out of that shame but seem to fill in missing pieces in your own story can seem like godsends. These meetings are especially compelling when they include the kinds of coincidental features and mutual transformations found in the story of Philip and the eunuch. Those abound even more in the next chapter.

Chapter 3

PILGRIMAGE, PROZAC, AND PENTECOSTALS: SYNCHRONICITY ON GOD'S PATH

housands of years before sports pervaded popular culture through cinema, music videos, and television programming, the anonymous writer of the New Testament letter to the Hebrews focused on a controlling theme: Keep running! Don't Quit! In order to motivate a weary and battered community, the writer narrates a host of harrowing stories about forerunners. Those ancestors endured cruel treatment on their journeys. Despite their perseverance and trust in God, they did not reach their destination. Now they cheer wholeheartedly for a new generation. In that enthusiastic role, they comprise a "great cloud of witnesses." Having set the stage for the main point, the writer offers a rousing speech that sounds as likely to take place in a locker room as a church setting.

> Do you see what this means—all these pioneers who blazed the way, all these veterans cheering us on? It means we'd better get on with it. Strip down, start running—and never quit! No extra spiritual fat, no parasitic sins. Keep your eyes on *Jesus*, who both began and finished this race we're in. Study how he did it. Because he never lost sight of where he was headed—that exhilarating finish in and with God—he could put up with anything along the way: Cross, shame, whatever. And now he's *there*, in the place of honor, right alongside God. When you find yourselves flagging in your faith, go over that story again, item by item, that long litany of hostility he plowed through. *That* will shoot adrenaline into your souls![1]

These running passages from Hebrews fit the criteria for what some scholars call religious and athletic "pilgrimages."

In *Religion and Sports in American Culture*, Scholes and Sassower detail the universality of pilgrimage. They write, "In a sense, we are all on a journey or a pilgrimage of sorts. A life consists in experiencing a series of events, both important and mundane, that often seem to be teaching us a lesson, even transforming us in some ways, as we are led to a destination."[2] The scholars place hardship at the heart of pilgrimage and thus clarify, "If a journey does not involve the difficult crossing of certain thresholds along the way, it may merely be a trip, but not a pilgrimage."[3] They identify both "internal" and "external" elements of such arduous crossings.[4] They stress the importance of inward changes as much as the changing landscape of a pilgrimage. From both internal and external perspectives, a pilgrimage entails a degree of "uncertainty." There are no guarantees a pilgrim will have the wherewithal to overcome obstacles on the path—whether those come from inside or out.

In this chapter, I consider various examples of pilgrimages relevant to sports, disability, and global Christianity. I examine that intersection, for instance, in the life of a young woman named Kayla, who took up the sport of cross-country running as a teenager, after she was diagnosed with multiple sclerosis (MS). Her story is relevant not only to pilgrimage, but to globalization, which Anthony Giddens defines as the "intensification of worldwide social relations which link distant localities in such a way that local happenings are shaped by events occurring many miles away and vice versa."[5] Kayla has an enchanted love story that involves U.S. Christian missionary work in Australia. People have not only shared her story across geographic borders, but also between nondisabled people and people with disabilities.

As a teenager, Tim Tebow went on a missionary pilgrimage to the Philippines, where he discovered a young boy with a disability who had been hidden from the visiting North Americans. That interaction not only shaped Tebow's understanding of the purpose of his life in general but also influenced the specific ways he would play sports and use them as a platform. While the reference to a "great cloud of witnesses" in Hebrews refers to people who have died, throughout Tebow's playing career, his foundation paid for many people with disabilities to witness his games.

Tebow began his college career at the University of Florida while I commenced my PhD in religion at the same institution. He ultimately had a profound effect on my faith. By the time I graduated from that program and began teaching at the University of Tennessee, I was also learning life lessons from another athlete, a player who had pitched at the University of Tennessee in his college years. Knuckleball pitcher R.A. Dickey not only stirred my faith, but he also modeled a path for my mental health. His pilgrimage involved a journey from suicidal urges to inner healing and spiritual wholeness. The mix of Spirit and therapy in his account prepared me for life-saving meetings with a woman from Nigeria. When she prescribed me both Fluoxetine (known more popularly by its brand name Prozac) and glossolalia (the technical term for speaking in tongues), she helped dismantle a dangerous separation I had internalized between faith and medicine.

The immediate aftermath of her hybrid concoction also led to jaw-dropping coincidences. Those serendipitous events, in turn, sent me on a pilgrimage back to my native country of Canada and my home province of Nova Scotia. I was searching for information about a Christian healer, who was also a former coal miner and boxer. He died several years ago but he is very much alive in my great cloud of witnesses. He arrived in that orbit through story. The late Tobin Siebers would not be surprised: "For human beings make lives together by sharing their stories with each other. There is no other way of being together for our kind."[6] An ESPN E:60 short documentary called "Catching Kayla" is the kind of story of pilgrimage, faith, disability, and athletic determination that people share far and wide.

At fourteen years of age, Kayla Montgomery was a soccer player in Winston-Salem, North Carolina. After falling on the field, she underwent tests which revealed she had MS. It was eight months after her diagnosis before she regained feeling in her legs. She switched sports and began a high school running career under the tutelage of Mount Tabor's cross-country coach, Patrick Cromwell. Her early results were less than spectacular.[7]

Kayla began as a "mediocre" runner but eventually found her impairment gave her a unique advantage: after an extended period of running, she did not feel leg pain or muscle tightness. If this could be deemed a "benefit," it was offset by an agonizing corollary: While running only on muscle memory, Kayla could not come to a coordinated stop. At the completion of competitive races in high school, she would collapse into Cromwell's arms. Scholes and Sassower place "long-distance running" alongside "mountaineering" and "cycling" as competitions that "are actually pilgrimages in themselves."[8] They explain, "The race is the pilgrimage—a onetime test of commitment, willingness to sacrifice, stamina, and determination. Athletes competing in these races experience both the uncertainty and the dangers that accompany any pilgrimage. . . . "[9] Kayla's flailing, wobbly finishes brought a rush of sensation back to her legs. In those moments, Kayla felt like they were on fire. She would thus plead for immediate assistance to cool off, a jarring ritual for viewers, and one to which the ESPN feature "Catching Kayla" repeatedly returns. An early portion of the piece shows Kayla falling as Cromwell scoops her up. He places her gently off the track, where Kayla pleads for an immediate cool down. The screen fades to a white gleam, over which Kayla's desperate words appear in stark black letters: "my legs . . . my legs . . . where'd they go? Where'd they go?"[10] Scholes and Sassower explain, "Often, a part of the pain that accompanies a pilgrimage involves physical hardship that attends the traversing of vast geographical distances and subjecting oneself to the deprivation of basic needs."[11] In the ESPN video, Cromwell acknowledges the significant deprivation Kayla experiences at the end of her races, observing, "She needs help because she's somewhat helpless there for a few minutes."[12]

The feature closes with the North Carolina State Championships for Outdoor Track, a race that takes a devastating early turn. Kayla falls after the first lap and all looks lost, including her devastated coach. Cromwell's belief rises when Kayla gets back up. She quickly closes the gap. Like the passage from Hebrews, she has both a loud cheering section and must fix her eyes on someone else to complete the race. In the Hebrews passage that someone is Jesus. In Kayla's case, her coach plays that role. On the last stretch, Cromwell screams final rousing instructions: "Drop the hammer!" Kayla throws it into highest gear and at the finish line, she falls familiarly into his arms. In first place.[13]

Disability and Christian Hope

Kayla used the ESPN piece to mix Christian proclamation with MS advocacy. When, for example, she announced on Facebook that an extended thirty-minute version of that feature was going to run on the 4th of July on ESPN News, she punctuated the note with sacred gratitude: "So glad God has given me yet another platform to help raise awareness #msawareness."[14] That overarching purpose sustained her when things did not appear to be working together.

In 2015, while running track for Lipscomb University, an institution connected with a Protestant denomination called the Church of Christ, she put some dispiriting results into cosmic perspective. Returning to Facebook she wrote, "Slower start to my season than I had hoped but God has a plan!"[15] Scholes and Sassower explain that each "self-denying action is a sacrifice itself, but in order for each small sacrifice to be worth it, it must fit into a bigger picture in the life of athlete. If sacrifices, as well as the triumphs that follow, are situated in the wider context of a long-term pilgrimage, the struggles encountered can be more easily justified and surmounted."[16] In the same post in which she wrote about her setbacks, Montgomery reminded readers of the biblical basis for her wider context: "Romans 5:3–4 'We rejoice in our sufferings, knowing that suffering produces endurance, and endurance produces character, and character produces hope.'"[17]

Lipscomb also covered Montgomery's story in a seven-minute video that focuses on the explicit Christian elements only implicit in the ESPN piece. She shared the Lipscomb video on her Facebook page. In the video, Kayla details various thresholds she has crossed in her journey.[18] Scholes explains, "The ritualistic quality of a pilgrimage requires the traveler to pass through different stages, endure trials, and change in the process in order to arrive at the destination."[19] She recounts how the initial diagnosis was a devastating test of her faith. She admits, "I couldn't see why [God] would allow me to go through so much pain and uncertainty, and so much confusion. How could such a loving and good God allow something so horrible to happen?"[20] She was "bitter and alone for years" before she had an emotional and spiritual breakthrough at a Christian youth retreat.[21] Unlike the ESPN documentary, the Lipscomb video centers faith.

Others repurposed the ESPN piece to proclaim a message of faith. Max Lucado, a Christian pastor and writer who has been called "America's Pastor" and "The Best Preacher in America," drew on the ESPN video in a book published during the global pandemic of COVID-19. In *You are Never Alone: Trust in the Miracle of God's Presence and Power*, Lucado writes that Jesus is like Kayla's coach, fulfilling a solemn vow to never let us down, especially at death. Other Christians found the video an instructive and inspirational representation of disability. After an Australian woman with multiple sclerosis saw "Catching Kayla," she decided to share it with a young American man name Tucker, whom she was hosting in her home. Tucker was a strapping, hockey-playing, missionary. The video seemed like a useful bridge between the two since it combined the host's difficult illness and the guest's athletic interests.

Years later, Tucker was playing frisbee on his college campus when a pretty co-ed walked by and stopped him in his tracks. Tucker tried to leverage his leisure activity into an impromptu date. He asked the attractive stranger to play catch, but she was meeting up with friends and declined his invitation. Tucker had more success the second time they met, securing a first date and another after that. One day he was sitting at her side while she scrolled through Instagram. Tucker noticed she had over 300 messages. She clarified to her wide-eyed suitor that she was responding to a bevy of fans from around the world, a pattern of communications that began after "Catching Kayla" first aired on ESPN. Tucker was dumbstruck by a sudden recognition:

he was dating the girl he had watched in the ESPN video while he was on his missionary pilgrimage to Australia. "Oh my gosh! I had been on a couple of dates with her before I realized who she was," he later admitted. Kayla completed a psychology degree at Lipscomb while running on an athletic scholarship. She became Kayla Keen when she took Tucker's surname on their wedding day, June 15, 2019. In Kayla's words, "The journey continues, and God's plan unfolds."[22]

When Tucker watched the video of Kayla on a missionary pilgrimage, he could not have imagined that he would marry her one day. Neither could a fifteen-year-old Tim Tebow conceive of the televised opportunities he would have in the future to share about a boy named Sherwin whom he would meet in the Philippines. In Tebow's words, Sherwin's "feet were on backwards." On that trip, Tebow learned the principal of the local school wanted to keep Sherwin hidden from the visiting U.S. missionaries because the educator shared the prevailing village belief that disability is a curse. In defiance of those attitudes, Tebow lifted Sherwin from the obscurity of a bamboo hut and carried him into the public assembly, confident that "the narrative started to change in their heads."[23]

My own first meeting with Tebow was much less dramatic. When Tebow walked past me and a colleague on a part of campus called the America's Plaza, I had no idea who he was. As a Canadian primarily interested in basketball, I did not know anything about star recruits in U.S. college football. I, accordingly, did not understand why my colleague gave such an enthusiastic greeting to a passing student. She was incredulous about my ignorance. "That's Tim Tebow!" she announced animatedly. The name did not a ring a bell. Eventually, though, Tebow re-enchanted my faith.

In his sophomore season, Tebow won the Heisman award for the best college football player in the country. Then in his junior year, he came up with a succinct means of translating media attention into Christian evangelism. As he states, "I was getting ready to put on eye black before the game and . . . I thought maybe I could use a Sharpie to write a Bible verse on the eye black. . . . The first verse that came to mind was one of my favorites, Philippians 4:13: 'I can do all things through Christ who strengthens me.'"[24] When the Gators reached the 2009 BCS Championship Game against the Oklahoma Sooners, Tebow decided to mix things up. To the initial consternation of his superstitious coach, Tebow switched the verse in his eye-black to John 3:16. Coach Urban Meyer initially protested the idea of changing verses mid-season, but eventually agreed "that's a great one too."[25] The Gators won, Tebow shined, and the viewing public Googled. The next day, while Tebow had lunch with his father and coach, a PR person for the college approached and informed them that during the broadcast over 90 million people Googled John 3:16. [26]

The following year, Tebow's last in college, the Gators failed to make it to another national championship game. Still, Tebow was spectacular in their bowl game. In Chase Heavener's documentary *Tim Tebow: Everything in Between*,[27] viewers are immersed on the field in the celebration that follows the Gator victory. Confetti falls while he and his teammates hoist the Sugar Bowl Trophy. Tebow then runs to the center of the field where he kneels next to a young boy in a wheelchair who is wearing his number 15 jersey.[28] In another portion of the film, Tebow visits an accidental gun-shot victim in the hospital. Tebow prays that God will give the boy "the strength of a warrior." My own prayers were less fervent.

It is no surprise that doctoral study in religion is a mainly cerebral activity. I did not lose my faith during that rigorous process, but my zeal dwindled. Due to the decidedly conceptual focus of my studies, I did not have as many strong feelings about my faith. I slowly adopted a kind of arid rationalism that made me less expectant of God's presence in everyday life. That is, until Tebow completed his storied career at UF and graduated to the professional ranks of the NFL.

When analyzing the upcoming NFL draft, most football analysts believed it would be difficult for Tebow to effectively translate his unique skill set at the professional level. They especially doubted his passing accuracy. Nonetheless, the Denver Broncos selected Tebow in the first round of the 2010 NFL Draft. He had some standout moments in his rookie year, filling in as a backup when the starter was injured, but it was not until the sixth game of the 2011 season that Tebow became a starter. In that game against the Miami Dolphins, he lit a firestorm of national attention. Tebow played horribly for three quarters but began consistently completing passes with less than three minutes remaining. With the Broncos trailing 15–0, he connected on two passing touchdowns and ran in a two-point conversion to tie the score. A field goal in overtime capped a historic comeback that one source called a "Miracle in Miami."[29] Tebow never got on track in his next game against the Lions, and the Broncos lost, but the rest of the season generally followed the pattern of the game in Miami; Tebow would play poorly for three quarters, and then catch fire in the fourth, benefitting from timely and seemingly inexplicable miscues from his opponents.

A colleague and I were enraptured by Tebow's unlikely run of professional success. Although I focused on Christianity in the Americas and he primarily studied Buddhism in Asia, we had common interests in pilgrimage. In the

Latin American context, many Catholics in particular go on pilgrimages, and as Scholes and Sassower point out, "Buddhists, while relying primarily on meditation to achieve enlightenment or nirvana, are instructed by the Buddha to make pilgrimages to several of the important places in the Buddha's life."[30] After Tebow led a game-winning, 95-yard drive against the Jets, my colleague and I celebrated by going on our own pilgrimage. Scholes and Sassower give the example of traveling to Halls of Fame as "sports-related pilgrimages" for fans.[31] They point out, "Artificial light emanates from the edges of bronze busts of the NFL Hall of Famers on display that lends an almost ethereal (holy?) feel to the men depicted in the sculptures."[32] In our case, we were heading to a sculpture in front of the "Lee Chira Family Heisman Plaza."

We left the Gainesville bar where we had watched the game, hopped in our car, and drove over to the Heisman statue of Tebow on campus. There, we paid homage by dropping to one knee. We were replicating a ritual called "Tebowing," which was part of the national craze of "Tebowmania" at the time. This was a jubilant, child-like pilgrimage characterized by genuinely ecstatic emotions. It was also, however, an act filled with irony. We were experiencing the joy of acting *as if* Tebow's comeback were a cause for religious celebration, even though we considered it trivial in the grand scheme of things. According to Kevin Craft of *The Atlantic*, Tebow is an "irony-free individual who seems uninterested in developing an athletic persona based upon rehearsed machismo or wink-wink self-awareness."[33] Nonetheless, Tebow exemplifies a different kind of irony. I am referring to an attitude he has found easiest to adopt when he is conscious of his "great cloud of witnesses." Tebow provided pilgrimages for many of those witnesses.

Inspiration, Disability, and the Ethics of Sports

During the improbable string of six consecutive victories in his second season with the Broncos, Tebow also continued a philanthropic pattern he established through his foundation: covering travel expenses each week for chronically ill and disabled young people deemed "W15H" kids. This moniker was a play on the term "wish" and Tebow's jersey number. He met with W15H kids before and after games. The on-field meetings prior to the game became conspicuous and were not always popular. Tebow later wrote about the criticism,

> I got a lot of flak for spending time with many W15H kids and others pre- and postgame. Some critics said it made me a distraction to the team and even

made me distracted on the field. I disagree. I believe these kids helped keep my spirit in check. Though I performed just as competitively, most times keeping the right perspective allowed me to handle the pressures of winning and losing. Of not feeling like if I didn't score a touchdown, my life would be over.[34]

Hence chronically ill and disabled young people helped Tebow achieve what ethicist Randolph Feezell believes is the "appropriate attitude for the reflective sports participant," which he calls "irony."[35] Feezell explains,

> What I have in mind refers neither to ironic uses of language nor to the irony of unexpected events. Rather, irony refers to 'an attitude of detached awareness of incongruity.' Irony is a way to regard sports participation, including the pursuit of athletic excellence and the desire for victory, *as if* it really matters, while at the same time recognizing that it is relatively trivial in the larger scheme of things.[36]

It would only take a few minutes viewing highlights of Tebow's post-touchdown celebrations to become skeptical that the game ever seemed trivial to him. He flexes and screams to the crowd as if nothing were more important than crossing into the end-zone. Indeed, Tebow was ultra-competitive even as a child. Nonetheless, Feezell argues sporting activities are enriched and enjoyed when players maintain this paradoxical abandonment and detachment. They should, like Tebow, abandon themselves to the contests, treating the activity and its outcomes *as if* they were crucial features of life. But they would also benefit by stepping back as Tebow claimed to do, with a more detached appraisal that a game is indeed "only a game." That commitment was tested on Christmas Eve.

In the last three games of the regular season, Tebow's well of late-game heroics dried up. After a putrid performance against the Buffalo Bills on December 24, 2011, comedian and outspoken atheist Bill Maher wrote a crass tweet to mock the idea God had been helping Tebow win games for the Broncos. In the face of the Bronco loss, Maher sarcastically rued Jesus's holiday trick on Tebow, "Wow Jesus just fucked #Tim Tebow bad! And on Xmas Eve!" But Tebow did the same thing before and after that loss that he had done before and after his victories: he met with a young person specially flown out for the occasion. Days before the game, his foundation announced, "This Christmas Eve, the Tim Tebow Foundation's Wish 15 (W15H) program, in partnership with Dreams Come True of Jacksonville, is bringing holiday joy to a high school junior whose football dreams were ended earlier this year."[37] As the starting quarterback for Woodberry Forrest, a private school in Central Virginia, 6-foot-3, 215-pound junior Jacob Rainey had received several scholarship offers from major Division I schools. But a freak tackle severed one of his arteries, leading to amputation above the knee. Tebow met him before his game against Buffalo and in its disappointing aftermath.

The Rainey family was touched by the authenticity they saw in Tebow after his poor performance. "He walked in and took a big sigh and said, 'Well, that didn't go as planned,'" Jacob Rainey remembers. "Where I'm from, people wonder how sincere and genuine he is. But I think he's the most genuine person I've ever met." Far from being dispirited by Tebow's poor performance, Rainey cited Tebow as inspiration to "keep fighting" for his own football comeback. In the cover image of an online ESPN article entitled "I Believe in Tim Tebow," Tebow is helmet-less, in his Broncos gear with his arm draped around Rainey. Both are smiling widely.[38]

Despite Tebow's uninspiring play in the final three games of the regular season, the Broncos made the playoffs, where they would face the Pittsburgh Steelers. Although banged up with some injuries, the Steelers had the top-ranked defense in the entire NFL. Tebow may have had faith despite the overwhelming odds against him, but the Broncos were hedging their bets. Given Tebow's notorious difficulties completing passes on third down, the Broncos planned for the possibility of inserting backup Brady Quinn for those pivotal plays. Since Quinn had not played in a game the entire season, the strategy was potentially humiliating for Tebow—it would move him from the spotlight to the sidelines. Peterson's paraphrase of Jesus's words in the Gospel of Matthew sounds written for Tebow's situation: "If I make you light-bearers, you don't think I'm going to hide you under a bucket, do you? I'm putting you on a light stand. Now that I've put you there on a hilltop, on a light stand—shine!"[39] Tebow was about to unintentionally proclaim the gospel to his largest audience yet, and in a way he could not have imagined.

Tebow threw several long successful passes throughout the game, and the Broncos scrapped their backup plan. Tebow's most momentous pass came on the first play of overtime when he connected with wide receiver Demaryius Thomas. Thomas took the ball the length of the field for a game-winning, 80-yard touchdown. At that peak moment of Tebowmania, I was prostrate on my friend's living room carpet, with his young daughter clinging to my back in excitement. Meanwhile, my friend stood and screamed an expletive in celebration. Later he called me to ask whether I had heard about the sacred meaning people were attributing to various statistics in the game. When the final touchdown yards were added to Tebow's passing total for the game, the sum was an auspicious figure, evocative of events from three years prior. Just as he had on that other occasion, Tebow learned about the statistical connections from an excited PR person:

> Do you know that it was exactly three years since you wrote 'John 3:16'? [Tebow did not know.] And during this game, you threw for 316 yards. Your yards per completion were 31.6. The time of possession was 31:06. The ratings for the night were 31.6 million. And during the game ninety million people Googled 'John 3:16'?[40]

As improbable as it might seem that a deity would intervene in a game like this, and not in much more serious matters, I found the timing of the statistical pattern compelling. Indeed, when the Broncos lost to the heavily-favored Patriots in the next game, thus ending Tebow's electrifying season, I felt both deflated and hungry. The wild season gave me an appetite for more enchanted sports stories.

In the summer 2012, I was leafing through an issue of *Sport Illustrated* when I noticed an intriguing selection from a recent book called *Wherever I Wind Up: My Quest for Truth, Authenticity and the Perfect Knuckleball*, by R.A. Dickey. I bought it shortly afterward. In July 1983, the summer before fourth grade, Dickey was raped by a female babysitter. She abused him on repeated occasions throughout the summer and into the fall. At the end of September of the same year he was raped again, this time by a teenage boy. Dickey fought back by pushing the pain inward. "I become good at compartmentalizing things, boxing them away into secret places forever."[41] He carried the shame everywhere, but kept it locked away from anyone's view, including his wife. I was never abused, but Dickey's descriptions of self-loathing and shame and his journey to healing and wholeness resonated so deeply I could not put the book down. I was especially struck by the ways his anomalous body seemed at one point to confirm his worthless soul.

In 1996, the Texas Rangers selected Dickey in the first round of the MLB draft. A team doctor noticed something troubling about a picture of Dickey alongside teammates from the USA baseball team. Compared to the others, his arm was bent at an awkward angle. The team ordered an MRI that revealed he was a medical anomaly: Dickey was missing the Ulnar Collateral Ligament (UCL) in his elbow.[42] This ligament is often injured by the repetitive strain of pitching, which leads to a common operation for pitchers called Tommy John surgery. The doctor had never seen or heard of the ligament being absent altogether. Dickey should not have been able to turn a doorknob without a UCL, much less pitch countless innings from the mound. With that information, the Rangers pulled their lucrative contract off the table, and returned with a comparatively measly offer.

Dickey was despondent and disillusioned by his sudden shift in fortune. He also felt exposed on an emotional level. "The whole thing taps into all my old wounds about being different from every other kid, being damaged in a deep way even if the world can't see it. This just confirms it. I am different. I am damaged."[43] Dickey does not have BDD, but I had never read anything up to that point that came closer to describing the mix of physical and internal worthlessness I felt. As I read, I thus felt personally invested in Dickey's search for grace.

Theologian Matthew Fox defines "grace" as "the unconditional love of the universe for us and of the universe's maker for us."[44] He believes this loving grace is abundant and ubiquitous, and that if people act like it is a scarce resource only certain groups and individuals can access, that misunderstanding can be calamitous. He asks, "If we succumb to a theology of the scarcity of grace, are we not condemning ourselves to addictions, especially the addictions of overarchievers?"[45] In hindsight, Dickey recognizes he was an addicted overachiever in desperate need of grace.

He was in Iowa, playing in the minor leagues, when he was struck with an adventurous whim: to swim across the Missouri River. The idea sprung from a root of emotional desperation: a "notion that achieving these audacious feats will somehow make me worthy, make me special, as if I'd taken some magical, esteem-enhancing drug."[46] He was not in the river long before a strong current and sweeping undertow made it clear that this was not courageous; it was foolhardy. He summoned strength for a desperate retreat but began to drown.

> I am underwater and I begin to cry. It's a very odd sensation, weeping in water. I am filled with contrition. I know I'm not getting to the surface again.
>
> It is time to say good-bye and to make amends.
>
> Anne, I am so sorry that I am leaving you and the kids alone. I am so sorry about my stupidity and recklessness, that I'd allow an asinine attempt to prove something—I don't know what—to take me away. I am so, sorry.
>
> God, please forgive me. Forgive all my trespasses and all the ways I've fallen short. Please give me peace. Please, when You take me, make it not so painful.[47]

When his feet hit the bottom, he felt a sudden surge of adrenaline and shot up through "probably eight feet of water."[48] After desperate flailing Dickey made it to the banks where an Australian teammate, who was gathered with others to watch the death-defying stunt, stretched and pulled him ashore.

Dickey was born again. "I jumped in the water thinking I was in charge. I found out He was in charge."[49] The terrifying ordeal led him to reveal to his therapist the full extent of his childhood trauma. The therapist helped him reframe the legacy of that pain as a potential gift of connection with God and other people—especially his family. After toiling for years in the minor leagues, Dickey made it back to the majors. In the same year that Dickey published his book, going public with abuse he had hidden from his closest confidantes his entire life, he earned the Cy Young honors for best pitcher in the National League.[50]

At the University of Tennessee, my wife Mallory and I attended several baseball games, including the one in which they gave out commemorative R.A. Dickey t-shirts. The souvenir has become like a relic for me, which Scholes and Sassower define as "a material object that can be endowed with *religious* significance."[51] Scholes and Sassower clarify that since an athletic jersey "stands little chance in a competition with God, placing excess significance on a sports item could not properly be called idolatry."[52] As strange as it may sound, I feel a connection to God when I wear the shirt. I have continued to wear it over the years when I need a reminder that through faith and therapy Dickey made it out of his mental anguish, and I can too. After all, I have also been tempted to achieve a sense of worthiness rather than to accept the grace that is central to Christianity. Scholes and Sassower explain that people tend "to hang on to material objects when abstract ideas of the divine can be fleeting and doubted as to their truth."[53] Grace becomes most concrete for me when I watch an infant baptism. Seeing a baby doused in a ritual of love and approval—despite not having earned such acceptance through accomplishments—relieves me of my own pressure to achieve worthiness. Martin Luther enjoined believers to remember their baptism, especially when plagued with demonic thoughts. I not only heed Luther's advice, but I also remember Dickey's perilous transformation in the Missouri river. Scholes and Sassower clarify that "even the . . . the water [religious leaders] swam in can also act as relics. . . ."[54]

I moved on from the University of Tennessee to Miami University in Ohio during the same year Dickey was traded from the New York Mets to my favorite team, the Toronto Blue Jays. At that point, Tebow's football career was fizzling out. After his dramatic sophomore year with the Broncos, he was traded to the New York Jets, for whom he only played sparingly. He later signed with the New England Patriots and the Philadelphia Eagles, but in both cases he was cut after pre-season games. Though Tebow was unable to earn a spot on an NFL roster, he provided plenty of inspiration for others to make their own comebacks.

When ESPN followed up with a brief documentary on Rainey, the young man Tebow first met on Christmas Eve 2011, Rainey was attempting to play football again after his amputation. ESPN reframed the inspiration story, titling the feature, "The Kid Who Inspires Tim Tebow." Many E:60 features begin with a roundtable discussion among producers. In this one, Jeremy Schaap made a telling biblical allusion, "There is something about getting to touch the hem of his garment."[55] That is a reference to a biblical story of spiritual exchange. Three of the four New Testament gospels tell the story of a woman who struggled for twelve years with a blood disease. Mark and Luke both mention something omitted in Matthew's telling: that she spent everything she had on medical treatment, but none of it restored her to health. When she hears Jesus is in town, she pushes past crowds, convinced that if she can just "touch the hem of his garment" she will be healed. When she reaches him, Jesus, who does not even see her, perceives an exchange of power. "Someone touched me; for I noticed that power had gone out from me."[56] Tebow continued to have mutually enchanted encounters when, after several failed attempts to make NFL teams, he tried his hand at baseball.

On July 31, 2017, when Tebow was playing in the minor leagues, a young boy showed the same persistence as the woman from the story to grab hold of an esteemed hero. Given that the short journey required emotional risk and uncertainty, it was a pilgrimage of sorts. The young boy's mother claimed it sparked an exchange of power. Nine-year-old Seth Bosch is autistic and has neurofibromatosis, which makes it difficult for him to play sports himself. Nonetheless, when he recognized an opportunity to connect with his favorite minor league baseball player, Tim Tebow, Seth moved with athletic alacrity. Tebow was warming up for his next at-bat when the opposing team commenced a short conference on the mound. With the break in action, Seth hustled down the bleachers behind the mesh separating fans from players. He waved his hand in a summons. Tebow smiled and walked toward Seth to shake his hand through the mesh. The crowd, many of whom had come to see the former NFL quarterback, loudly cheered the exchange. Overwhelmed by the moment, Seth returned to his seat next to his mother, Illeana, and began to sob.

Illeana comforted Seth and assured him Tebow would "hit a homerun now." And late in his at-bat, that is exactly what he did. Illeana was sure all this was more than coincidence. On the cell phone video she took of the unlikely sequence, she explains to someone in the stands that Seth is on the autism spectrum: "[The handshake] made me cry. Then he hit the homerun. That's a spiritual connection right there." In an interview, she is more specific about who she thinks orchestrated the spiritual connection, "When Seth came back to his seat, he was crying. And then Tim hit the homer. I started crying, too. How does that happen? I think God brought Seth and Tim together."[57] That is how I feel about the circumstances that led to me finding my therapist.

As I mentioned in the previous chapter, working as a hospital chaplain during the pandemic was emotionally grueling, and my mental health deteriorated in the process. The suffering I was seeing (and not just related to the pandemic) was so searing that I often felt dizzy with confusion, anger, and anxiety. One morning I woke up at 3:00 a.m. in such a thick cloud of depression that I knew I needed to get help soon. The first result from my Google search for a therapist was not only a former staff psychologist and adjunct professor at TCU, where I had taught, but also someone who had credentials from where I studied. Harry (Hap) F. Klinefelter III has a PhD in Psychology from the University of Florida. Matthew Fox asks, "[A]re not our trips to therapists often a kind of pilgrimage in search of grace? A graced listener, a graced presence, a graced caring, a grace-ful soul, a graceful heart?"[58] I found all these channels of grace in my pilgrimages to Hap's office, but there was still one avenue I refused to explore. In an early therapy session, Hap asked gently whether I had ever considered medication for my BDD symptoms. I told him the same thing I had told my wife: "Medicine does not work for me." My posture changed when I read about the role of medication in Drew Robinson's recovery from suicidal ideation, which I recounted in the previous chapter. I was subsequently committed to finding medication that would work for me. That readiness led me to a divine appointment.

When I first met with Njideka (NJ) Domrufus, I only knew that she was a Psychiatric Mental Health Nurse Practitioner. Although I was not familiar with any of her titles, I was about to find lifechanging common ground. In a second meeting with NJ, I asked her if she followed a religious tradition. She explained that she was Pentecostal. I told her about my mixed background. I then asked if she could share some spiritual advice with me. She squirmed a little in her chair and explained that faith is not something she normally talks about with her patients, but she was open to doing so since I made the request. "You said you are a Pentecostal?" she asked. "Well, my mom is Pentecostal and that is an important part of my formation," I clarified. "But I'm more like Charismatic Catholic, even though I'm not Roman Catholic." She was familiar with Charismatic Catholics in Nigeria, so she felt comfortable with a follow-up question about my prayer life: "Do you speak in tongues?" "Yes," I said. "Okay, speaking in tongues is a way you can strengthen your inner spirit. I would like you to start doing that an hour a day." I had never spoken in tongues for even half of that duration, but I agreed to all her suggestions, which included taking Prozac. Since it is sometimes prescribed for OCD, a cousin of BDD, she thought it might help. I admitted that I seemed to have some internalized stigma about taking medication for mental health. I explained that aversion might have been a product of my Pentecostal formation. I had heard people talk about depression and anxiety in such circles, but I had never heard any Pentecostal mention taking medication for those problems. I had at least subconsciously concluded that this omission signaled a contrast between trusting the Spirit and relying on medicine. NJ looked at me intently, and with a compassionate tone, she proclaimed, "Medicine is God's mercy." A few days later, I read the following Verse of the Day on the Bible app: "Now that we know what we have—Jesus, this great High Priest with ready access to God—let's not let it slip through our fingers. We don't have a priest who is out of touch with our reality. He's been through weakness and testing, experienced it all—all but the sin. So let's walk right up to him and get what he is so ready to give. Take the mercy, accept the help."[59] (Hebrews 4:14–16). When NJ prayed for me, at my request, I felt a weight lifted off me. I left feeling lighter than I had in weeks.

Now it was time to do something I was dreading. Earlier in the pandemic, CNN had published an article about how people with BDD felt some relief about being able to hide their appearance in socially acceptable ways, since masks became the order of the day.[60] By contrast, the pandemic exacerbated my BDD. Many of my new friends and colleagues only new me in a mask. Hence for me, being masked for both work and leisure compounded my sense of external and internal worthlessness. I was terrified of dropping the mask in public—not because of COVID, but because of the intensity of my BDD self-consciousness. But having had the breakthrough in the morning with NJ, I decided to try to take a first step and drop the mask while I worked out. (For context, at that time, the worst of COVID seemed to be over here in Fort Worth, Texas, and by that point I never saw anyone besides me wearing a mask to the gym.) When I got in the car to drive to the gym, one of my CDs was sitting halfway in the CD drive. I pulled it out completely and realized it was *Synchronicity* by The Police. That is a concept that comes from psychologist Carl Jung. Superficially (and in the amateurish way I tend to think about it), "synchronicity" captures the mystery and meaning of coincidence. The concept of coincidence and synchronicity is such a longstanding source of intrigue and encouragement for me that my wife even bought me a shampoo called "Amazing Grace" with this message on the bottle: "grace is like a magnolia petal whirling in the wind, guiding your journey; it's the quiet whisper urging you forward when you're hindered by uncertainty. it's support and inspiration when you need it most. it can disguise itself as coincidence or synchronicity, but no matter what you call it, grace will always light the way forward." So given the coincidence of finding that *Synchronicity* CD right before heading out, while feeling uncertainty about dropping my mask, I thought maybe God would bring me a meaningful coincidence at the gym. I remembered how several years earlier I had met a man in a Canadiens t-shirt when I was heading for the exit in the gym. As I wrote about in an earlier chapter, his birthday was the day after mine. That coincidence had led me to be in the right place at the right time so that I could meet someone else whose family member had been hit by a car in a crosswalk.

I was wearing my mask when I entered the gym, but no one else was in the basketball courts, so I removed the mask and continued to shoot around by myself. It felt a little liberating but mainly scary. I developed enough positive psychological momentum, though, that after shooting for a while, I walked into the crowded weightlifting section without my mask. This time, I felt closer to the liberating end of the spectrum than the scary side.

By the time I left the gym, I felt like I was floating. As I began to walk to my car, a tall handsome man in his late 20s was walking toward the entrance. He was wearing a Blue Jays hat. I stopped, and blurted out, "Bro, you are a Jays fan?!" He smiled, with a look of confusion, and responded, "Yeah." I asked, "Where are you from?" He said, "Nova Scotia." I felt drunk now. "Nova Scotia? I'm from Halifax!" He was from Cape Breton. We both had a kind of stunned daze. I even sputtered something about "synchronicity" and the CD I was listening to on the way to the gym.

He did not know, and I did not tell him, that he was one of the first strangers in months whom I had talked to without my mask, or that I was only an hour into this liberating step of dropping it in public. I am not sure if he peripherally noticed my scars, but his focus was clearly on the moment, not my appearance. And then he asked, "What's your name, man?" I said, "Sean." He shook his head in disbelief. I said, "No way, bro." He laughed and confirmed, "Yeah." He explained that he spells his name "Shaun." We exchanged contact info before I got in the car and blasted *Synchronicity* the entire way home.

When Shaun and I met a second time, I was not sure what I would share or how. Mallory and I met with him at a bar before the gold medal women's soccer match between Canada and Sweden. For Shaun to grasp the height of my joy these days, he would need to know my previous depths of despair. Also, how would I possibly explain about the meeting I had with NJ immediately before we met, especially the part about speaking in tongues? Surely, most people think of speaking in tongues as a decidedly foreign, if not weird, phenomenon, I thought to myself. Disclosing both mental health problems and bizarre religious devotions is not the usual first step in a long-term friendship. When we broached the topic of religion, Shaun mentioned that he was raised Catholic but that he never felt a strong connection to the Mass. His grandfather, though, was not only devout, but also an extremely formational figure in Shaun's life. Casually, Shaun, added, "He even spoke in tongues when he prayed over me." I was flabbergasted. "He spoke in tongues?" I asked in disbelief, sure that I must have misheard him. "Yeah, and he had a healing ministry too. God really moved in that man's life." I had the same intoxicating feeling I experienced during our first coincidental meeting.

I breathlessly recounted these events with both NJ and Hap in our respective therapy sessions. NJ was unsurprisingly thrilled to hear about the positive turns in my life and the way the Spirit seemed to be moving. I was not sure what Hap would make of it. In our early meetings I had always tried to speak in subdued and rational tones when discussing my faith, wanting to assure him that I could maintain a detached and reasonable approach to spirituality. Now, though, I gushed about the Spirit. His reaction made me wish that I had been more forthright at an earlier stage. He and NJ helped me integrate my faith journey with my commitment to Cognitive Behavioral Therapy (CBT) and medication. I felt more whole than I ever had in my life. Hap had me fill out a form in which I ranked my feelings concerning various issues we had addressed in early stages of therapy. When Hap compared the most recent numbers to the earlier ones, he said, "This is a miracle." He gave me the sheet so I would have a tangible reminder of my progress. I drove home from the session with the paper on the passenger seat. A song came on the radio praising God for profound inner change. In "Look What You've Done," Tasha Layton sings,

> Look what You've done, look what You've done in me
> You spoke Your truth into the lies I let my heart believe
> Look at me now, look how You made me new
> The enemy did everything that he could do
> Oh, but look what You've done

I looked down at the paper next to me, which mirrored every lyric of the song.

I also talked to Hap about our church. We were a small community to begin with, but the pandemic dwindled our numbers even further. Some congregants moved. Some had debilitating health crises. I was not sure how to proceed. I talked to Hap about my desire to make a connection with a well-established denomination in the area, perhaps the Evangelical Lutheran Church of America (ELCA), since our small church network encouraged such collaborations. I also explained that I longed for an older spiritual mentor. Mallory and I did not lack ideas, but we needed help with practical advice. It was difficult to grow the church since we were hosting meetings in our home, so we were exploring options for a public space, like a bar.

Hap said it sounded like we were ready to "operationalize" some ideas. "That's perfect," I said. "I needed a word that would help focus some of my scattershot thinking right now." "That just came to me," Hap admitted. "I don't normally use that word. Maybe it was the Holy Spirit."

That evening I watched a PBS documentary about a small organization accused of terrorism. In a talking head, one of the interviewees clarified, "I don't think they were operational." There it was again: operational/operationalize. I determined to put some of my ideas in practice.

The next day, I did a Google map search for Lutheran churches in our area. Various virtual flags appeared on a map of Fort Worth. When I clicked on one of the flags at random, it came up with the website for Kyrie Pub Church. I read a description that matched what Mallory and I wanted to do with The Ark. This was another stunning moment in a serendipitous season. I called the church right away but was informed that the pastor was out of town. The woman I spoke with asked me to send an email with my contact information and the reason for my call. I hoped this would lead to a fruitful connection, but there were a couple of potential obstacles. While our affirming stance on LGBTQ people would be in line with this Lutheran church, I thought the "Charismatic" element of our faith might be a turn-off. Still, I wanted to be upfront and honest about who we are.

Having been forwarded the email, Pastor Phil Heinze called me that night. Although Kyrie had a larger group than The Ark, their numbers had also shrunk during the pandemic. Indeed, just that past Sunday he had been thinking seriously about possibly shutting it down. Then he received my email. Far from being turned off by our Spirit-centered faith, he was intimately familiar with the Charismatic movement. His father, Rudolph W. Heinze had been a professor of history before he and his wife encountered the Charismatic movement. They ministered in England, championing such gifts of the Spirit as healing, speaking in tongues, and prophecy. Like me, Pastor Phil was not sure what the connection between Kyrie and The Ark would ultimately entail, but he believed it was birthed by the Spirit. After our first Sunday visit, I joined the preaching team at Kyrie, where Mallory has also since preached.

The day before my first sermon, I started the morning playing basketball. I played terribly in the initial stages. I shot multiple airballs, which elicited some snickers from the sidelines. Then, a teammate gave me some pointed encouragement. "I am going to pass you the ball in the same spot, and I want you to shoot again. Keep shooting." I had always found it hard to maintain confidence when my shot was off. Nevertheless, I had been listening to a song lately with an athletic message of determination. In "My Champion," Alter Bridge calls for resilience in the face of failure, as they sing,

> Sometimes you fall before you rise
> Sometimes you lose it all to find
> You've gotta keep fighting, and get back up again
> My champion
> Oh, my champion

After my teammate's encouragement, the next time down the floor, I launched a three-pointer from the corner. I made that one and nearly every other shot I took the rest of the morning. Jeers turned to cheers and I left the gym on a high. I was thus prepared for the exhilarating news my wife was about to give me when I arrived home.

Mallory was pregnant again. I was ecstatic. I wanted to tell the world, but of course at this early stage, we were not telling anyone yet. I could not have been in a better mood to put the final touches on the sermon. I planned to illustrate my points with the story about how Shaun and I met. I texted Shaun to ask him his late grandfather's name. I had now come to think of this man I had never met as part of my great cloud of witnesses, and I wanted to ask him to pray for me for the sermon. Shaun texted back, "Earnest 'Champ' Hannigan." I was struck by the coincidence of the nickname given the champion song I had been listening to and thinking about that morning. I was even wearing champion socks, so I texted a picture to Shaun and explained the coincidence. He responded enthusiastically: "Oh man, God works in incredible ways! He lived many lives, and at one point in his young years, he was a professional boxer. The nickname stuck ever since." When I did a Google search, I found "Champ's" obituary. I was astounded by another coincidence. It had been exactly four years to the day since Champ's passing. I was not sure what to do with the coincidence, so I revisited Tebow's story.

Tebow's "316 game" with the Broncos occurred three years to the day after he wore John 3:16 in his eye black in the college championship game. Tebow got years of evangelistic mileage out of that coincidence. In 2017, he appeared on Harry Connick Jr's eponymous talk show. While addressing the unusual confluence of 316 statistics in his football career, he grinned and said like a schoolboy, "Some people say coincidence; I say big God." The fan reaction to the Tebow segment was so enthusiastic that the producers invited him back. He seized the second opportunity to tell the story about meeting Sherwin as a fifteen-year-old on a missionary pilgrimage to the Philippines. I wanted to make sure to find purpose in my coincidence as well.

I thought about Shaun's close relationship with his late grandfather and meditated on the opening lyrics to "My Champion":

May this be your victory song
A song for you when I am gone
Reminding you of what you're meant to be.

I sent Shaun the full lyrics and wondered if he might be able to receive these words as a message from his grandfather on the anniversary of his death. He replied, "Those words really hit home. [They were] things he would often say." With Shaun's permission, I incorporated these latest coincidences into the sermon the next day. Later he sent a link of the sermon to his mother, Maureen, who lives in Cape Breton. She wrote back that it had moved her to tears.

I soon after went on two pilgrimages. First, I drove 30 hours from Fort Worth, Texas to Washington state to visit my sister and her two children. While I was in Washington, Mallory called and tearfully shared that she either had an ectopic pregnancy, in which the fetus develops in the fallopian tubes, or that she had miscarried again. Between the two distressing scenarios, the first was the most worrisome. By the time, I started the return trip to Texas, medical staff were able to confirm that she had miscarried. It was a long drive.

I took the second pilgrimage two weeks later. This time, I flew to Nova Scotia to see my family in Halifax. I also embarked on a pilgrimage within a pilgrimage. I drove four and half hours from Halifax to Cape Breton to visit Shaun's mother and uncle. They showed me Cape Breton hospitality, filling my plate with more delicious food than I could eat, and more fascinating and hilarious stories than I could fully digest. They told me about Champ's prayer life. He would sometimes get impressions from the Holy Spirit. One time he sensed a child in the neighborhood needed urgent prayer. When he knocked on that neighbor's door, the parents confirmed the dire circumstances. Maureen told me how exhilarating it was to listen to her father's side of the conversation when those same parents phoned later to announce that Champ's prayer had worked. Their child was healed. These were not just bygone stories relevant to a yesteryear. Shaun's uncle David told me he was personally not religious, a point he made while liberally interspersing expletives, but that he was nonetheless having visions of his late father. Maureen added that one day she was "praying in the Spirit" (speaking in tongues) very quietly when she had the strongest sensation of holy presence she had ever experienced. She felt like she was going to pass out, or "rest in the Spirit," as she referred to it in Charismatic terms. At that moment, without knowing what Maureen was experiencing, David had a vision. He told her that Champ was sitting next to her with his hand on her leg, saying the rosary. It was surreal for me to close the evening by laying hands on and praying for both Maureen and David. I felt thoroughly bonded to a family in Nova Scotia that I knew because of a brief coincidental meeting at an L.A. Fitness in Fort Worth, Texas.

Nevertheless, connections across far reaches of territory can also produce new expressions of conflict within the same faith. When a medical student named Bennet Omalu traveled from Nigeria to the United States, he expected to arrive at a Promised Land, "the country that was closest to what God wants us to be."[61] Instead, he discovered a nation beset by racism,[62] and one that treats its sports heroes with a vexing mix of adulation and contempt. He found fans idolized football players as gods when they performed well, but that the fan devotion quickly waned when players' bodies broke down. As a neuropathologist and Christian, Omalu considered players who ended their lives—after enduring psychological torment and physical pain—as key people in his great cloud of witnesses. Shaun's Uncle David claims to have realistic visions of his late father, and Omalu similarly believed that deceased players visited him after death in palpable spiritual form. Accordingly, he felt buoyed in his own battles to prove the physical, psychological, and spiritual perils of football. In short, Omalu believed God was calling him to counter the sport because of the ways it was disabling its players. Meanwhile, Tebow believed God had called him to use football to valorize people with disabilities. Hence Tebow and Omalu represent a collision of callings at the globalized intersection of sports, disability, and Christian pilgrimage.

In this chapter, I used the descriptions of pilgrimage that Scholes and Sassower apply to both religion and sports—a difficult, uncertain, and

obstacle-laden journey—to consider various internal and external pilgrimages related to disability. For an autistic person like Seth Bosch, traveling to
and attending a game of his favorite player requires persistence on a journey
that involves a host of potentially overwhelming stimuli. That pilgrimage
becomes even riskier when it includes an attempt to meet the player during
a break in the action. As a parent of a child with a disability, Ileana also experienced pilgrimage with her son. After a religious pilgrimage, some people
share with others about the power of their journey. In this case, it was Ileana
who testified to the connections between Tebow and her son. I also sought a
spiritual connection through physical means when I began wearing a souvenir t-shirt of R.A. Dickey. To me, it symbolized Dickey's therapeutic journey
and my desire to experience similar grace. The shirt was also a reminder of
God guiding my steps, since both Dickey and I were journeymen: I was an
academic on full-time but short-term contracts, just as Dickey's peripatetic
movements included stints for various minor league and major league teams.

   I am a little over three months older than Dickey. Shaun's Uncle David
was also born in the same year as us. Furthermore, we are all white men.
In the next chapter, I consider connections of difference: not only between
disabled and nondisabled people, but between people of different races. By
drawing on Jordan Peele's horror film *Get Out* and Bennet Omalu's memoir
Truth Doesn't Have a Side, I demonstrate the social dangers of inspirational
sports stories for minorities and people with disabilities. While Tebow was
long known for his chaste reputation, he continues to hear charges of "inspiration porn." Those criticisms are also part of the broader context of the
next chapter.

Chapter 4

THE PERILS OF BLACK ATHLETIC SUCCESS: WHAT *GET OUT* GETS RIGHT ABOUT INSPIRATION PORN

As a pilgrim traveler—journeying in common, I believe, with many others of my generation—I have found that a lot depended on the God we were looking for and the gods we were willing to let go.

— MATTHEW FOX —

How can Americans idolize football players, yet seem to care so little about the toll the game takes upon their heroes. It seems like such a contradiction. Yet as I learned after moving to Harlem in June 1995, America is a land of contradictions. I am truly an American, because my time in Harlem revealed the contradictions deep inside of me as well.

— BENNET OMALU —

I think everybody, even white liberals—especially white liberals— appreciate exposing the dark side of what we think is the most politically correct type of white person.

— JORDAN PEELE —

Jordan Peele's horror comedy *Get Out* (2017) plays with the longstanding profit people have made off the black athletic body (in addition to other sources of black entertainment). At one point, the black protagonist seems to find a refuge of understanding with a blind white man. I argue that what Peele decides to do with this relationship reflects an awareness that inspiration porn can not only obscure ableism but also the racism embedded in social structures. Bennet Omalu's critiques of how the brutality of contact sports reveal racial dimensions of the socioeconomic disparities in the U.S.

is one of the important ways in which his story connects to Peele's film. The other is his representation of loving kindness in the medical sphere. Whereas Omalu treats the dead bodies on his slab with respect and spiritual dignity, U.S. medical professionals have not always shown living black people even a modicum of that respect. In the "Tuskegee Study of Untreated Syphilis in the Negro Male," which began in 1932, poor black men were lured into a study for which they were promised financial assistance and food subsidies. What the participants did not receive was clarity. They were never told what they had or what syphilis was. Even when penicillin was discovered as a treatment for syphilis, the antidote was withheld from the study's subjects. The clandestine research lasted forty years until the *New York Times* broke the shameful news.[1] Peele imagines not only cruel, white medical experts sacrificing black bodies for the sake of enlightenment progress, but a surgeon and psychiatrist whose motivations are also fueled by an enchanted cosmology.

A white family, the Armitages, belong to a religious order descended from the Knights Templar.[2] As medical experts in the order, they use black bodies to create genetic perfection and eternal life. Their operations are steeped in clandestine rituals, which they cloak with an attractive facade. The sexy, sophisticated, and funny twenty-something daughter, Rose, lures her black romantic partners and friends from the city to their more rural home. The mother, a psychiatrist, hypnotizes them and buries their consciousnesses in a "sunken place." The neurosurgeon father subsequently oversees transplantations in which the will, mind, and emotions of eager white parasites are grafted onto the now docile black bodies. Essentialist notions of black athleticism are part of the allure for the white captors and transplant recipients. We learn early in the film that the grandfather lost a race to Jesse Owens in a qualifying round of the Berlin Olympics. Later we realize he now lives on through a spry black body that races ominously in the night, obsessively pursuing Owen's record time. In a director's commentary, Peele connects the grandfather's obsession with black bodies to that character's belief in the interplay of race, religion, and sports; namely, the grandfather believes "that black people have more God-given advantages."

The Historical Power and Commodification of the Black Athlete

It may be surprising for some to learn there was a time when white people were thought to be better athletes than black people. Black people, it was thought, lacked the physical stamina to endure the rigors of the ring. When African American Texan Jack Johnson defeated white Canadian Tommy

Burns in a bout held in Australia on December 26, 1908, he dislodged that significant prong of racial ideology. A film of that spectacle (the medium having recently been invented) carried Johnson's counter-message far and wide. When he handled white American James Jeffries with even greater ease than he had done Burns, white society was so threatened by Johnson's exploits that white people began attacking celebrating black people and race riots broke out throughout the country. Sociologist Ben Carrington believes that when Winston Churchill cancelled a bout between Johnson and a white Briton, ostensibly over concerns about the violence of the sport, the politician really feared a Johnson victory could subvert the ideology of white supremacy that sustained, at least in part, the far-flung Empire.[3]

Jesse Owens built on Johnson's social impact through his own spectacular performance in the 1936 Berlin Olympics, sometimes nicknamed in retrospect, "Hitler's Olympics." The African American sprinter and long-jumper triumphed over the "Aryan" competition with a singular achievement of four gold medals. By the time Jackie Robinson broke into integrated baseball in 1945, the old stereotype of black physical inferiority had been inverted on its head. As Carrington notes, "By the 1930s this logic had been significantly challenged, such that by the middle of the twentieth century, blacks were generally viewed as physically *superior* to whites."[4] Douglas Hartmann argues that this sporting success contributed to the growing popularity of the apolitical color-blind ideology, a belief that through talent and hard work people of any race or ethnicity could achieve success in U.S. society. In Hartmann's view, black athletic success produced genuine racial progress. It also, however, came with a significant social cost. Color-blind ideology "suddenly became an obstacle for activists who had achieved numerous formal, legal victories and yet still found themselves up against cultural and institutional inequalities that were both deeper and more persistent than they first imagined."[5] This required a change in athletic activism. No longer could African Americans contest racism simply by excelling in integrated fields of sport. They would now need to speak out. None were more vociferous than the man born Cassius Clay, who became even more famous when he converted to the Nation of Islam (NOI) and became Muhammad Ali.

After he won a gold medal in boxing in the light heavyweight division at the 1960 Olympics in Rome, Cassius Clay thought his achievement would forge new paths of equality. He was surprised to still find formidable roadblocks. He was thus fertile soil for the Nation of Islam's message about "Black pride and independence."[6] Although he disagreed with the most incendiary claims in the movement, even the demonizing language grabbed his attention:

"The Nation of Islam taught that White people were devils. I don't believe that now; in fact, I never really believed that. . . . But when I was young, I had seen and heard so many horrible stories about the White man that this made me stop and listen."[7] He found that Elijah Muhammad, the movement's leader, offered a compelling account of historical theft. White people stole black identity by giving enslaved Africans the names of their masters. They also created religious amnesia by imposing Christianity on Africans who previously had their own robust religious traditions, including Islam. Clay analyzed his own surroundings, with a Baptist mother and Methodist father. His father earned money painting murals of various Christian scenes, and Clay found the white European imagery especially troubling when held up to the light of Elijah Muhammad's critiques.[8]

As his spiritual journey toward the NOI accelerated, Clay also trained for his first heavyweight title bout. Many thought it would take a miracle for Clay to defeat the reigning champ, Sonny Liston. Liston's thick frame made Clay look slight by comparison. The odds were seven to one in Liston's favor. The David and Goliath story is shorter in the Koran than in the Hebrew Bible, but the underdog theme is central to the Koranic version as well, along with the movement from dispiriting doubt to resilient hope. When the underdog doubters complain, "There is no power for us today against Goliath and his soldiers," they are reminded, 'How many a small company has overcome a large company by permission of Allah. . . .'"[9] As he does in the Hebrew Bible, David fells the giant in the Koran. When Malcolm X joined Clay in his Miami training camp, the charismatic spokesman for the NOI roused Clay's spirit with that story.[10] The big-muscled, hard-hitting Liston proved no match for the big-talking, quick-moving Clay, who in victory declared himself an adherent of the NOI. Elijah Muhammad renamed him Muhammad Ali.

Ali soon courted controversy when he was drafted to serve in the Vietnam War and refused to enlist. "No Viet-Cong ever called me a nigger," he defiantly declared. Other prominent black athletes rallied around him, joining Ali in a summit that raised the profile of a growing movement of black athletic activism. Stripped of his title, Ali spent over three years in professional limbo until the Supreme Court decided he could reclaim his boxing career.

The Thrilla in Manilla is an HBO documentary released in 2008 about the famous 1975 fight between Muhammad Ali and Joe Frazier. It revisits the complicated racial dynamics of the period, the brutality of the sport of boxing, and the unforgiving religious interpretations of disability. The documentary suggests progressive whites who cheered Muhammad Ali as a heroic black liberator and bought into the portrayal of his perennial opponent as an "Uncle Tom" chose a simplistic narrative over nuanced reality.[11]

Disability As Punishment and Gift in the Life of Muhammad Ali

The aftermath of Ali's reinstatement in professional boxing included three grueling fights with Frazier, none more physically devastating than that last one in the Philippines. At the time of the *Thrilla*'s release, Ali's image had softened with the slowing speech and lumbering gait he acquired from Parkinson's Disease. Scenes of Ali resiliently trembling while lighting the 1984 Olympic Torch in Los Angeles had long ago cemented his status as a lovable and patriotic U.S. icon. When the HBO documentary revisited Ali's rivalry with Frazier, they instead portrayed a villain.

In the film, various commentators explain and debunk the popular belief at the time that Frazier was an Uncle Tom and Ali was an authentic black man. The stereotypes are difficult to square with reality. It was Frazier, not Ali, who could identify best with the grueling economic struggles of black people throughout U.S. history. Frazier grew up in poverty, picking cotton well into his youth, but "Ali never worked a day in his life." It was Ali, not Frazier, who was sponsored by a group of white millionaires. But many people saw the situation from Ali's point of view, leading schoolmates to bully Frazier's children because of their father's image. In the press, Ali mercilessly berated Frazier, dramatizing his contempt by pummeling a gorilla doll he used as a stand-in for his darker-skinned opponent. Ali proclaimed himself pretty and Frazier ugly. The film makes Ali's colorism look despicable. Ali later regretted how he treated Frazier, admitting all the taunting got out of hand. He was especially regretful about the negative impact the mocking had on Frazier's family.[12] Ali declared Frazier a more than a worthy opponent; he called him "a great warrior, marked with respect and pride."[13] In the documentary, though, a slow-walking, slurred-talking Frazier has not let go of Ali's cruel vitriol.

Frazier beams while alluding to Ali's symptoms of Parkinson's disease, "You see him now, don't you? I did that to him." Although Ali is not interviewed for the film, in another source he dismisses the notion boxing caused his Parkinson's. "I would have had Parkinson's if I had been a baker. There aren't many boxers that have Parkinson's, and there are lots of people who have Parkinson's who've never even seen a boxing match, let alone been in one."[14] Even before their final fight, Frazier warned of divine punishment for

Ali's taunting, "I think God gonna slap the hell out of him one of these days."
Interviewed years later for the documentary, Frazier sees Ali's disabled body
as confirmation for the prediction he made decades before. Ali also considers that God might have chosen to give him the disease but for redemptive
rather than punitive purposes. "I think maybe my Parkinson's is God's way
of reminding me of what is important: for example, how we treat each other.
It slowed me down and caused me to listen rather than talk."[15] Frazier's comments fit at the most negative end of the symbolic paradigm: the idea that
disability is a curse. Ali's words carry the lingering hope on the opposite side
of that ancient spectrum: that disability brings gifts. Ali hoped to pass his to
others. He was intentional about destigmatizing disease by appearing with
his Parkinson's symptoms on full and unabashed display. "By living my life
publicly, I hope to show people who are suffering from illnesses of any kind
that they don't have to hide or be ashamed."[16]

Even if Ali's illness was unrelated to his boxing career, the film demonstrates the unrelenting punishment the sport inflicts on the body. The opening
scenes show people gambling on a cockfight in the Philippines. Ali's longtime
ring physician waxes philosophical about the animal instincts revealed in
boxing. Ali made a similar connection when acknowledging his own mis-
givings while watching others duel in the ring: "These two men are like two
roosters at a cockfight whose owners have strapped knives to their spurs
and had them fight each other to satisfy the crowds who bet on them."[17] Ali
believed his approach was more cerebral and dignified. "I didn't want to be
seriously hurt, and I didn't want to do that to anybody else either."[18] But in
their final fight, Ali inflicted so much damage Frazier could not see out of
one eye by the final rounds. Frazier landed so many powerful blows himself
that Ali later admitted "it was the closest I'd ever come to dying."[19]

That kind of brutality is what leads Bennet Omalu to say that "boxing
cannot be made safe."[20] More controversially, he also does not think that
"football as we play it today can ever be made safe. . . ."[21]

Omalu As Enlightened Enchanter

In 2002, when Bennet Omalu was working at the Alleghany County medical examiner's office, he did not know about the socioeconomic factors surrounding sports. He barely knew anything about American football at all.
He saw the sport on television once as a youth in Nigeria but found it both
incomprehensible and bizarre.[22] He was always fascinated by the United
States, though. Growing up in Nigeria, he envied and admired the foreign
country, imagining it as far superior to his own. He idealized it as a land of

spiritual authenticity and accomplishment. "I believed it to be the country that was closest to what God wants us to be as His sons and daughters, a place where you can be whatever you want, a place where you can be yourself."[23] Omalu felt out of place as a child, even in his own family.

Omalu was small for his age and worried about his short stature. In response, his mother offered a maternal spin on the myth of individual opportunity, "Bene, do not worry that God made you short because if you work hard, you can become anything you wish, even the tallest man in the world in whatever you choose to do."[24] Omalu also had a spiritual awakening to his own beloved uniqueness: "As I sat on my balcony, crying, I felt the Spirit of God speak to me. *Yes, you are different,* I felt the Spirit impress upon me, *but that is okay. You are who I made you to be. You are Bennet Ifeakandu Omalu, and there can never be another.*"[25]

Decades later, while studying medicine in Nigeria, he dealt with various bouts of severe depression, but he continued to pray and hope for a better tomorrow.

When he came to the United States for additional study, he initially found confirmation of the American Dream: "I learned that opportunities for education are more abundant and easier to take advantage of here than in most parts of the world. As a fairly new arrival in the United States, I did not have any money, nor did I have social connections. But I discovered that if I was willing to work hard and apply myself, doors would open."[26]

Omalu, however, was soon stunned to find rampant racial inequality. While doing his residency in Harlem, the myth of individual opportunity began to look transparently fictitious. "I talked with very strong people who had been bruised and battered by a system they felt locked them out of any meaningful opportunity."[27] Still, it took a disillusioned African American man to decisively challenge Omalu's uncritical acceptance of the American Dream. When Omalu tried to encourage him to further his education and opportunities, the man countered, "'If you had been born here in this neighborhood, you never would have become a doctor. From day one, people would have you pegged. You never would have had the chance to become a doctor. Never."[28] Upon reflection, Omalu agreed. "He spoke of a reality, where your slot in society is already set from the day of your birth before you do anything. I know there are exceptions and that opportunities can be found, but the core of what he said to me has not changed."[29] Omalu found "contradictions" not only in the U.S., but in his own lifestyle.

During residency, Omalu worked hard and prayed little. To escape resurgent depression, he frequented clubs, hunting for a multitude of sexual partners. He partied on Saturdays and went to mass on Sundays. He remembers one embarrassing encounter at the altar rail when he received the Eucharist from a woman he had slept with the night before. She offered a flirtatious wink along with the body of Christ. Omalu believed that God subsequently punished him with impotency. He later viewed it as a blessing in disguise. Muhammad Ali surmised that God gave him Parkinson's to "slow him down" and appreciate life,[30] and Omalu believed God imposed a period of impotency on him to restrain his sexual appetites. As Omalu put it in his memoir, "God had done this to me to put an end to my contradictory lifestyle."[31] By contrast, when Omalu learned about a Hall of Fame NFL player who died after years of pain, he did not posit a disciplinary divine hand behind the turmoil. Neither did he think it was self-inflicted. Speaking to the man's unseen spirit, Omalu insisted, "Something did this to you."[32] Omalu believed he encountered the man's death so he could protect the lives of others. He concluded God chose him for a controversial discovery that would elicit a bold religious claim: "God did not intend for human beings to play football."[33] Omalu learned that from the first football player he ever met.

When Mike Webster died at age 50 of a heart attack, Omalu was prepared for a unique case; in fact, he believes he was providentially guided to this case. Omalu did not usually watch television, but he happened to that morning and so heard a newscaster chronicle the late Pittsburgh Steeler's anguished final years. Even in life Webster's body evidenced physical disrepair. In his final season, before he retired at age 38, he "played with three broken ribs, a fractured right heel that never properly mended, and bulging discs in his back that his kids could see when they splashed around in the pool."[34] Nonetheless, it was what the report mentioned about Webster's disordered mind that Omalu found most relatable. "When I heard he suffered from depression, my heart went out to him because I had suffered from it myself."[35]

Omalu intuited a complex set of circumstances, suspecting "that more than heart disease was at play here."[36] Addressing Webster's spiritual presence, which Omalu sensed was with him, he promised medical skill in exchange for mystical help, "I'm going to use all of my skills and all of my knowledge and all of my education to find out what has happened to you, but I cannot do this alone. Come with me. Walk with me. Guide me to the light of the truth."[37] To the annoyance of an impatient assistant, Omalu decided to have the brain preserved` in a process called "fixing," so that he could study it microscopically. When he did so, he found a curious tangle of tau proteins. He unraveled that discovery in a series of papers about football and brain damage that rankled the NFL and its most supportive physicians. Omalu continued to study the brains of other retired players who died, many by suicide, after final periods of pain and confusion. He called the pattern of trauma he found in their brains Chronic Traumatic Encephalopathy (CTE). Whereas Tebow was an American exposing and undermining a religious narrative about disability in another country, Omalu was a Nigerian who happened upon microscopic evidence that challenged the narrative about what he considered a dangerous U.S. religion. Omalu's discovery suggested the very platform Tebow so enthusiastically celebrated was pulverizing players—leading to long-term disabilities and even deaths. This is a compelling case of a "reverse mission."

Reverse Mission

Anthropologist Horace Miner wrote an article in the 1950s defamiliarizing the familiar. He described strange rituals among an unusual people group called "the Nacirema." Nacirema is "American" spelled backward, and Miner used the exoticizing style of academic prose to make common American customs seem like bizarre behavior. It is meant to remind Americans of the power differentials in so many supposedly neutral accounts of foreign people groups outside of the U.S. Omalu did not need such a thought experiment. In his words, he was "like an anthropologist who stumbles upon a ritual ceremony in a clearing in the middle of a rain forest under a starry sky."[38] After watching his first football game in the U.S., he had the feeling he "had just witnessed some sort of an odd religious sect or a cult," and the devotion was unrivaled. "The emotions and passion in the room surpassed those I observed at any ordinary church service." As he learned from a colleague when he was "neck-deep in [his] fight with the National Football League, football truly owns a day of the week—the same day the church used to own. God no longer has any claim to Sundays, at least not in Pittsburgh, between Labor Day and Valentine's Day. Sundays belong to football."[39] Whereas European and American Christian missionaries historically called Africans to abandon their traditional religious practices in total submission to Christianity, here was an African accusing Americans of idolatry.

Scholars have noted a seismic shift in the locus of Christianity from the global North to the global South.[40] The center of the faith was long thought to reside in Western Europe and North America, but the areas of greatest Christian growth are now in Africa, Asia, and Latin America.[41] Not only have these territories had an upsurge in total numbers of Christians, but different streams of faith have converged there. Understanding the present mixture requires exploring divisions in Protestant Christianity.

At the turn of the twentieth century, Modernists (also known as Liberals) reinterpreted Christianity according to new historical and scientific findings like Darwinism. They generally considered miracle accounts as allegory, and they focused less on Jesus's death as an atonement for sins and more on his message of love for the common good. Fundamentalism developed in vigorous opposition to these reinterpretations. A series of books published in 1910 called *The Fundamentals* summarized a non-negotiable core of Christian doctrine. In the broader culture, Fundamentalism lost esteem with a much-publicized court case in the 1930s over the teaching of evolution in public schools. The Scopes Monkey Trial, and the later play (1955) and movie (1960) about those judicial events, stamped the image of the fundamentalist in American popular culture as a bumbling, reactionary anti-intellectual. Fundamentalists increasingly turned their attention inward to the purity of doctrine and morality of its own churches and institutions.

A younger group of disaffected Fundamentalists, however, such as the popular preacher Billy Graham, wanted to engage more directly and persuasively with the broader culture, even while maintaining aspects of fundamentalist doctrine. Graham and others revived the term "evangelical," which had been used in the 18th century for Christians who emphasized a "born-again" experience. Evangelicals, according to a famous definition offered by historian David Bebbington, have historically stressed a quadrilateral of beliefs and practices: "conversionism, the belief that lives need to be changed; activism, the expression of the gospel in effort; biblicism, a particular regard for the Bible; and what may be called crucicentrism, a stress on the sacrifice of Christ on the cross."[42] Graham used sports for his preaching in packed stadiums around the world. Star athletes took the stages of his international campaigns and displayed the vitality of born-again life through testimonials and athletic performances.

By the second decade of the second millennium the combination of evangelical Christianity and sports was most often associated with one iconic figure, Tim Tebow. He fits in all four corners of the Bebbington quadrilateral of evangelicalism: He believes the Bible is the ultimate authority in all matters of faith and morals, and he stresses the atoning work of Christ on the cross as a payment for the sins of humanity. He also believes that people must have a personal experience of salvation, as evidenced by his multiple retellings of his childhood conversion story. And, finally, he agrees the gospel should be expressed in effort. In Tebow's case, this involves testifying to his faith and carrying out charitable acts for the poor, sick, and disabled, both abroad, in places like the Philippines, and at home in the United States. To understand

Omalu's relationship to faith and football, we need to revisit a bridge movement between evangelical Protestantism and Roman Catholicism. That starts with a son of formerly enslaved parents.

William J. Seymour was born into poverty in Centerville, Louisiana, and later moved peripatetically. While ministering in Cincinnati, Ohio, he developed smallpox, which left him facially scarred and blind in one eye. He traveled to Houston, where he met a man named Charles Fox Parham who was preaching about an empowering experience a person could have after the initial evangelical stage of being "born again." Upon an invitation to preach in Los Angeles in 1906, Seymour adapted Parham's teaching about the "Baptism of the Holy Spirit" to fit his own style. In an abandoned warehouse on Azusa Street, a multiracial, transnational cohort flocked to the site to hear him preach; many in attendance claimed to receive "gifts of the Holy Spirit," like speaking in tongues, healing, prophecy, and other spectacular phenomena. The movement splintered in different directions, giving birth to various "Pentecostal" denominations and influencing similar movements in far-flung regions of the world.

In the 1960s, professors and students at various U.S. Catholic universities became intrigued by the Pentecostal phenomena and soon Catholic priests and laypeople were doing things once mainly associated with Pentecostal churches. The Catholic interest sparked wider ecumenical enthusiasm, starting with Episcopalians and spreading to other non-Pentecostal Protestant denominations. Charismatic Christianity has thus blurred some theological boundaries, especially in places like Africa. Philip Jenkins claims, for example, "If you talk to a Nigerian Anglican and you try to pin him down, saying, 'I cannot figure you out, are you evangelical, are you Catholic, are you charismatic?' The immediate answer is yes. And they mean it."[43] The Charismatic Renewal has also influenced the Catholic Church in Nigeria, where "by the late 1980s born-again neo-Pentecostalism was widespread in [the southern region] and the notion of charisms or spiritual gifts was intriguing to many Protestants and Catholics, with numbers of adherents skyrocketing during the 1990s and the movement highly mediatized by the 2000s."[44] The impact of this Charismatic milieux is evident in *Truth Doesn't Have a Side*, Omalu's most recent memoir.

In the North American context, outside of Charismatic circles, the mysteries of the Holy Spirit are sometimes considered so opaque, the third person of the Trinity is barely mentioned. In Omalu's book, by contrast, "Spirit" or "spirit" appears thirty-three times. In one of those instances, he recounts a family prayer he had in Nigeria before leaving to study in the

United States. His evangelical sister's prayers for her Catholic brother were mediated through the ritual of laying on hands, a practice often associated with Charismatic Christianity.

> Right before I left for the airport, my two sisters, Winny and Uche, along with my brother Ikem, gathered in Winny's living room. A couple of years earlier, Winny and Ikem had become evangelical Christians. We worshipped together in their living room, singing songs of praise. They also read Scripture passages over me and laid their hands on me, asking God to cover with the blood of Jesus as I went out on this new adventure. . . . When I rushed out the front door, I felt the presence of the Holy Spirit.[45]

A Nigerian Interruption of the American Sports Dream

In the 2015 Hollywood film that dramatizes portions of Omalu's journey, Will Smith captures Omalu's warm attentiveness to both the Spirit and spirits. By contrast, the NFL appears like a cold and uncaring bureaucratic institution. The film's screenwriter Peter Landesman acknowledges, "If there is a villain in the movie, it's the corporation, the National Football League."[46] People at various levels of the corporate hierarchy dutifully and unquestioningly meet their specific job demands in service of an overarching goal—the wealth of the NFL brand. This streamlined efficiency leaves no room for compassion or compensation for its disposed commodities, those retired players whose brains are now furiously rebelling from all the hits to the head that helped make the league so well-heeled. The absence of concern and help literally drains their life, as one after another dies in despair. Their hero arrives not from the cold currents of Enlightenment progress, but through the re-enchanting channels of globalization.

Christianity and Globalization

Proponents of globalization theory recognize that people have been borrowing, trading and moving across boundaries since time immemorial. Nevertheless, "Despite extensive trading networks, translocal integration was weak with limited impact over the lives of the vast majority of inhabitants in the heterogeneous cultures and societies subsumed by early world empires."[47] What makes contemporary modes of mobility and exchange distinct, according to such theorists, is the pace and intensity with which these processes now take place.

Nederveen Pieterse "argues for viewing globalization as a process of hybridization that gives rise to a global mélange."[48] In the film, the Nigerian-born coroner, reenchants this "rusty" world, suturing the land of the dead and the living with a globalized medical kit of jazz, Catholicism, and spirit-centered faith. He sticks out. His instincts run counter to the dehumanizing hyper-rational treatment of life and death in a corporatized world. Omalu lavishes care on his patients using clean instruments for each one. He protects their individuality, acknowledging their unique imprint as the image of God. Regarding the set for the autopsy scenes, screenwriters Peter Landesman explains, "It was a very church-like place we built. I asked for these windows over the slab to feel like a church, like a cathedral because it was Bennet's church, it was his place of spirituality, it was where he brought God together with death. I wanted the light to be breaking and quiet, as it would be in a church."[49]

In *Truth*, Omalu confirms that when he performed autopsies, he felt like he was "treading on holy ground."[50] Both book and film also confirm that Omalu plays music as he works, which seems to keep his movements slow and his focus steady. For Omalu, the morgue is literally enchanted with spirits of the dead. His awareness of this realm creates clashes with people more conscious of material concerns. In the film, when Omalu orders, "Fix the brain!" he is rebuked on financial grounds, "You know we don't have the budget." There is cruel irony here: the NFL rakes in billions on the backs of disposable players, whose postmortem testimony to the violence they endured is silenced because of a restricted budget. Omalu shines an intimate light that also exposes the limitations of proximity. Fans may feel near all the action through close seats in person, or via amplified sounds and High-Definition visuals on screen, but they do not see what he sees. Omalu has a literally microscopic view of the effect of that pounding, and it is devastating.

In the opening scenes of the film, Landesman sought to capture the religious feelings he had in his youth while watching mammoth players who seemed indestructible. An image of Webster in his playing days looks "just like a Greek god that would come out on Sundays and just mythologically lift us up. We'd cheer. They'd be impenetrable, these guys. They'd be omnipotent, so what would happen to these guys would be almost impossible to believe."[51] Omalu found this religious aura surrounding football kept people from giving his findings a fair hearing. In the world of the film, the NFL's reach is extensive and ominous.

Omalu was a protégé of famed pathologist Cyril Wecht, and in *Concussion* the FBI pressures Omalu by going after Wecht with corruption charges. Landesman explains,

This scene is supposed to suggest the long arm, the long reach of the NFL and corporate interests and not necessarily directly with the FBI but through the cultural field office of the FBI, these are still Pittsburgh men who live here and work here. The idea that culture and religion, government, sports, economic interests, corporate interests, all combine into one force, one force-field against one individual, one David versus all of that Goliath, just try to tell the truth. David vs. Goliath, whistleblower tales, are very much a part of the American fabric and the American culture; the notion of telling the truth, the desire to tell the truth, the need to tell the truth is such an American moment.[52]

In his memoir, Omalu also found the David and Goliath story suitable for expressing the daunting challenges he faced as "the little man from a faraway land who dared threaten the giant's greatest love."[53] In the film, Omalu's insistence on telling the truth destroys his American dream. Most tragically, his wife miscarries from the relentless pressure. They also must leave behind their dream home. In an earlier scene, that spacious abode looked like the realization of what Landesman calls a "Horatio Alger tale of rags to riches, of a man with his own hands making good on the back of his work and his honesty."[54] But Omalu's honesty now cost him dearly, giving the lie to the myth of individual opportunity. While the cinematic catalysts were exaggerated, the family did lose their dream home and his wife, Prema, had a very real and painful miscarriage. All this took place while Omalu struggled to defend the research he believed God had guided him to author.

In his book, Omalu ties his critique of the violence of football to the economic disparities of race. He realizes his revulsion with the on-field collisions of the sport might make him sound weak. "Yet strength does not mean watching young men, primarily young black men, inflict possible lifetime mental and psychological problems upon themselves for the sake of the entertainment of the thousands in the stands and the millions watching on television."[55] He extends the connections between race and disability to religion and the American Dream when he discusses the suicide of former NFL player Andre Waters. "For his mother, Andre's making it to the NFL was an answer to prayer. A descendent of slaves, the entire family saw Andre's achievement as an opportunity to rewrite their family's history and grab hold of the American Dream."[56] Omalu calls the promise of making it to the NFL to achieve the American Dream one of the "greatest fallacies of professional football." He stresses the short span of the average NFL career, and details the assorted deductions that cut the seemingly exorbitant salaries down to a less impressive size.[57] Omalu felt personally connected to players with CTE because of his own struggles with depression. He was keenly aware that money is not sufficient compensation for a player or his family when that athlete's thinking is so distorted that they cannot enjoy what they have.

Omalu criticized the myth of the football version of the American Dream for poor black men, but *Slate* columnist Daniel Engber complained Omalu (especially the movie version) was himself contributing to deceptive myths—"pervasive national myths about head trauma." Engber thought *Concussion* failed to acknowledge the inchoate stage of the science on brain injuries and football.[58] In his view, that modest voice was drowned out by Omalu's grandiose spiritual claims. "When Omalu's character says, at one point in the film, that 'God did not intend for us to play football' and later warns that as long as we do, 'men will continue to die,' he's appealing not to fact-based objective truth but to an alternate reality—an emotional, spiritual one—that has come to dominate the enlightened person's understanding of the NFL."

Engber wanted to tone down the outrage with a more sober consideration of facts.

> Here's a more sedate and honest formulation: Omalu really did discover an unusual pathology in the brains of former NFL players, and the NFL's corrupt administration really did attempt to discredit his research and then for half a decade ignored this important line of inquiry (only caving under congressional scrutiny). But these facts have been spun out, in this film and elsewhere, into a melodrama wherein Omalu's deadly brain pathology drives football players crazy and destroys their minds. Eventually it leads to suicide.[59]

Engber's pointed criticism of *Concussion*—and, by extension, Omalu's contribution to a supposedly misleading narrative—was tame compared to an article published on January 22, 2020, in the *Washington Journal*.[60] In that piece, national sports reporter Will Hobson did not downplay the severe effects of head injuries in football, nor Omalu's pivotal role in bringing the concussion crisis to national prominence: "A Nigerian American pathologist portrayed by Will Smith in the 2015 film, 'Concussion,' Omalu is partly responsible for the most important sports story of the 21st century." Nevertheless, with ample quotes from leading experts on CTE, Hobson calls into question both Omalu's competency and, arguably, his integrity. He notes that in contrast to Omalu's continually strident claims, "Among CTE experts, many important aspects of the disease—from what symptoms it causes, to how prevalent or rare it is—remain the subject of research and debate." The thesis is as scathing as it is startling.

But across the brain science community, there is wide consensus on one thing: Omalu, the man considered by many the public face of CTE research, routinely exaggerates his accomplishments and dramatically overstates the known risks of CTE and contact sports, fueling misconceptions about the disease, according to interviews with more than 50 experts in neurodegenerative disease and brain injuries, and a review of more than 100 papers from peer-reviewed medical journals.[61]

There are similarly critical articles of Tebow's relationship to disability. In the previous chapter, I mentioned that Tebow talked about "changing the narrative" of disability in a village in the Philippines. In a *Vice* article, Ariel Henley suggests Tebow is exacerbating a pernicious narrative about disability in the U.S. She points particularly to the Night to Shine proms his foundation organizes.[62] Like Hobson in his Omalu article, Henley draws on various experts to bolster the case.

In a statement released by Link20—a Ruderman Family Foundation initiative that brings disabled and nondisabled activists together—the group objected to the segregated nature of the event. "We encourage you to create a night where teenagers are celebrated and loved regardless of their differences. An inclusive prom where teenagers with disabilities are dancing alongside those without disabilities is the kind of event that can change individual lives and make an impact on our society as a whole," the statement read.[63]

John Altmann, a Disability Studies scholar who lives with cerebral palsy in New Hampshire, compares the Night to Shine events with media images that ostensibly celebrate people with disabilities but are designed for the inspirational gratification of able-bodied people. In his view, The Night to Shine proms magnify that pattern: "It's large-scale inspiration porn that able-bodied people consume so they can feel like they're good people."

Alaina Leary, a disabled editor and writer in Boston living with autism and Ehlers-Danlos syndrome, expresses similar concerns. "I'm also really wary of the media coverage of events like Night to Shine—it's set up in a way where readers and viewers are supposed to feel some combination of inspiration and pity because disabled people are able to participate in something that non-disabled people take for granted, like attending a prom," she says.

Disability and Spiritual Compensation

David Mikkelson believes that both an essentialist belief about the inherent purity of people with disabilities and a hope that the world is fair help explain the popularity of inspiration porn. He proposes, "We find comfort in the notion that the disadvantaged are blessed in other ways by a benevolent God who works in mysterious fashion to keep all things in balance, hence our desire to believe deficiencies in intelligence are compensated for by unfailingly sweet natures and a way of looking at the world in childlike wonder."[64]

Early in Ali's career he was considered a vocal patron saint of black athletic activism, but when he developed Parkinson's disease, he was treated as a quiet paragon of disabled and religious inspiration. One man experienced him as a muse for his spiritual growth and incidental profit. After Ali's death on June 3, 2016, renowned writer Davis Miller eulogized him in a television interview: "He changed my life. He made me a writer when I'd been a video store clerk. He saved my life as a kid when my mom died unexpectedly and I was depressed, and I saw him for the first time and started living vicariously through him."[65] Miller had offered similarly exultant testimony when he wrote his first article about Ali while in a financial panic. "Time with Ali is loaded—everything feels weighty, important. He's sort of a walking metaphor. Or maybe he's more like a haiku, a vessel of momentary enlightenment. Visiting with Ali is like church is supposed to be."[66] Carrington argues that the "recuperation" of Ali as an "American hero within the United States" required a "profound act of historical amnesia."[67] While a disabled black body can provide spiritual uplift for white people, more often black athletic bodies have symbolized power and strength in popular culture.

Eventually, the thorough commodification of the black athletic body in popular culture drained the symbolism of its erstwhile progressive power. "The black athletic body is repeatedly used by contemporary advertisers to signify power and strength, the crouched black sprinter becoming a standard trope for 'performance,' thus allowing those who 'buy into' the products a form of mastery and control over the black body itself."[68] As Carrington points out, some black artists critiqued this trend. Michael Ray Charles, for instance, depicted black athletes chasing fame and ignoring social ills as duped and blind. Charles's "'After Black (To See or Not to See)' plays with the ambiguous imagery of the blindfolded black subject, literally unable to see due to the dollar-sign-printed blindfold."[69] And there are horrifying undertones. "The position of the 'basketball player' is . . . caught in mid-air, underneath the hanging tree branches metonymically invoking the space of other types of 'hangings' that the literally darker companion piece 'Before Black' more directly plays on and off."[70] Charles's "After Black" came out in 1997, and twenty years later a film was released with similar themes and message.

Charles made his black sporting caricature blind via a "dollar-sign-printed blindfold," but Peele created a white blind villain to oppose his black sighted hero. The blind white man seeks to acquire the black protagonist's vision.

Chris, a black man, is a photographer and the blind white man an art dealer; his envy of Chris's sight thus exists on both a basic sensory level and a loftier aesthetic plane. The blind white man wants to see the world through black eyes. Chris's attempts to escape the dastardly procedure make for the bloodiest and most horrifying scenes of the film.

Peele was concerned about a symbolic blindness, the "denial of the reality of the African-American experience and the horrors attached to it."[71] He was especially worried about the illusory effect of electing a black person to the highest political office in the United States. "Obama was elected and all of a sudden we weren't addressing race or there was this feeling like, if we stop talking about it, it will go away."[72] That he wrote the film while Obama was still president means the absurdist comedic elements are not meant as a sendup of self-declared bigots but rather of self-congratulating liberals. I thus examine another relevant instance in popular culture when a person used the inspiration of disability to mask the persistence of white supremacy.

The Peanut Butter Falcon and Inspirational Distraction

The Peanut Butter Falcon is relevant to this chapter simply because it includes sports entertainment, Down syndrome, blindness, and Christian faith. It is even more pertinent since actor Shia LaBeouf found religious inspiration in his co-star with Down Syndrome after a well-documented, drunken, and racially charged screed. I begin with the film's plot and content.

The Peanut Butter Falcon is about a man with Down syndrome named Zak (Zack Gottsagen) who is obsessed with professional wrestling.[73] He is especially fascinated by a wrestler who goes by the name "Salt Water Redneck" (Thomas Haden Church). Zak obsessively watches his videos and mimics his moves. Zak lives in a care facility with people of varying ages and impairments and his elderly roommate helps Zak escape so he can pursue his dream of professional wrestling. Zak hides in a boat of a fisherman who is on the run. LaBeouf plays Tyler, the unlicensed fisherman who has run afoul of some local crabbers and burned $12,000 worth of their equipment. Tyler does not realize Zak is sleeping in his boat and is furious when he discovers him. He cannot afford tag-alongs, but after leaving Zak on shore, Tyler sees some boys bully him. He agrees to take Zak to the wrestling school of the Salt Water Redneck. Tyler is heading to Florida and this adventure will not be far off his route. They hit a detour when they nearly collide with another boat and find themselves without a means of transportation.

Tyler is a resourceful thief and Zak is a willing protégé, but when they think they have found another boat to take, the owner emerges with his pistol drawn. "Blind Jasper" cannot see, but he can shoot. When the black man asks them their race, and neither answers, he fires in their direction, narrowly missing Tyler. Zak yells, "White!" By the time Jasper asks if they are "Godfearin,'" Tyler has learned his lesson. "Yep," he answers immediately. Jasper is pleased to hear this.

In the next scene Jasper prepares the men for baptism in the river. In a pre-baptismal sermon, he distinguishes between sheep and wolves and assures Tyler and Zach that they are "sheep who have strayed from His flock." He warns them that "a wolf might hunt ya down, just by smelling your past sins." A gospel song about Jesus washing sins in his blood accompanies the images of Jasper baptizing Zak. Jasper offers them various materials to build a raft and get back on their journey. He sends them off with a closing benediction, "Today is the first day of the rest of your life. Nothing can touch you now under the grace of the Lord. Accept his blessings. Let all the wolves of your past be laid to rest." Some might have argued that was what the troubled LaBeouf needed to hear in real life, but he was not listening to it. In the scene, his character politely declines the baptismal invitation, explaining, "I'm more a baptism by fire kind of guy." Offscreen, he had faced more than his fair share of those.

As a child, LaBeouf heard a man raping his mother and then overheard her description of the rapist in a counseling session. It led to PTSD. Childhood and adolescent acting success did not relieve the stress. In his twenties, LaBeouf gained a reputation for being irascible and unstable. He was also, by his own admission, "a drunk." He was in one of those stupors when he was arrested in Savannah, Georgia, at 4:00 a.m. on a Saturday. *Esquire's* Eric Sullivan reviewed tapes of the ugly tirade that ensued.

> In one, he brags about his "millionaire lawyers." In another, he belittles a black officer for being "stuck in a police force that doesn't give a fuck 'bout you. So you want to arrest, what, white people who give a fuck?" He suggests that a white officer's wife watches porn involving "licking a black dick," continuing with "Don't you feel like, 'Fuck, man, I ain't got all the goods?'" One can lose track of the number of times he calls various officers "bitch" and "whore."[74]

LaBeouf is not explicitly racist with the black officer, but he fits the condescending liberal image Peele parodies in *Get Out*. He acts like a self-congratulating woke white man who thinks he can arouse the consciousness of a black Uncle Tom in blue.

The other part of LeBeouf's rant fits longstanding fear and fascination about pairings of black men and white women. Carrington explores the contemporary legacy of colonial anxiety. "Black men with white women becomes *the* taboo sexual pairing that has invoked the deepest fears of white, male voyeuristic mastery and scopic control by the desire to watch and to see, turning both the black male body and white female form into sexualized objects."[75] Hence the worst insult LaBeouf can devise for a white officer is a cuckolded scenario, in which a black man supplies the "goods" the white man has only in short supply. That kind of thinking can be fodder for insult, but it has also represented threat. White male anxiety of black men spoiling the purity of white women has motivated racist violence in both historic and more recent circumstances. David Rosen explains, "Although the wave of rabid racism may be considered to have abated somewhat in the late twenties, it is incontestable that the nation was still affected by the same racial preoccupations. In March of 1931 the infamous Scottsboro Boys case began, in which nine black youths were accused of raping two white girls."[76]

The internet provided new access and virtual recycling for these preoccupations. One such cyber reader went into the historic Mother Immanuel AME church in Charleston, South Carolina. When he entered the building, participants in that Wednesday night Bible study invited him to join them. He sat with them for nearly an hour before rising and shooting. Every shooting victim, including the nine who died, were black. At one point, one of the church members pleaded with Dylan Roof not to kill them. Roof explained he had no choice, "Y'all are raping our women." That was June 17, 2015. LaBeouf's rant took place on July 8, 2017.

To juxtapose those dates would create false equivalency if the point were to suggest similar scale of malice. That is, of course, not the goal. I have placed them in proximity to highlight Peele's point that the unmistakable evil of the first kind of atrocity exists within the same historical orbit as the second kind of drunken revelation. Peele refuses to create a foil for violent white racism. The blind white villain and the sighted black hero do not unite in an inspiring multiracial revolt. *Get Out* is not interested in setting up duels of good whites versus bad whites anymore than it is in reviving the more obviously racist trope of the good black versus the bad black. The film requires deeper focus than that. In LaBeouf's case, disability did offer at least a moment's distraction from the complexities of his racial tirade.

At the time, LaBeouf was in Georgia to shoot *The Peanut Butter Falcon*, and while others on set were reticent to address his public disgrace, Gottsagen was not. Directors Tyler Nilson and Michael Schwartz wrote the movie after meeting Gottsagen at a camp for actors with "special needs," and Gottsagen refused to allow LaBeouf to derail his personal project. "You're already famous. This is *my* chance. And you're ruining it," he insisted to LaBeouf. LaBeouf was converted. "To hear him say that he was disappointed in me probably changed the course of my life," he says.

> "We were getting ready to do a scene and Zack said, 'Do you believe in God?' And I thought, *No fuckin' way are you about to explain God to me, Zack.*" LaBeouf tries to keep it together. His voice jumps an octave. "Zack said, 'Even if He's not real, what does it hurt?'" He turns his face away. He takes a breath and continues.
>
> "I don't believe in God . . . But did I see God? Did I hear God? Through Zack, yeah. He met me with love, and at the time, love was truth, and he didn't pull punches. And I'm grateful, not even on some cheeseball shit trying to sell a movie. In real life. That motherfucker is magical." LaBeouf's posture is all right angles, as if the memory alone has straightened him. "Zack allowed me to be open to help when it came."[77]

Gottsagen convinced him to clean up his act. Their spiritual bond is reflected in the film and its surprising box office success.

Could the inspiration LaBeouf found in a co-star with Down syndrome be a good thing? Could it provide the kind of "external experience that upon being internalized leads to behavior change"?[78] This is how Cottingham, et. al summarize "inspiration," a decidedly positive experience that can create "increased creativity." They draw on Avramenko's research to make a claim germane to the inspiration Omalu drew from deceased football players, and which Tebow found in a boy with a disability in the Philippines: "Inspiration seems to be a cross-cultural phenomenon and occurs in various settings."[79] Cottingham et. al point out, "research suggests that those who are inspired can only be inspired by those with whom they identify."[80] I wonder whether Bennet Omalu would find the same inspiration in a retired Hall of Fame football player whom I admire. Like Omalu, and unlike me, Brian Dawkins is black. Like both of us, Dawkins practices a Spirit-centered faith. All three of us also all share a common history of mental health problems. Dawkins says, for instance, that faith and psychiatric care saved him from suicide in early stages of his career.[81]

Omalu might find it puzzling to learn that during his playing career, Dawkins's spoke in tongues on the field in preparation for games. He would probably be more appalled than intrigued to find out that Dawkins was calling for the Spirit to fuel his aggressive tackles on defense. In addition to Pentecostal practices, Dawkins also used pre-game rituals to transform into a character from popular culture called Weapon X/Wolverine. Grantland's Chris Ryan observed, "I know now that part of the 'transformation' Dawkins made himself go through—to go from mild-mannered, deeply religious Brian Dawkins to speaking-in-tongues, berserker 'Weapon X'—was probably necessary for him to play the game the way he did. He was basically a human ICBM. God knows how many head injuries he doled out or accrued himself."[82] In the next chapter, I examine a unique cinematic depiction of the character Wolverine, one which shows the physical, psychological, and spiritual cost of violent interactions. I compare that character to other fictional and real-life athletes who have been called "superheroes." I analyze their fragility and failures to demonstrate that while inspiration may be exhausting in some contexts, it has not yet been exhausted as a dynamic and context-dependent subject.

Chapter 5

UNMASKING AND HEALING SUPERHEROES: FROM A PUNT BLOCKER TO "THE BLADE RUNNER"

> We like clear heroes and clear villains. We like things black and white.
> We like to simplify and categorize people into good guys and bad guys.
> That's why we like stories. That's also why we like court cases.
> Because it's clear. It's the good against the evil. It's justice. That helps us
> to make sense of this crazy world around us.
>
> —THE LIFE AND TRIALS OF OSCAR PISTORIUS—

I am sitting in a movie theater thinking about the red track running down my forehead to the tip of my nose. I am so self-conscious about my scars they seem luminous in these dark confines. The trailer for a new James Bond movie shows a villain with ample facial scarring. The feature presentation that follows includes a pivotal transition when a character moves from the dark to the good side of "the force"—losing his facial scars in the process. Since most people in real life look comparatively pristine, my scarified kind stand out on film. I do not find solace in their company. Others also balk at such imagery: "The film industry has such power to influence the public with its representation of diversity, and yet films use scars and looking different as a shorthand for villainy far too often."[1] In this chapter, I study heroes with evident limitations and imperfections, which include the scars normally reserved for the bad guys.

There are two decorated athletes in this chapter. Steve Gleason is a former NFL football player with ALS. He is also a disability advocate who was awarded the Congressional Gold Medal—"the highest honor Congress gives civilians"—on January 15, 2020. The second athlete, Oscar Pistorius, won a total of six gold medals as a Paralympic runner. Nicknamed "the Bladerunner," the double-leg amputee helped garner unprecedented attention for the Para-lympics. Pistorius's renowned athletic career also included a singular achieve-ment: In 2012, he became the first amputee to compete against able-bodied competitors in the Olympics. He was not only considered a hero but also a "superhero," a label he embraced.

Pistorius, though, had a dramatic fall from grace. On February 14, 2013, he fatally shot his girlfriend Reeva Steenkamp. He claimed he mistook her for an intruder. "Bad shit happens to people I care about"; that is the warning Logan, a fictional superhero, gives in a movie with some emotional parallels to Pistorius's life. Despondent over his violent past, Logan's dwindling powers match sinking spirits. In previous films, Logan, known as "Wolverine," had larger-than-life attributes, like self-healing powers, associated with super-heroes. Hugh Jackman's final portrayal of Logan, however, was based on the emotionally burdened and physically strained Randy "The Ram" Robinson (played by Mickey Rourke) in the movie *The Wrestler*. All four of the "he-roes" in this chapter struggle psychologically as they grow more dependent physically. More optimistically, their stories demonstrate the healing poten-tial of interdependence. This is especially true with respect to dynamic and flexible depictions of "family." Exclusively "nuclear" conceptions of family prove too narrow for the people and characters in these settings. They ex-pand their associations and allegiances in search of a broader view of the world and their place in it. Though filled at times with grueling emotional struggle and misunderstanding, the best family moments in these cases have a collaborative, musical quality. I thus examine songs and cinematic scores associated with each story.

Consider, for instance, the stylistic mashups and cultural mélange that rocked the Superdome on September 25, 2006. That Monday night was the first NFL game back in the Superdome after the devastation of Hurricane Katrina. Irish band U2 teamed up with the American band Green Day, along with local brass musicians. At one point in their performance of "The Saints are Coming," Bono, the lead singer of U2, yelled, "Rebirth!" After the music, one New Orleans Saint evoked that hallowed concept in a way no one could have expected.

Steve Gleason and the Religion of Sports

The Falcons received the ball first, but the Saints defense quickly stifled that opening drive, forcing the Falcons to punt after only three downs. As Falcon kicker Michael Koenen was receiving the ball, Saint safety Steve Gleason raced through a gap. Koenen went into his kicking motion, and Gleason hurled his body like a projectile. In flight, he slapped the ball to the ground, sending it wobbling toward the end zone where teammate Curtis Deloatch recovered it for a touchdown. In a retrospective from NFL Films, the narrator explained, "For nearly a minute after Gleason's punt black, the television broadcasters remained silent as 75,000 Saints fans gave their city back its voice."[2] The ensuing frenzy in the stands looked like a revival. Testimonials confirmed the religious power of football.

Tony Kornheiser, one of the television commentators, explained his silence in that ecstatic moment. In his view, the punt-block unleashed a healing flow with even farther reach than the ruinous flood waters of the hurricane. This was not just local renewal. The rush of excitement resonated nationally. "This is a shared experience in the body politic of the entire country and you don't want to trump it by trying to believe that you can say something more important than what you are watching. You are hearing this noise, you are watching these people. You are watching what so many people in that place thought was an absolute rebirth."

The Saints storied quarterback Drew Brees confirmed the lofty assessment: "I have, to this day, never heard a sound more meaningful than that football hitting Steve Gleason's hands when he blocked it."[3] Roy Mouledous, the project manager for the Superdome Reconstruction, began to cry while trying to put words to emotions. Once he composed himself, he drew religious comparisons to the ecstasy and heartache: "It was like anything that ever happened good in your life, all at one time. It was your First Communion. It was your birthday. It was your graduation. It was your first date. Getting married. And then in the back of your mind, it was the people you lost. It was the trials and tribulations that the city went through. To have that kind of emotion on a high, you've got to have a great loss; so I'll be very happy if I don't have that high again."[4]

New Orleans musician Frenchy Frechette was likewise tearful in his interview, and his comments had a striking biblical parallel: "It was like getting a new heart. It was like getting a heart transplant, you know."[5] In Ezekiel 36:26, it is God who performs this transformation: "A new heart I will give you, and a new spirit I will put within you. . . ." In the video, the healing power of football reaches the bleakest of places. "Even those watching in a FEMA trailer that night, like Shelton Alexander and his family, felt the power of the rebirth."[6] Wearing a t-shirt emblazoned with "Destiny's Team" across the front, Alexander testifies, "From that moment, that was us taking our stand, you know, where nothing is going to stop us."[7] Clearly, for many, the game represented a sacred rebuttal to the hurricane's devastation. In retrospect, it made Bono's earlier yell of "Rebirth!" seem prayerful—prophetic, even.

Anarchic Spirit and Healing Rituals

In Ireland, Bono was in high school when he came across a Charismatic ministry called Shalom Fellowship. They made a rigid distinction between the secular and the sacred. The conservative organization nearly convinced Bono and his friends to abandon their then fledgling rock band, U2. Bono eventually embraced the Holy Spirit as an unpredictable border-crosser. As he puts it, "God's Spirit moves through us and the world at a pace that can never be constricted by any one religious paradigm. I love that. You know, it says somewhere in the scriptures that the Spirit moves like a wind—no one knows where it's come from or where it's going. The Spirit is described in the Holy Scriptures as much more anarchic than any established religion credits."[8]

That is in keeping with Gleason's spiritually eclectic perspective. He connects to the divine more fully through nature than homilies in a church. After Gleason was diagnosed with Amyotrophic Lateral Sclerosis (ALS) on January 15, 2011, he continued to testify to the spiritual power of nature. Speaking to a public Catholic assembly, he clarified, "More recently, because ALS has trimmed the boundaries of my adventures, I find the Creator's voice in the youngest branches of the oldest most mysterious oak trees in the neighborhoods of this wonderful city."[9] What Bono might affectionally call Gleason's "anarchic" view of God developed despite his father Mike's conservative Charismatic faith.

It was only months after Steve faced the darkness of an ALS diagnosis that his world was brightened with joyful news of his wife Michel's pregnancy. Steve recorded videoblogs for his unborn son, footage which comprises a significant portion of the documentary *Gleason*.[10] In the film, Mike stands before Steve and Michel explaining an "Old Testament" notion of "generational sin": the idea that sins of the fathers can be passed on to multiple generations until someone consciously breaks the pattern. Mike attempts to persuade the two of them to frame their experience of Steve's ALS in biblical terms and to seek physical healing in Christian circles. Even if Steve resents his father's expectations, he still heeds one of his suggestions. By the time Mike convinces Steve and Michel to attend a service of faith healer Kevin Dedmon, they feel uneasy but hopeful.

Dedmon asks people to touch areas of their body that need healing. With

his hands behind his head, Steve joins with other congregants in gentle singing of an adapted R.E.M. song: "It's the end of my pain as I know it, and I
feel fine." Dedmon encourages people who sense a stirring in their bodies to
step out in faith and attempt to move that area. Gleason informs the group
he will try to run in the sanctuary. He moves to the front of the congregants
and asks them, "Who wants to see me run?" With their encouragement, Steve
incorporates sports into the religious space. He crouches down in the three-
point stance he used to adopt while on the field before he would catapult
toward the opposing offense. In the church, he launches from that position,
takes three unsteady strides, and lands in a heap. Michel is crestfallen. She
has seen enough. "This is bullshit," she declares. When Mike rebukes her,
insisting, "Michel, you're his partner. You need to trust and believe with
him," Michel seethes in shock. "I am with him so much, Mike. Don't you
dare say that to me," she responds. There is no indication in the film about
any religious beliefs Michel holds, but it is clear she finds the faith healing
service repugnant. In a commentary on the film, she mentions that her favorite ritual took place on the field with Steve when he led a "Who Dat?"
chant. At that point, Steve could still walk with assistance, but he was obviously weakened by the disease.

Gleason exchanges greetings with Saints players in preparation for that on-
field ritual. When he makes his way to the field, he is flanked by two former
teammates, his hand perched on quarterback Drew Brees's right shoulder
pad for balance. Gleason's eyes are raised toward the crowd as he makes each
deliberate step. His head suddenly sinks with obvious emotion and possible
muscle strain. He readies himself and summons a surge of strength before
turning to Brees and saying, "Ready." Brees takes two steps backward and
Gleason throws his right arm to the sky, fixing it for a moment in the air.
He drops it like a hammer unleashing a fan roar of the "Who Dat?" chant.

In a video blog before Rivers was born, Steve admits to the intoxicating and
dangerous power of those cheers: "When you are good at something, it's fun
to see other people admire you. And I think that's a good thing to be so good
at something that people admire you, but I think it can become dangerous if
that becomes obsessive. And I certainly struggled with that when I retired.
If you're not doing something where there's tens of thousands or millions
of people that are admiring you, can you still be happy? Tough question."

Randy "The Ram" Robinson winces with that same unspoken question
in *The Wrestler* (2008). Rourke stars as the middle-aged professional wrestler with an esteem linked to his ability to entertain fans. He relishes years

of adulation for his high-performing body. With the physical decline of age, however, he has trouble inhabiting his stage persona. Fan responses dwindle as his body crumbles.

The Wrestler and the Body of Christ

In the First Letter to the Corinthians, Paul compares the Christian community to a body, which requires multiple functioning "members" to maintain total holistic health; in the bloodiest match of the film, the idea that the fans, along with the wrestlers themselves, represent different members of the same social body is made tangible by a prosthetic leg. Randy is wrestling another aging opponent who compensates for his lack of mobility by employing a cornucopia of blood-spurting props. In the ring, the opponent adopts the persona of a vicious villain as he staples Randy's torso and drives fork tongs into his forehead. Blood gushes down Randy's face. The crowd reactions mirror what Paul writes to the Corinthians, "If one member suffers all suffer together with it; if one member is honored, all rejoice together."[11] Fans are furious and distraught by Randy's pain and vicariously ecstatic when he counters the cruelty.

Randy smashes a pan full of glass against his opponent's face and drives him over the ropes next to the frenzied crowd. A fan hands Randy a garbage can, the dirty contents of which Randy pours over his fallen opponent. Randy then covers the opponent from head to torso with the can. Randy picks up a chair and is about to hit the can-draped man, but a passionate fan interrupts with a vivid appeal to anatomical and social relatedness. To convince members of the church in Corinth that they are all indispensable parts of the body of Christ, Paul writes, "The eye cannot say to the hand, 'I have no need of you,' nor again the head to the feet, 'I have no need of you.'"[12] When a fan screams, "Use my leg!" as he holds his prosthetic leg up in offering to Randy, the wrestler is reluctant and confused. The fan insists emphatically, "Come on. Use my leg!" to a now resounding crowd chorus of "Use his leg! Use his leg!" Randy takes the leg, swings it through the air with an exaggerated windup, and smashes it against the can. The opponent falls forward. Randy triumphantly raises it in the air, smiling widely and soaking in the glee of the crowd.

When he is not performing as a wrestler, he enjoys observing the performances of strippers. In a club, he finds his double in "Cassidy," the stripper moniker for a woman named Pam. When Cassidy notices a cut on Randy's head, she exclaims in concern, "Oh Jesus, you're bleeding." Randy touches his forehead remembering the self-inflicted cut he made earlier in the night to heighten the drama of the wrestling spectacle. He proceeds to map out the various injuries on his body, providing Cassidy a travelogue of their origins. Cassidy tenderly traces the scars as she listens wide-eyed. She makes the subtle biblical parallel explicit: "He was pierced for our transgressions. He was crushed for our iniquities. The punishment that brought us peace was upon him, and by his wounds we are healed." Pam knows the words from a movie she saw, *The Passion of the Christ*, in which the biblical text, as inter-title, introduces the action of the film. "You have the same hair," she insists while clutching his long locks, "You've gotta [see the film]. They throw everything at him—whips, arrows, rocks. They beat the living fuck out of him the whole two hours, and he just takes it." Randy smiles with a knowing nod as he confirms the identification, "Tough dude." Cassidy responds with one more biblical connection for Randy (and the viewer). "The sacrificial ram," she blurts out, laughing with surprise at the realization that Randy shares a nickname with Jesus, who in Christian tradition is called the lamb of God.

Randy is compared to other animals, besides a ram, in the Golden-Globe winning song that plays during the film's closing credits. In his acceptance speech for "Best Original Song—Motion Picture," Bruce Springsteen explained the song's genesis. Mickey Rourke called him and "told [him] a little bit about the character. [Rourke] said, some people invest themselves in their pain and they turn away from love and the things that strengthen and nurture their lives, and he said this was a guy that hadn't figured that out." With his characteristically hoarse vocals, stripped-down piano, and acoustic guitar arrangement, Springsteen captures the pathos of a man turning inward and missing out. To do so, he mentions both animals and disability. The references progress from a cautiously hopeful note about a "one-trick pony in the field so happy and free" to a pitiable litany of impaired figures: "a one-legged dog making his way down the street", "a one-armed man punching at nothing but the breeze", and finally, "a one-legged man trying to dance his way free." If you have seen any of those sights, the song's sad protagonist insists, "you've seen me." David Marchese of *Spin* thinks it is the viewers' intimacy with Randy that gives the lyrics their poignancy: "We feel like we know 'the Wrestler,' and that makes us care that he feels like a 'one-legged dog.'"[13] Indeed, many reviewers raved about Rourke's deft emotional touch in the film. Just as *The Wrestler* revived Rourke's career, it inspired another actor seeking a fresh angle for his superhero character.

Mutant Cage-Fighters and Their Disfiguring Scars

Moviegoers were originally introduced to the cinematic character of Wolverine in the first X-Men film in what ended up being a lucrative franchise. In *X-Men: First Class*, Wolverine is a cage-fighter in "Laughlin City," Alberta, where he mercilessly decimates all challengers. When a sore loser attacks him after the official fights, we learn Wolverine is a mutant. He unleashes three blade-like claws from his left fist and pins the disgruntled loser against a beam. The bartender cocks a shotgun and aims it to the back of Wolverine's head, insisting, "Get out of my bar, freak." Wolverine swipes backward, unleashing his right claws and slicing through the shotgun like butter. Thus begins a saga that culminated in a genre-bending finale seventeen years later, one with multiple links to *The Wrestler*.

The surprising success of *X-Men: First Class* catapulted a then-unheralded Australian actor named Hugh Jackman into Hollywood stardom. Though he diversified his roles in a variety of other popular films, the character of Wolverine continued to fuel Jackman's star power. This included appearances in the slew of X-Men films that followed the first, as well as the related stand-alone blockbusters that carried Wolverine's name in the title. Seventeen years later, as Jackman was searching for a fitting finale for his popular superhero character, he had a flash of insight: "I've got this idea, we do something more like 'The Wrestler' or 'Unforgiven' and [director James Mangold] mentioned 'Shane' and I said, 'We're gonna stick to that and do that.'"[14] Jackman knew *The Wrestler*'s director, since Aronofsky was initially slated to direct the second Wolverine movie. Aronofsky gave Jackman tips for *Logan*: For example, the scars. [Aronofsky] said, 'You know, mate, I get that he heals, but if you're a human, your scars are with you your entire life. The scab might go within a month or two weeks, but that scar is there for life, so even if he has accelerated healing, that scar is with him for a good ten, fifteen years, so he should be completely disfigured."[15]

The idea that Logan could wear his struggles on his skin made Jackman realize, "Oh, there's a whole other way to do this character; there's a whole other way to get into it."[16] Viewers got an intriguing, if enigmatic, glimpse of how Jackman decided to inhabit the role during a commercial for the NFL's biggest cultural attraction.

Gleason and Logan at the Super Bowl and Behind the Glass

Sometimes even more than the game, the commercials for the Super Bowl generate keen anticipation and lively post-game discussion. 20th Century Fox thus released the trailer for *Logan* to a massive audience. Fuschia Kate Sumner, Sting's daughter, provides the haunting spiritual soundtrack for the violent and explosive images. She only sings the first two lines of "Amazing Grace," but they are soul-stirring and intriguing. What "grace" will be found in this carnage? Who is the "wretch" in this case? Who will save that wretch and how? It is clear there are several children in distress. As they run through the woods, one looks behind her in terror. In the frenetic montage, we see a brief image of her claws, and she leaps and flips over adversaries. The trailer closes with an image of a child tenderly grabbing hold of a muscular man's wrist. We cannot see their faces. Steve Gleason's face, however, is unmistakable in another commercial that ran that evening.

It begins with a man painting lines on a field. Academy Award-winning actor Forrest Whitaker narrates football footage from the field that speaks to social progress off it. The "fight to move forward" includes the image of a female referee. That season President Donald Trump had railed against players who were taking a knee during the national anthem to protest police brutality and systemic racism. Trump called them "sons of bitches" who deserved to be "fired." In a nod to the protests, the commercial showed white and black players and coaches from the Seattle Seahawks standing with locked arms. And then there is Gleason. When he raises his arm for the "Who Dat?" chant, Whitaker reframes an illness that might have been caused by the sport he played as one of the NFL's inspiring "victors." The image zooms out at the end to reveal the man was painting the outline of a U.S. map on the field. This is another example of how Gleason's story has been incorporated into national healing.

It is unlikely Bennet Omalu saw the trailer or the commercial that night since he does not throw Super Bowl parties. He explains, "Too often our sports heroes are not human beings in our eyes. They are gladiators, putting their bodies and minds at risk for our entertainment. When I begin to see them through the eyes of God, I cannot . . . be a party to their pain."[17] James Mangold also wanted viewers to recognize pain. As the director and co-writer of *Logan*, he wanted to make a movie in which neither the powers nor the bodies of superheroes are boundless: "I'm more comfortable making a film in which the violence has very real implications for the very fragile flesh that holds us together."[18] Mangold thus joined Jackman's vision of a superhero character like Randy the Ram, and with striking parallels to *Gleason*.

In contrast to most summer blockbusters, but like the documentary *Glea-son*, Mangold allows scenes to breathe in an unhurried fashion. Viewers witness interactions that do not advance the plot in any dramatic way but which enhance the intimacy between the characters. Just as caretakers lift Steve's body in *Gleason*, Logan physically carries his father figure Charles, which in at least one case inadvertently draws attention to the structural barriers that stairs can pose for wheelchair users. In both a surprisingly funny and unnervingly raw scene in *Gleason*, a nurse helps alleviate what feels to Steve like a "football-sized" bowel obstruction. Similarly, Logan must help Charles use the bathroom. Charles angrily asks him to turn around, which Logan gruffly confirms he is eager to do.

On June 25, 2016, several months before the release of *Logan* but just days before *Gleason* came out to the public, Hugh Jackman tweeted, "Just saw @GleasonMovie. Incredibly powerful. If you get a chance—check it out." In 2020, Gleason hosted Jackman on an interview series called "Behind the Glass."[19] Gleason pressed the *Logan* actor about real-life vulnerabilities, "Where would your teenage kids and wife Deb acknowledge your vulnerabilities and weaknesses as a father?" Jackman smiles while shaking his head at the profundity and difficulty of the question: "We should be asking ourselves this question all the time, and as you can see by my reaction, it is a tough one." He admits his wife would say he works too much, and his children think his disproportional worries take him out of the moment.

There is unspoken understanding in this exchange that Gleason has already revealed his many vulnerabilities in his documentary. In one of his video journals for Rivers, Gleason rails about his failures to live up to heroic expectations and his disgust with his own limitations: "Rivers, I'm having a bad day. I'm an asshole to people, and I don't care. I can't talk. I think the last of my talking days are here. The drugs I take don't work. I have no faith that I can heal. None! No hope. I want to punch something, but I can't! The only thing I can do is scream!" After screaming, Gleason moves slowly out of frame in his motorized chair before a jump cut to Gleason wheeling through the tunnels of the Superdome in preparation for the dedication of his statue outside the stadium. Drew Brees reads the statue's inspirational text, "On Monday, September 25, 2006, Steve Gleason was responsible for one of the most dramatic moments in New Orleans Saints history. He blocked a punt in the first quarter of the team's return to the Superdome following Hurricane Katrina. That blocked punt that season symbolized the rebirth of the city of New Orleans." Brees then looks to the sky as he says, "Amen." The film undercuts this ethereal glance to the heavens with the earthy messiness of

Gleason's life. Gleason talks about what happened after the ceremony, "Yesterday, about five minutes after I got home, I pooped all over myself and my wheelchair. And I think it's crazy that I can go from people saying, 'You're my hero,' to having to be helped on to the toilet with my pants full of shit. It's an incredible example of polarities, and dichotomies, and juxtapositions that is my life."

That kind of dependency is a terrifying prospect for the protagonist in *Logan*. Mangold explains, "Love scares [Logan]. Intimacy scares him. Being dependent on others scares him. Being vulnerable scares him. So I sat down and started to construct a story that would somehow subject him to this most frightening of prospects, which is family, having a father he had to care for and even a child who he would have to own paternity for and ultimately love."[20]

A documentary about a famous real-life athlete with similar emotional scarring as the fictional Logan includes the fractured family among its introductory themes.

Oscar Pistorius and the Revival of Hope

An unidentified woman with a South African accent softly enumerates the manifold pain that plagues her nation: "I like many of you have become saddened and tired of the circumstances and situations we find ourselves in as a people and as a nation. The troubles in marriages around us, the unemployment, the women abuse, the crime, and the poverty." Just as Gleason's punt-block unleashed what some called a local and national "rebirth," this announcer envisions a sweeping turn for South Africa. "I believe that revival will be a time when God will visit South Africa. It will be a time when he will sweep away the works of the devil." After this pronouncement, she turns the broadcast over to another interviewer. "Joy" speaks to a woman named Sheila about her "special son" Oscar. Sheila explains, "I have three children, Carl, Oscar, and Aimee. Oscar's my middle son, and he was born with missing bones in the legs. This was a very difficult time, but with God's help, he has gone from strength to strength. He's been a tremendous source of encouragement to many people, and he's just a very popular well-respected boy, and I certainly deem it a privilege to know him and be his mum."[21]

Sheila Pistorius died after a misdiagnosis and an infection. Oscar was only 16 at the time. Even though Sheila tried to instill indefatigable drive in her son, it would have been impossible to imagine the stunning heights of his adult success and the vast geographic reach of his inspirational image. "But as it is written, 'What no eye has seen, nor ear heard, nor the human heart conceived, what God has prepared for those who love him.'"[22] A woman in Iceland was shocked when the universe brought her Sheila's son.

Learning her unborn son had a condition doctors had "never encountered before in Iceland" left Ebba Guðmundsdóttir feeling distraught and achingly alone.[23] In her anguish, she hoped for a miscarriage. (The thought is so painful in hindsight she whispers the word.) But when her husband Googled "double amputee," they found a startling image of hope: "Oscar Pistorius running in Athens." They learned Pistorius was born with "fibular hemimelia," the same condition as their son, Haflidi. Ebba's description of that moment evokes Bono's reference to the Holy Spirit moving like an unpredictable wind. Ebba makes a whooshing sound and a wind-swept gesture declaring decisively, "It changed everything." It was as if Pistorius had blown through their home at warp-speed, turning everything right side up. Ebba says, "It captured a moment of triumph for him and for us it was a moment we moved not just from despair to hope, but to knowing our son would be just fine."[24] Ebba's mother reached out to a reporter who had interviewed Pistorius. She shared the hope Pistorius brought the family. Pistorius contacted the family by email and later met them in person when he traveled to Iceland, where the company that made his running blades was located. They continued connecting over the years. After a first place-finish at a race in Manchester, Pistorius jumped the fence, ran into the stands, and placed his gold medal around Haflidi's neck. He said, "It's for you, champion."[25] There were no cameras in the vicinity of that exchange, which Ebba's mother believes is indicative of Pistorius's unfeigned generosity and kindness. In one visit, Ebba asked if Pistorius would remove his prosthetics so Haflidi could see the similarity in their feet. Pistorius was happy to do so. Later, when Ebba's mother showed Haflidi the picture and asked what he was thinking in that moment, he replied, "I knew I was okay."

The Religion of Sports and the Biography of Saints

Although on a different scale, I feel similar assurance when I look at a woman with a red scar down her forehead. After my surgery, and while my scars were still bright red, I bought a St. Rita statue. I placed it prominently on the fireplace mantle. I also use other material means to bring her to mind— especially during despairing moments triggered by my BDD. I wear her image on a chain around my neck, and, more playfully, we have placed her cartoon caricature on one of our dog's collars. For more serious devotion, I keep her prayer card nearby and in view.

Ebba's mother drew on similar material devotions, but from the religion of sports, not the biography of saints. "I printed out pictures of [Oscar], many pictures, and I glue it on my fridge, on the wall of my office, and in my wallet, so every time I was a bit worried, I took them out or looked at the pictures. And that helped me to [Exhales] . . . not stop worrying, but less worry."[26] I find other connections between St. Rita and Oscar.

Margherita Lotti was born in Roccaporena, Italy, in 1381. As a young girl, her parents rebuffed her desire to enter the convent. Instead, she had an arranged marriage to a man who ended up being abusive. After his death, and that of her two sons, Rita joined the convent where she was marked with an unmistakable sign of devotion. She miraculously received stigmata, a lifelong and painful forehead wound associated with Christ's own suffering. Pistorius also bled sometimes while living in "professionally monkish solitude"[27] in Italy. In his case, it was a product of the "intense training" he carried out as an "ambassador" of a small town called Gemona. While St. Rita, with her forehead scar, is the patron saint of impossible causes, the mayor believed Pistorius, with his running blades, stood for the town's indomitable spirit.

New Orleans is often still associated with Katrina, and Gemona was known for its calamitous earthquake. In 1976, 400 people died in that disaster, and thousands of others were displaced from their homes. Many of its ancient buildings were reduced to rubble. Given the obstacles Pistorius faced in his life, the town's mayor, Paolo Urbani, saw him as a kindred spirit.

> His desire to be normal despite his disability was not unlike the struggles that our community faced since we suffered our own 'disability' if you will. But we wanted to go back to our normal everyday lives. The city wanted to move on 35 years after the earthquake. We wanted to show everyone that the earthquake was in the past and that thanks to our determination we were able to recover. In that sense, I see similarities with Oscar's story. Thanks to his persistence and determination, he managed to achieve so much.[28]

This represents a different kind of disability symbolism than New Orleans chose after Katrina.

The Catholic Church was left with an important symbolic decision about what to do with three missing fingers on Jesus's left hand. A statue of Jesus in Jackson Square in New Orleans was improbably well-preserved after the storm, except for digital amputations. The statue lost the forefinger and thumb of its left hand, and part of the pinky on its right. Some imagined the missing digits were a sign of sacrificial power: Jesus had flicked the storm away (at least from that sacred space). Ten years later, in his ESPN article on the complicated tributaries of sports, disability, and Catholicism after Hurricane Katrina, Wright Thompson noted, "After Katrina, the church said it would leave the statue broken, out of solidarity, until the city had recovered. This year, on the anniversary, the archdiocese is reattaching Jesus's fingers."[29] Hence to symbolize the city's new birth, Jesus was restored to physical wholeness, which is arguably the kind of symbolism Nancy Eiesland warned "perpetuates the belief that disability is inherently 'un(w)holy.'"[30]

In *The Disabled God*, Eiesland searches for a "reconception of wholeness."[31] She imagines not "an omnipotent, self-sufficient God, but neither a pitiable, suffering servant."[32] Instead, she finds an emancipatory symbol in the resurrected Christ, especially because of the impairments preserved on his glorified body. In the New Testament accounts, Jesus still has the scars of his crucifixion after his resurrection. "In the resurrected Jesus Christ they saw . . . the disabled God who embodied both impaired hands and feet and pierced side and imago Dei."[33] This provides a relatable image. "It suggests a human-God who not only knows injustice and experiences the contingency of human life, but also reconceives perfection as unself-pitying, painstaking survival."[34] In explaining why the people of Gemona saw their story reflected in the Blade Runner's, Pistorius biographer John Carlin uses some of the same words and sentiment as Eiesland: "They were *survivors*. Not given to *self-pity*, they had overcome the consequences of natural disaster by dogged persistence" (emphasis mine).[35] Aronofsky proposed to Jackman that Logan should be "completely disfigured" and, before his season in Italy, Pistorius had a boating accident that according to one commentator left his face "deformed." Nevertheless, despite breaking "seven or eight bones in his face," and receiving "a hundred stitches" inside and outside his skin, there was no obvious evidence of the accident when Pistorius was back in the public eye. His symbolism for Gemona notwithstanding, the Blade Runner was not usually a scarred symbol of difficult circumstances, but a pristine "god" of unrivaled glory.

Looking Like a God

Sports journalist Gareth Davies notes that when he burst onto the Paralympic scene as a teenager, Pistorius looked otherworldly: "There was a light around him. He literally glowed. It was like seeing something mythical."[36] The aura was manufactured as well. In one advertisement, Pistorius is floating in the sky, wearing only white shorts and his running blades. The low angle of the shot elongates his sleek frame. He peers down at the viewer with serene confidence. Debora Patta observes, "There he was with his blades looking like a god." Over a futuristic and regal image, with Pistorius sitting on a throne holding a star, Patta adds, "This wasn't a disabled man by any stretch of the imagination. This was a man of the future."[37] Still, some feared what Pistorius's running blades augured for the future of sports. To explore the wariness about his perceived technological advantage, it is useful to revisit the role of technology in *Logan* and *Gleason* and to consider what Jackman and Gleason had to say about the subject in their conversation during the pandemic.

In *Logan*, Charles claims he is telepathically receiving signals from new mutants and that they want Logan's help. Logan scoffs at the suggestion. Charles agrees that Logan makes an unlikely rescuer in his self-destructive condition: "Oh, yes, that's how fucking stupid they are." He means that as a pointed barb against Logan, not the mutants sending telepathic distress signals. Their situation is indeed dire, and it has to do with technological advancement run amok and without virtue.

Technology As Help and Threat

In *Logan*, a biotechnology company called Transigen created children as weapons from mutant DNA. The children are powerful but unruly. They are deemed disposable once the corporation finds alternative weaponry. They plan to kill the children, but several nurses help them escape. One of the nurses finds Logan hiding in obscurity as a limo driver and asks him to transport a young girl named Laura to refuge. Charles and Logan find out Laura was made from Logan's DNA. A high-ranking member of Transigen's security force relishes technological threat; he points to his bionic hand, noting ominously that he has been "enhanced."

Andy Crouch reflects theologically on technology by examining both popular culture and classical writing. With respect to the former he explains why the tv series *The Six Million Dollar Man* stays with him after all these years: "For the children of the 1970s, Steve Austin (played by Lee Majors) was our first cyborg, fitted with a 'bionic' eye and limbs after a nearly fatal accident. Every episode began by retelling his origin story, as a voiceover intoned: 'We can rebuild him. We have the technology. We can make him better than he was. Better, stronger, faster.'"[38]

Crouch lauds the "rebuild" portion of the origin story, explaining how it is in keeping with what Enlightenment philosopher Francis Bacon identified as the noble application of technology: namely, "the relief of man's estate."[39] Crouch elucidates implications that resonate with a wide swath of people. He mentions "the treatment of injury and illness and the end of material poverty."[40] The first point is especially relevant to athletes, and the combination of illness and material poverty fits the situation of many people with ALS, who cannot afford the often exorbitant adaptive and lifesaving equipment associated with the disease.

In the documentary, Team Gleason struggles to help people acquire expensive speech-generating devices. Their efforts to raise political awareness are rewarded in the passing of the Steve Gleason Act. Cultural and political dimensions of disability technology are also evident in Amazon's *Pistorius*. Oscar's prosthetist, Trevor Braukman, points out that at the time Pistorius became an infant amputee, countries around the world were protesting South Africa's racist apartheid policies with economic boycotts. He explains, "It was in the time of sanctions, they weren't all lifted yet. So to get materials and latest technology, it was not that easy. It is not like you could just go and buy a little foot like that. You had to make a little foot like that." For all its "rebuilding" promise, though, technology can also create peril.

It is the "enhancing" part in the opening portions of the *Six Million Dollar Man* that worries Crouch. "Already our smartphones are very nearly an extension of ourselves," he says.[41] Jackman expresses similar concerns about the disorienting pace of technological growth. In his interview with Gleason, he mentions Oliver Sacks's gloomy assessment of people walking around "the West Village of New York" with "heads buried in their cell phones." In Sacks's view, as Jackman relates it, these people appear like the many institutional psychiatric patients he witnessed in a "disassociated state." Conversely, Jackman also recognizes great potential: "Technology, in general, if you have some self-discipline, is phenomenal." In their interview, Gleason offered a similar mix of testimony and caution. On the one hand, he says, "In many ways technology has cured my ALS. Without technology, I would be dead." On the other, "I also see the problems, and dangers, and side effects that technology has caused for our civilization."[42] It is not Gleason, but Pistorius, who Crouch mentions when discussing such concerns: "And we are moving beyond repair to enhancement, not just in the dubious results of elective cosmetic surgery but in the realm of speed and strength. The prosthetic replacements now available for human limbs are sufficiently capable that many athletes believe that amputees who employ them, most famously the South African sprinter Oscar Pistorius, have an unfair competitive advantage."[43]

The Pistorius documentaries show the tests Pistorius underwent in hopes of disproving that idea. He is strapped to various devices evaluating the energy return of his blades. He must give full effort. At one point, Pistorius frantically removes a mask and vomits into a bucket. His efforts seemed futile when the International Association of Athletics Federations (IAAF) ruled in 2008 against Pistorius, declaring they found confirmation he had a competitive advantage over able-bodied runners. The Pistorius camp ultimately prevailed upon appeal to the Court of Arbitration for Sport in Switzerland, however, and paved the way for Pistorius to compete in both the Paralympics and Olympics in London, 2012.[44]

Alongside Olympic sprinter Usain Bolt, Pistorius was the star attraction of those Games. Known as "the Blade Runner," Pistorius was asked about the Paralympic promotional tagline, "Meet the Superhumans," which was plastered around the city. A television interview observed, "The media have sort of labeled the Paralympic athletes as superhumans. How do you feel about that label? Is it putting too much pressure on you?" Pistorius was categorical and unhesitating in his reply, "No, not at all. Not only myself, but I think every athlete is a superhuman."[45] Some have argued in hindsight that this verbal denial was also indicative of a more profound psychological kind. While traveling with Oscar as his teammate, Samkelo Radebe saw Pistorius's emotional devastation over disappointing results. "Seeing Pistorius break down on that bus in New Zealand gave Samkelo a glimpse of the vulnerability behind the superhero façade. Yet, he said, it made him value his friend's virtues all the more."[46] Once Pistorius became associated with vice, people looked back on earlier times surmising that Pistorius was terrified all along that someone would unmask his superhero image. Some were eager to do so in the wake of Reeva's death.

Arnu Fourie, another of Pistorius's teammates, said, "The media are seizing on the bad stuff now to confirm the monster image, just as before they looked to confirm the superhero image."[47] Radebe noticed the same thing but was defiant about Pistorius's heroic impact: "Everyone wanted a piece of his story before and now they don't want it anymore. They shun him. But he is the biggest South African hero since Mandela."[48] Many began to suggest two sides to Pistorius. A South African reporter explained and wondered, "We'd seen flashes of it before, but took no notice, so desperate were we for a hero to inspire us. But was it that dark side that came to the fore in the early hours of Valentine's Day?"[49] Revelations in the trial of an irascible, hot-headed Pistorius conflicted with his winsome, soft-spoken image. This is another instance when the film *Logan* provides useful comparison with Pistorius's story.

Logan and Pistorius in Comparative Perspective

Unbeknown to Charles or Logan, Transigen created a clone with DNA taken from Logan during his years as a warrior called Weapon X. The clone, X-24, is a haunting reflection of "what bad [Logan's] done in his life, the blood that is on his hands." Mangold uses explicitly religious language to describe this mirroring: X-24 "has no speech to give, has nothing to say about the past, but just embodies [Logan's] *own sin*, his own darkness" (emphasis mine).[50] Before Logan confronts his dark side, he experiences domestic bliss with acquaintances, just as Pistorius did in Iceland and Italy.

Ebba noticed that with their family Pistorius could "really put down his guard and could always be himself. He could feel that we genuinely loved him for who he was, not for his fame or anything. We were just like meeting a good friend."[51] In Gemona, at the family-run hotel where he stayed, many women expressed "maternal instinct" toward him and "pampered" him to his satisfied delight. In their view, they were the "family he never had."[52] These were pictures of domestic bliss he never experienced in his own broken home. Logan has a similar experience of found family. In one scene, Charles says, "You know, Logan, this is what life looks like. A home, people who love each other. Safe place. You should take a moment and feel it." In that case, they had met a black Christian family, the Munsons, who exude peace and offer dinner.

For the first time in the film, like Pistorius in Iceland and Italy, Logan lets down his guard. He smiles easily and jokes good-naturedly. There is also an athletic tie between Pistorius's life and the scenes of the Munson family. Oscar's brother Carl suggests, "[My father's] dreams for my brother were really ambitious. He could be a hard man and strict. . . . I think there was a lot of pressure as Oscar's career developed." Similarly, in *Logan*, we learn the teenage Munson son, Nate, is feeling some sporting pressure from his father. He has many horse-riding trophies on his wall, but he explains to Laura that they have more to do with his father's wishes than his own desires: "Those are for breakaway roping. Those are for barrel racing, and right here is for pole bending. They're all second, third place. I'm not so good at it, but my dad makes me." The most terrifying connection between the film and Pistorius has to do with the Munson family's gruesome demise.

The clone, X-24, slips into the Munson house and kills Charles and the entire Munson family. Mangold explains, "The film almost enters the emotional and style space of a horror film."[53] A week after *Logan's* U.S. theatrical release, another U.S. movie came out that challenged the longstanding pattern *Logan* perpetuated. Jordan Peele admitted he was tired of seeing black people killed off in early stages of horror movies, a frustration that fueled the creation of Chris, the smart black survivor of *Get Out*. In South Africa, there is a reverse racial terror to the home invasion depicted in *Logan*.

Nomboniso Gasa points out that many white South Africans "fear an imagined intruder" that is concocted from their "fantasies of black men."[54] Both the ESPN and Amazon documentaries contextualize home intrusions with a broader historical lens, suggesting a tie to violent repression and resistance during apartheid. Nevertheless, the bulk of real footage they use reinforces the imagined black intruder—gun and machete-wielding black men break into residences with white occupants. In defending Pistorius, his lawyers stressed not the widespread white fears about black intruders, but Oscar's particular anxieties as a man with a disability. At sentencing, defense attorney Barry Roux asked Oscar to do what he had done in a much more inspirational setting in Iceland: remove his prosthetics. This time the act was not meant to encourage a young boy, but to dispel assumptions about Pistorius's vast capabilities. As he inched his way to the center of the courtroom, Pistorius grabbed the backs of benches. Oscar was transformed from the superhuman who eschewed the term disability to a short weeping and wobbly man. He appeared so unstable without his prostheses that a woman walked forward and grabbed his arm, seemingly to hold him up. Tears streamed down his face as Pistorius hung his head.

That physical undressing reinforced the psychological unmasking the defense attorneys had attempted during the trial. Multiple psychologists testified to an internal conflict between the powerful image Pistorius presented in public and the lingering sense of deficiency he had carried since his childhood. Dependency in this context was meant to look pitiable, to spur the most lenient sentence possible. There is, however, a remarkably moving and complex scene in the Amazon documentary that combines images of interdependence and athletic accomplishment, without irony or dichotomy. It is an intertextual scene that draws subtly on feminine imagery of God.

Intertextuality and Liberating Dependency

The Book of Isaiah promises a maternal kind of divine support: "As a mother comforts her child, so I will comfort you."[55] Grace Noll Crowell was recognized as the "American mother of 1938," and one of her nominators explained that the prolific poet "expresses the spirit of motherhood in her breadth of human sympathy, and in the fact that literally thousands of people write to her every year because she draws from them a desire to confide, as a child to its mother."[56] Crowell began writing poetry while convalescing after giving birth. She worried her immobile condition might be permanent. One of her poems valorizes stillness and appears in modified form in the Amazon documentary on Pistorius. The original poem reads:

> Dear Heart, God does not say
> today, "Be strong!"
> He knows your strength is
> spent, He knows how long
> The road has been, how weary
> you have grown:
> For He who walked the earthly
> roads alone,
> Each bogging lowland and each
> long, steep hill,
> Can understand, and so He
> says, "Be still
> And know that I am God'"

The emphasis on stillness in this first portion of the poem is also a prominent theme in a poem Gleason wrote and shared on social media during the pandemic. That poem includes the lines, "Come Sit. I'm Listening," and, "Stay With Me As the Secret Becomes Known. Stay in Stillness." Crowell's poem transitions from the theme of stillness to rejuvenation.

> The hour is late
> And you must rest awhile, and
> you must wait
> Until life's empty reservoirs fill
> up
> As slow rain fills an empty,
> upturned cup.
> Hold up your cup, dear child,
> for God to fill,
> He only asks today that you be
> still."

In the documentary, footage of Pistorius's Olympic 400m heat against able-bodied competitors combines the original sounds of the broadcast with audio of Sheila reading a portion of Crowell's poem. As Oscar readies himself in the starting position, an announcer comments, "You can sense, Tom, that [Oscar] knows how long this journey has been to get to these starting blocks, and he appreciates not just the opportunity but the moment." From that point on, the sounds of the broadcast are mixed with a soaring score and Sheila's calming voice. She reads snippets of Crowell's poem and elaborates with her own reflections.

Sheila abbreviates the original opening lines, "Dear child, God does not say to you, 'Today, be strong.' He knows that your strength is spent. He knows how long the road has been, how weary you've become, and so He simply says, 'Be still. Be still and know that I am God." At that moment, the live action footage of the preparations for the race is replaced with a still image of Oscar on the track. After the sound of the starter pistol, we see him running in motion. A still image follows of Oscar as a young boy crying with mud all over his prosthetic legs. Sheila comments on the first lines of the poem, "I'm so glad I don't have to be strong. He is strong." Footage of the race is once again interrupted by a broader shot of the earlier picture of young Oscar crying. Now Sheila is in view holding Oscar up while Oscar looks down at the mud on his prosthetics. Again, Sheila reflects on the personal resonance of the poem, "I'm so glad I don't have to be good. I will try my best, but never be perfect." We are back to the earlier childhood moment, but now we see an image of the young Oscar looking at his mud-covered hands. The images shift again to the race. When the next photo shows Sheila helping Oscar wash off his prosthetics, we hear her reflections about imperfection. She closes by paraphrasing the final lines of Crowell's poem, "I don't have to be a specimen in the museum of perfection, just to rest at His feet and let him fill your cup." In the last picture in this sequence, she holds Oscar's leg with the prosthetic now removed. Oscar is turning a tap with water gushing onto the ground. His left prosthetic is still dirty. When Sheila says "fill your cup," she is holding the prosthetic to the spout. We return to the adult Oscar arriving in second place of his heat, thus qualifying for the final.

In this scene, the documentary undercuts Pistorius's image of invincibility with a reminder of his childhood dependencies. But the purpose is not to evoke the pity his lawyers tried to arouse during sentencing. It is rather to paradoxically highlight the strength of stillness alongside the footage of movement. The stillness is not literal, of course. This scene celebrates God's loving intervention, embodied symbolically by a mother's tender assistance. It makes the running footage look less like striving for achievement and more like receiving grace. That is what Logan gets in his dependent final moments.

Mangold suggests Logan thinks he is "cursed," that anyone who gets close to him dies; Logan, like Randy in *The Wrestler*, tries to turn away from intimacy, from vulnerability. In *The Wrestler*, Randy eventually chooses the imagined community of the wrestling world, instead of accepting Pam's real offer of a relationship. Logan makes a similar decision: he refuses to accompany Laura and the other young mutants into Canada, where they have been assured a "safe haven." This will mean parting from Laura and perhaps following through on his plan to kill himself, a plan which Laura found out about and which he admits to her. Laura protests, but Logan barks that he has done enough for Laura by reuniting her with her friends. He continues a vehement defense, but his eyes water through cracks in his angry veneer: "And it is better this way because I suck at this. Bad shit happens to people I care about. You understand me?" Laura responds with an angry dejected barb from her own pain, "Then I'll be fine."

In their conversation during the pandemic, Jackman talked with Gleason about the "hero's journey," a concept he acknowledges they are both familiar with from reading comparative anthropologist Joseph Campbell. Campbell claimed, "There is but one archetypal mythic hero whose life has been replicated in many lands by many, many people." Jackman believes "there is some kind of grace, universal consciousness that calls to us," and Campbell suggested heroes heed that call. As Campbell put it in discussion with Bill Moyers, "A hero is someone who has given his or her life to something bigger than oneself."[57] Jackman describes its affective dimension as "that feeling that there is an inner journey in life being the most fulfilling and ultimately the right path for us." In summarizing structural elements of the myth, Greg Garrett points out that the hero undergoes "an Ordeal" that leads to "a reward the hero brings back to society."[58] This is Randy the Ram facing his bloody ordeal in the ring, before joining the ranks of fans in the audience. It is Gleason returning to the Superdome to lead the "Who Dat?" chant, after undergoing the initial stage of his ordeal with ALS. It is Pistorius returning triumphant from the ordeal of Paralympic competition and meeting with a proud Nelson Mandela, a man with well-known interest in the power of sporting heroes to heal a nation. Logan, though, no longer wants to be a hero for something "bigger than himself." With Charles's death, he is lost without a peer to help him find his bearings. Berger explains "that the individual appropriates the world in conversation with others and, furthermore, that both identity and world remain real to himself only as long as he can continue the conversation."[59] The X-Men world in which mutant powers are put to life-giving services has lost its plausibility for Logan. But when Laura and the other young mutants face an overwhelming assault from Transigen forces, Logan feels compelled to intervene.

He races to their rescue and faces his greatest nemesis—his "dark self." In battle, X-24 impales him on a fallen tree. As Garrett points out, "Our American superheroes are equal parts demigods from Greek myth, strongmen and prophets from Judeo-Christian tradition, literary lions and folktales, and pop-culture traditions".[60] Laura plays a part in Logan's life that resembles Jesus in Christian theology, especially the idea of "*Christus Victor.*" Many early church leaders used the metaphor of Christ as a liberator to explain that, through his death and resurrection, Jesus defeated the powers of evil, releasing sinners from their bondage. This is what Laura literally does for Logan. She shoots X-24 while he has Logan in his death grip, and she runs and cuts the branch of the tree from which Logan is suspended in agony. A root remains lodged in his stomach and he is still in extreme distress, but in a spiritual sense he is free to glimpse something new. It is not only Laura's triumph over X-24 that liberates Logan from his guilt, shame, and sin. It is the invitation of her hand. Pam offered real love in *The Wrestler*, and now it is Laura extending it to Logan.

Throughout the film Mangold uses a motif of interlocking hands, which is the tender image in the otherwise violent Super Bowl trailer with "Amazing Grace." Laura and Logan grip one another's hands while he dies. Logan sputters to get final words out to Laura, breathless instructions that she does not need to fight any longer, that she should just run with the others, that she does not have to be what Transigen created her to be. And then a deep confidence washes over his face, catching him by surprise. His scowl finally relaxes into a blissful grin. Logan does not receive this grace through his superhero strength. He finds it in his immobilized weakness.

There was earlier foreshadowing of this moment when Logan is sick and weary. He is hoisted to a mountain by the mutant children. In that instance, he could not move. He could only stay still and let himself be lifted. It is a picture of the kind of grace that dispels hubris. "For by grace you have been saved through faith, and this is not your own doing; it is the gift of God—not the result of works, so that no one may boast."[61] Logan could not brag about getting himself up that mountain, and neither can he move in his final moments as he senses, perhaps for the first time, that he is enveloped in love. In his dying moments, basking in the love of a daughter he has effectively adopted, he declares, "So this is what it feels like." In Romans, Paul writes that there is a "spirit of adoption" that bears "witness with our spirit that we are children of God." The manifestation of that witness-bearing spirit is a cry, "Abba! Father!" Abba is an Aramaic word often translated "Daddy" in English. In Logan's dying moments, Laura looks tenderly at a man she found so frustrating on other occasions, and says softly, "Daddy." Amazing grace indeed.

In *Gleason*, there are similarly touching moments as Steve grows more dependent on the help of others. At Rivers's first birthday party, another man feeds Steve a piece of Rivers's cake. Meanwhile, Rivers digs out globs from his own piece, stuffing his mouth and painting his chin with liberal splashes of frosting. These are warm and pleasant shots, with Steve gazing lovingly at his son's cake-covered face. A slow piano score adds a tinge of sadness, and so too does a twilight shot of the "rebirth" statue, meant to dramatize the "polarities, dichotomies, and juxtapositions" of a hero needing help.

Later, as the couple continue to navigate Steve's increased physical limitations and related dependencies, Michel places Rivers on Steve's lap in his wheelchair. Steve slurs his affections. "I love you," he drawls to Rivers, who, to Michel and Steve's wide-eyed amazement, repeats it back. Steve brims with joyful laughs that emerge as delighted groans. Rivers presses his head against his father's immobile chest for a magical moment: "Daddy, I love you."

There was no such pleasing resolution for Pistorius. While he inherited Christian faith from his mother, it seemed to wax and wane in intensity throughout his life. Still, he and Reeva had connected on a spiritual level. They enjoyed listening to the worship music of Hillsong, a Charismatic global network of churches based in Australia. Reeva would also pray for Oscar at night. In the aftermath of the shooting, Oscar prayed desperately, promising God total consecration in exchange for a miracle. One observer on the scene testified at trial, "Oscar was crying all the time. He prayed to God to please let her live, she must not die. He said at one stage that he will dedicate his life and her life to God if she would just only live and not die that night."[62] While the audio of that testimony plays, there is a still image of Oscar from the trial with head cupped in his hands. He also grips a rosary.

Oscar reportedly felt like Logan did in his suicidal state. Family members worried the despondent Pistorius would take his life. Multiple ministers intervened at different times, offering extended spiritual conversation and biblical study. One Charismatic minister tweeted about his meeting with Pistorius and asked for prayers.[63] Pistorius himself now leads Bible studies in prison with some notoriously dangerous criminals. He has also sought the forgiveness of Reeva's parents. Reeva's mother is not interested in talking to him, but she has forgiven him internally. She explains, "I'm a Christian. God expects me to forgive. But He doesn't expect the person not to be punished. He's got to be punished. A lot of people don't understand that but it's true."[64] It is not Reeva's mother, but Oscar's who gets the last word in the Amazon documentary: "What I would like to say is that it doesn't go about our bodies, or how beautiful we are, or what has happened to us, but it goes about us fearing the Lord and that delights the Lord."[65]

In this chapter I have explored the contested symbolism of bodily whole-ness and holiness in Christianity and bodily wholeness and heroism in popu-lar culture. I found stories in both kinds of sources that granted heroic status to impaired bodies—whether with scars or disabilities. Nevertheless, hero-ism in such sources is redefined not as a spotless life of virtue but rather as a graceful path of help from people, God, or both. Recognizing our dependence helps us value interdependence. The teamwork of interdependence requires effort but also creates durable and meaningful reward. Many of us would probably rather keep our pain private while pursuing cures. "Cure suggests that one's painful life-altering experiences are left behind, while a nuanced understanding of healing appreciates how such life experiences are inte-grated into one's ongoing narrative, and indeed, one's entire life."[66] Gleason's descriptions of "exploration" sound strikingly akin to this integrated view of healing. Steve explains, "Exploration requires two simultaneous elements. A curiosity to gain knowledge and the admission of ignorance, which to my ears, sounds like when Jesus said, I told you that unless you change and be-come like little children, you will never enter the kingdom of heaven."[67] While exploration looks forward to something new, cure is an act of restoration to how things were. As the stories in this chapter demonstrate, sometimes there is no turning back.

To move forward, Michel and Steve extend the value of interdependence beyond just human relationships. Before Gleason's diagnosis he joined Michel in a hearty duet about the interdependence of nature and humanity. They belt out the chorus to "Rivers and Roads" by the indie folk band The Head and the Heart. It is a wistful song about friendship, family, and loss. It also hails collaborative work between nature ("rivers") and humanity ("roads") in forging our joyous and painful paths. In the next chapter, I discuss the role of nature in stories about Bethany Hamilton, who lost her arm in a shark attack while surfing as a teenager. Nature, especially non-human animals, plays an equally prominent role in stories about Brady Jandreau, a Lakota bronco rider who suffered serious head injury from the sport. In *Pistorius*, Dr. Jonathan Scholtz notes, "Cowboys don't cry. We are brought up that way. You don't break down, you don't give up, but how does the typical strong South African male even own up to the fact that he was afraid?" I explore the same questions with respect to the Christian Lakota cowboy in the next chapter.

Chapter 6

COWBOYS AND SOUL SURFERS: GENDER, DISABILITY, AND NATURE FROM BETHANY HAMILTON TO *THE RIDER*

O n October 31, 2003, a thirteen-year-old surfer named Bethany Hamilton was relaxing on her board off the coast of Kauai, Hawaii, when a fifteen-foot tiger shark bit off her left arm. On April 1, 2016, a Lakota cowboy named Brady Jandreau was in a rodeo competition when a bronco bucked off the twenty-year-old and stomped on his head. Hamilton "lost over half her volume in blood" and had life-saving surgery.[1] Jandreau went into a coma and received a titanium plate for his skull fracture. The athletically precocious Hamilton had started surfing when she was five. Jandreau could "actually ride and control a horse before [he] was potty-trained."[2] Hamilton's multi-mediated story includes a biographical movie starring AnnaSophia Robb and a more recent documentary called *Unstoppable*. Jandreau plays a fictionized version of himself in *The Rider*, a film that blurs the boundaries between both genres.

Although Hamilton and Jandreau had traumatic injuries from animals, they champion a divine-human relationship mediated through non-human nature. What is more, human interdependence is a striking feature in each of their stories. Finally, for both Hamilton and Jandreau life after traumatic injuries required reframing the gendered expectations of their social worlds—those identifiable spheres of social relationship they respectively inhabit; that is evangelical surfing culture in Hamilton's case and Lakota cowboy culture in Jandreau's. Together these two case studies help us reconsider our identities and connections within and across social worlds, species, and dis/abilities.

Good God and Wild Wondrous Nature

Not long after her traumatic injury, Hamilton and her family fed the broad appetite for her story through various media products targeted to diverse audiences. Most are related to *Soul Surfer* (2004), the book Hamilton wrote with Sheryl Beck and Rick Bundschuh shortly after the attack. The storytelling team addressed delicate faith questions. Suggesting a divine hand behind the traumatic events that befell Hamilton could evoke the symbolic paradigm of disability, which scholars often refer to as the most atavistic and disabling of all such models. Rosemarie Garland-Thomson warns, "It is the logic of theodicy: if something 'bad'—like having a disability—happens to someone, then there must be some 'good' reason—like divine or moral justice—for its occurrence."[3] In *Soul Surfer*, however, Hamilton resists this idea and preserves the mystery of misfortune: "I don't pretend to have all the answers to why bad things happen to good people. But I do know that God knows all those answers, and sometimes He lets you know in this life, and sometimes He asks you to wait so that you can have a face-to-face talk about it."[4] Instead of speculating about the answers, *Soul Surfer* reframes the "traumatic amputation" as a calling and opportunity. "I have this thought every second of my life: 'Why me?' Not necessarily in a negative way—like 'Why did this horrible thing have to happen to me?' But more 'Why did God choose me and what does He have in mind for me?'"[5] "Calling" then becomes a controlling theme of the book, but one which is entangled in the complicated task of imagining and describing a deity who permits, but does not orchestrate, traumatic circumstances.

Accordingly, Hamilton places greater emphasis on divine omniscience than omnipotence. In Hamilton's adolescent view, God knows everything even if God self-limits with respect to life's events. Nature in Hamilton's account has autonomy—both for a surfer's good and ill. For example, in discussing the best surfing techniques, she qualifies her tips with an acknowledgement of the disproportionate role nature can play in the sport: "But as skilled as you are, sometimes nature is smarter, stronger, and tougher. The wave may suddenly take control and completely envelop you, dragging you to the bottom (we call that a 'wipeout' or 'dirty lickings' in surfspeak). There are other times, however, when nature is on your side. The wave, the conditions, and the dance all come together into an experience that penetrates you so deeply that you find yourself talking about the ride over and over again."[6]

In this description, nature does not operate according to divine instructions but is unpredictable in its ludic whims; as Hamilton puts it, "nature can play games with you."[7] As Mitchell and Snyder point out, "Disabilities bear the stigma of a reminder that the body proves no less mutable or unpredictable than the chaos of nature itself."[8] Accordingly, Hamilton imagines God anticipating and responding to the attack, but not causing the trauma itself, which leads her to find tentative cosmic meaning that is decidedly hopeful: "So I think this was God's plan for me all along. I am not saying that God *made* the shark bite me. I think He knew it would happen, and He made a way for my life to be happy and meaningful *in spite* of it happening."[9]

Hamilton locates small signs of God's mercy through nature and via human interdependence: "It's a small miracle it was high tide. If it had been low tide, we would have had to go all the way around the reef to get to shore—a trip a quarter of a mile that usually takes ten minutes to paddle over reef that's twenty to thirty feet in depth."[10] God is also active in the community that rallies around her. Sarah, her youth pastor, asks for a message from God for the family and a verse from the Book of Jeremiah comes to mind: "For I know the plans I have for you, declares the Lord, 'plans to prosper you and not to harm you, plans to give you hope and a future.'"[11] Finally, the whispers of an abbreviated biblical passage from a paramedic on the scene of the trauma are not only of lasting comfort for Hamilton, but also signal ways her story was birthed in a space betwixt and between secular and religious space. "I remember most clearly what the Kauai paramedic said to me: He spoke softly and held my hand as we were pulling out of the Tunnels parking lot. He whispered in my ear, 'God will never leave you or forsake you.' He was right."[12] In this instance, as in many cases already discussed in this book, the secular sphere of medical trauma is enchanted with religious "moods and motivations." In *Unstoppable*, there is a remarkable hospitable scene of intimate connection. Earlier scenes showed Hamilton and her best friend Alana Blanchard engaged in frenetic surfing and inseparable frolic. (I even found it difficult to distinguish between the two in some of that footage.) In the hospital after her attack, Hamilton makes an astounding admission about the depth of their bond, "I'm glad it was me and no one else out there. I'd just rather have it be me than Alana because I love her so much."[13]

Hamilton was able to reconcile her conception of a loving God with the shocking attack, but at a subconscious level, in at least one stage of her life, she still felt powerless. *Unstoppable* shows a home video in which a teenage Hamilton recounts a recurring nightmare. Her legs are trapped inside the jaws of the shark, and she cannot escape its grasp. Still, she bounded back into the waters only four weeks after her attack. Her father helped her adapt to new challenges by grafting a handle to her board so that she could duck dive with one arm. She caught on so quickly that when she entered the national amateur competition at the age of 15, she astounded observers with a first-place finish. If she carries any reservations about the ocean and its potentially dangerous inhabitants, they are miniscule compared to her immense gratitude. At the end of *Unstoppable*, now as a married mother, she offers the following paean: "The ocean is so much for me. It's my passion and my love, but also my place of healing and reflection. And somewhere where I can just be me." That place of quiet contentment has not always been easy with the undulating media noise of praise and criticism.

Pick Yourself Up by Your Bikini Straps

Given its secular publisher, MTV Books, it is unsurprising that Hamilton, and her support team, narrate *Soul Surfer* with a keen consciousness of how it fits both within and without evangelical Christian culture. That straddling is exemplified in the explanation of the dual goal for the work: "I hope it helps people find faith in God and in their own strength and ability."[14] In one instance in the book, this combination of willpower and Christian faith is fused with an astounding claim:

> I see that God is able to use my story to help others. Once a girl (I never got her name) came up and told me that she had had cancer. When she saw my story it made her realize that she didn't need to give up; it made her want to fight hard too. She ended by saying, 'Now I'm cancer-free.' I don't think I had anything to do with curing her cancer—she did that herself. But if my story made her pledge to battle this disease and beat it with her own strength and willpower, than that would be enough for me.[15]

Readers, though, don't have to combine these elements to appreciate her story, since she sometimes segregates references to human agency and divine intervention. Her evangelical audience could be encouraged, for instance, by the following bold and explicitly Christian proclamation: "My strength came from my relationship with Christ and from the love and encouragement of my family and friends."[16] Non-Christians, agnostics, or atheists might focus on another aspect of Hamilton's identity as "living proof that where there's a will, there's a way."[17] This latter emphasis conforms to the supercrip pattern as described by RJ Berger: "'Supercrips' are those individuals whose inspirational stories of courage and dedication, and hard work prove that it can be done, that one can defy the odds and accomplish the impossible. . . . It is the myth of the self-made man."[18] Attention to her evangelical faith does not guarantee she will be cast in a role other than the supercrip. Writing for the twenty and thirty-something target audience of *Relevant Magazine*, an evangelical publication which frequently fuses pop culture and matters of Christian faith, Carl Kozlowski describes Hamilton as an extraordinary figure, and narrates her ordeal and recovery in terms that fit comfortably within the myth of individual opportunity.

> It was believed by many that she would never surf again, both out of fear of sharks and the ocean and as a matter of practicality since surfing normally requires both arms to paddle out against waves, as well as for balance once riding a board.
>
> But Hamilton quickly proved that she was *no ordinary girl*, and through a combination of outsized courage and her immense Christian faith, she was back on the ocean a month later and has since regained her status as a champion surfer (emphasis mine).[19]

To critique such a description for the way Hamilton is rhetorically removed from the "ordinary" is not to suggest her accomplishments are commonplace. I would contend, though, that the repetition and circulation of these kinds of descriptions do little to dismantle dominant perceptions of disability, "most often seen as bodily inadequacy or catastrophe to be compensated for with pity or good will, rather than accommodated by systematic changes based on civil rights."[20] In *Soul Surfer*, Hamilton rejects both pity and catastrophizing: "What I don't want is for people to pity me or think of me as a person who has had her life ruined."[21] In one portion of the revised edition of *Soul Surfer*, Hamilton attempts to link signifier and signified with an explicitly religious anchor. She seeks to secure the terms of her iconicity outside of the realm of inspiration. "I don't really want people looking to me for inspiration. I just want to be a sign along the way that points toward heaven."[22] Hamilton is not alone in rejecting, in a qualified way, the imposition of an "inspirational" role, since many disabled people in general and athletes with disabilities in particular find the term patronizing and reductive. Still, her early desire to be an evangelical sign "that points to heaven" was complicated by a small but vocal group of opponents. They did not see themselves as detractors of Hamilton, but rather critics of her representation.

When the movie *Soul Surfer* was released in 2011, the film was met with generally positive Christian reviews about its faith-affirming message, but dissent over the presentation of female bodies in the film emerged in some corners of cyberspace. A contingent of conservatives decried what they believed to be the film's flaunting of Christian modesty culture through a preponderance of scenes with young actors in bikinis. Stacy McDonald, a Christian blogger and author of the book *Raising Maidens of Virtue: A Study of Feminine Loveliness for Mothers and Daughters*, warned, "If a man would find it difficult not to lust sitting at a crowded beach watching beautiful women in bikinis walk by, then he will probably have a hard time with this movie."[23] And judging from the abundance of comments supporting McDonald's review, her warnings resonated with followers of her blog. Indeed, contrary opinions were so hard to find on the site that one commenter named "Jennifer" incorporated and then denounced comments that had been left at another (unnamed) Christian website. A nineteen-year-old at that other site had been untroubled by the image of young athletic female flesh on the big screen. He took issue with the backlash the movie was receiving in some conservative Christian circles. He wrote, "The user comments on this page very much sadden me. More or less because they can be summarized as follows: 'Men are animalist lust toads who cannot control their base desires and must be shielded from such filth.' That seems so condescending. I feel as though I deserve more respect than that. But, I, also, am sad for you—sad for all of the beautiful beaches that God created that you will presumably never see firsthand, out of your fear of sin."[24] After quoting him, "Jennifer" offered incredulous and pointed commentary: "EVERYONE suffers from lust and visual stimuli sometime; no need to act like you and a few others are lone snowflakes who don't. You're a young male and, while I usually would never presume to tell another what they feel, I'm not naïve; as Stacy said, if a male isn't in the least stirred in his mind by these kinds of things, I'd be concerned."[25]

The closing warning could be meant to shame a straight young man into believing he has a puny and abnormal libido, or to hint that if he can watch bikini-clad young women in an unaroused state, he is probably not straight. This exchange is pertinent to Debra Shogan's contention that "if someone does not perform . . . gender skills as a notification of one's sex in all situations, others are baffled or even angered."[26] Indeed, this is an example of vigorous, seemingly furious, policing at the borders of evangelical and secular culture and between male and female bodies, in which both are perceived to be "zones of danger requiring special ritual maintenance."[27]

McDonald's sharp distinction between secular and Christian worldviews also leads her to a perhaps surprising critique about the film's unspoken reliance on the myth of individual opportunity: "A secular movie review I read didn't seem to even realize there was supposed to be a 'Christian message,' and acknowledged what so many Christians are failing to see, that *Soul Surfer* has the typical 'athlete-overcomes-obstacle story line.'" In McDonald's view, Christian fans of the film are dupes, who are unable, or unwilling, to recognize that the film has more to do with "bootstraps" tenacity than being saved by grace. She lays out the recipe for pandering to a Christian audience: "In the case of *Soul Surfer*, all they needed were two verses, a female youth pastor, a worship song, and the flash of a Bible. Throw in a deeply moving (true) story about a sweet Christian girl who pulls herself up by her bootstraps (or bikini straps) and we're hooked."[28] McDonald is not only distressed that Hamilton's cinematic body is treated as an object of inspiration, but that it is accessorized in such (supposedly) titillating fashion.

Authoring and Interpreting Images

Most scholars studying female athletic imagery would not share McDonald's conservative evangelical and, arguably, overwrought concerns about the film in question. Nevertheless, her contention about the force of images on our quotidian lives echo what scholars have said, with more sophistical language, about the "hyperreality" we live in: "Media and its images . . . become not 'just' representations we can turn off but reality itself, indisputable facts of life within which we are inextricably caught up."[29] An evangelical Christian displaying her hard-earned bikini-clad physique while also publicly championing chastity is not a familiar character in many cultural scripts. "Indeed, so powerful is the cultural imperative to structure experience with absolute categories that figures who seemingly defy classification . . . elicit anxiety, hostility, or pity and are always rigorously policed. The rigidity of social order testifies to the destabilizing threat of ambiguity as well as the artificial, constructed quality of all social identities."[30] As a sexy, disabled, and evangelical surfer, Hamilton joined the list of those upsetting rigid social categories.

On November 12, 2014, Hamilton posted a rear-view bikini picture, presumably of herself, walking on a cliff overlooking a beach while cradling a surfboard under her right arm. With her hips angled to the left, the purple and yellow bikini bottom left much of the bottom portion of her backside very much in view. Her blond hair was wind-swept over the entire left side of her upper back, exposing only a slither of skin on her left shoulder, making it difficult to determine whether the woman in the photo had two arms or one. Hamilton's disability was not entirely legible in this scene, an ambiguity that could make her indistinguishable in the long line of sexualized female athletes. As Ellen Samuels points out about explorations of "real" and "fake" disability in American film, "portrayals of ambiguous identification are tolerable only if contained and ultimately resolvable."[31] At least one anxious commenter on Hamilton's photo demanded resolution: "Bethany. I hope this isn't you."[32]

Given the prominence of and focus on her backside in the picture, it was unsurprisingly the subject of most of the Facebook responses she received, whether positive or negative. Many commenters worried about the generous amount of flesh on display in the picture. Rebecca Elaine Nyce wrote, "Oh nice to have your rear hanging out. Yes, you are cute, very much indeed. But what about being modest?" Erika Lynn Beynon feared Hamilton had internalized an objectified view of herself: "You have so many more beautiful qualities about you than your bottom. Please don't reduce yourself to the need of flaunting your body for attention. God has created so much more in you."[33] Michelle Massey pushed back against this negative tide, attempting to expose a dichotomy in the process; she both defended Hamilton as a decidedly positive female influence and praised her physical attributes on display, arguing there was no contradiction between exemplary female character and overt sexiness. She wrote, "If I had a booty like that I'd be rocking that bikini too. I have 2 little girls and I am PROUD to have Bethany as their role model. She is beautiful inside and out."[34] These comments diverge in their assessments of the photo, but not in their interpretation of the picture itself. All three of the commenters agree this is a sexy picture that intentionally draws attention to Hamilton's curvaceous figure. They differ about whether that intentional sexiness is morally corrupting or physically admirable.

Hamilton's career in professional surfing has not only coincided with a complicated moment in the mass mediation and commodification of female athletes in general but also for female athletes with disabilities in particular. Drawing attention to a hitherto iconographic absence of sexually desiring and desirable women with disabilities, Thomson explains,

> While feminism quite legitimately decries the sexual objectification of women, disabled women often encounter what Harlan Hahn has called 'asexual objectification,' the assumption that sexuality is inappropriate in disabled people. ... The judgment that the disabled woman's body is asexual and unfeminine creates what Michelle Fine and Adrienne Asch term 'rolelessness,' a social invisibility and cancellation of femininity that can prompt disabled women to claim the female identity that the culture denies them.[35]

Accordingly, some female athletes with disabilities, have begun to seize new opportunities to demonstrate a combination of athletic achievement and sexuality. Several have appeared naked in various installments of *ESPN The Magazine*'s popular "Body Issue," for instance. Hamilton, though, faces a conglomeration of pressures: the social pressure for disabled people to present asexually, evangelical concerns for modesty, and the economic benefits of surfing sponsorship, an industry which has long profited from the sexualized image of the blond "surf girl."

Hamilton offered a linguistic signpost for her rearview photo that many commenters had missed or ignored. In the tagline she wrote, "comfy and cute in #mybikini," which only a few commenters accurately identified as the advertising hashtag for Rip Curl, Hamilton's surfwear sponsor. One might assume that recognition of the advertising context of the photo would reinforce the views of those who felt that Hamilton's body was being objectified, or commodified as it were. Nevertheless, all of the comments that mention the sponsorship do so to defend rather than critique the photo. Iona Hickman declared, "the hashtag mybikini is part of a marketing campaign for ripcurl. Bethany is a ripcurl girl. She's not posting to be 'sexy' and 'flaunt' herself . . . all you angry posters should go get a life! She also looks great and a woman in a bikini on the beach is pretty normal!!"[36] Jacinta Landa was even more adamant that her sponsorship should absolve Hamilton of guilt for any objectifying elements of the photo. She posted, "In case people haven't figured it out yet she is sponsored by ripcurl therefore she has to post pictures of herself wearing the bikinis as part of her sponsorship and advertising for the company she is getting sponsored by! Stop judging before you know the facts!"

There are indications that social class plays an intersectional role in the interpretation of these pictures. From the first iterations of her story in the book *Soul Surfer*, Hamilton connected the importance of financial gifts and the commercial revenue she received through interviews and advertising to her family's lower socioeconomic standing: "At the time, nobody knew how much the hospital bills would be, or even with the health insurance, how much the portion my parents would have to pay. (Remember, my dad is a waiter and my mom cleans rental condos, so we don't exactly have a lot of bucks in the bank.)"[37] Her humble beginnings seem to play a part in how some fans interpret her images. She married Adam Dirks on August 18, 2013, and her status as a married woman further complicates the interpretation of her presence in the public eye.

Continuity and Change Since Marriage

Since marrying Dirks, a youth minster from Indiana, Hamilton has narrated their relationship as redemptive fulfillment of youthful dreams once clouded in doubt. When she was interviewed as a teenager for the documentary

Heart of a Soul Surfer, she described both the challenges of and strategy for preserving self-esteem with an anomalous body: "Well, I realize I do get self-conscious sometimes. When I see all these beautiful girls with perfect bodies, perfect everything, it's like 'Ughhh.' The way I deal it with it: I know that beauty is not everything and in your heart you can be beautiful and just do your best to ignore the fact that you're not going to be perfect."[38]

Ruth Marie Griffith explains why evangelicals may be particularly vulnerable to pressure about body image. "The pressure to be thin and beautiful may be even greater for teens in the devotional world for the same reasons it is so considerable among their older female counterparts: the duty to serve as a glowing witness to Christ's transformative power. Straddling the norms of secular youth culture and the intense bodily disciplines of American Protestantism, Christian teens are as crushingly preoccupied with bodily control. . . ."[39]

Once partnered with Dirks, Hamilton explained retrospectively, "I always felt it would be hard for me to meet someone because I'm different. . . . To say I was completely comfortable looking at myself in the mirror and seeing one arm would be a lie. I just had to trust in God and know that he had someone special for me."[40] In the book *Soul Surfer*, Hamilton had been even blunter when describing the initial revulsion she felt about her appearance after the attack: "I thought I would be able to handle it okay. But when I looked at that little stump of an arm held together with long black stitches I almost fainted. 'Oh my gosh,' I thought. 'I look like Frankenstein's monster.'"[41] Thomson explains, "If the male gaze makes the normative female a sexual spectacle, then the stare sculpts the disabled subject into a grotesque spectacle."[42] It seemed that after the amputation Hamilton was not only staring into the mirror through her own eyes, but through the third-person standpoint of the male heterosexual gaze. She was viewing herself from the then elusive and hypothetical vantage point of "someone special for me."

When she appeared with Dirks on the CBS reality show "The Amazing Race," she giggled about how she considers certain activities more suitable for "guys," such as a task in which contestants had to fix a motorized bike, which her husband tackled with her vocal support. Also, in a questionnaire for the show Hamilton wrote, "I'm a girl and I'm more emotional," in response to the portion about the "Biggest challenge you and your teammate will face on the Race together." She then added, "Plus, I have one arm."[43] At first blush, it might be tempting to interpret Hamilton's reinforcement of gender roles and perceived gendered skills as a product of her evangelical Christian faith. After all, this a form of Christianity known to maintain "separate spheres" arguments through the discourse of complementarity—that is, the idea that men and women are inherently different but that their differences are complementary for male and female unity. Subsequent events, though, complicate that picture.

Even before the airing of the show, on his questionnaire, her husband listed his occupation as "Professional husband. Full-time support."[44] Indeed, in many ways Dirks's new presence significantly enhances the older focus on Hamilton. His repeated expressions of "pride" in all that Hamilton was accomplishing on the show even elevated her inspirational status. In the third episode, he testified, "Bethany has a gift of being able to see something that normally I would think would be really hard with one arm, but she makes it happen." During the fifth episode, he expressed similar sentiment while describing an arduous task at a tannery in Morocco when players had to strip hair from three hides: "Bethany's doing great. She's using her feet. She's using her hand, ripping all the hair out. I don't see what the other teams are doing but I think she's hanging with them pretty well. I'm proud of her." Other teams were equally impressed with Hamilton. Brooke, a professional wrestler, was in awe: "I cannot believe how awesome Bethany is at all of these challenges. I'm having difficulty with two arms and she has one." Hamilton completed competitive tasks with such tenacity that another female contestant, Kym, affectionately called her a "beast," a term most frequently used in popular culture for male athletes—and particularly African-American athletes—who display unquestioned strength in high collision sports like football. Hamilton's performance of gender, like many other facets of her persona is complicated, as is her husband's.

In *Unstoppable*, Dirks says he had an inkling of what he was getting into by "jumping on the Bethany bandwagon train." He was also eager to support Hamilton's surfing career, which like all professional athletic pursuits has a relatively short shelf life. Later in the film, he sounds wistful and uncertain as the provisional plan to step out of the traditional gendered bounds of evangelical Christianity starts to settle in as a longer-term reality. He says in this scene, "Being a guy, I want to provide. I want to be depended on. 'Cause that's how I grew up. That's how everyone I knew grew up. It's definitely like challenging. I started out thinking like okay, for this few years or something, I'm gonna support Bethany, and things will kind of like, phase out, and, um, then, like, I'll get a job."

After the birth of their son, Tobias, Hamilton initially struggled in surfing competition. By the time she entered the Fiji Pro as a wildcard, she had regained her form. And then some. The 26-year-old pulled off a huge upset, taking down the number one seed. She made it all the way to the semifinals.

Unstoppable revisits that feat and the revival of media interest it sparked. Fellow surfer Carissa Moore was shocked: "The craziest part for me is seeing her here in Fiji as a mom and multitasking between heats." Moore was also inspired, but not because of Hamilton's success as a one-armed surfer. She was impressed with how Hamilton modeled liberating options for female athletes in general. Moore had previously assumed she would need to wait to have children after her surfing career was over, but seeing Hamilton's success, she realized, "You can do both." The closing surfing scene of *Unstoppable* is awe-inspiring for any person in any stage of life. Hamilton takes on a gargantuan wave known as "Jaws" in the surfing world. An overhead aerial shot with soaring musical score captures her incredible balance and grace for a wave the film had already firmly established as notoriously fierce and unmerciful. Afterward, Hamilton beams with the adrenaline of success from a risk few people would ever dare.

When she was still an adolescent, Hamilton responded to a question many surfers hear about risk, even when they have not faced the kind of attack she survived: "What about sharks?" Hamilton wrote that dwelling on worst case scenarios sucks "the joy out of the sport."[45] As she pointed out, surfing has no monopoly on danger. "What if the horse throws you?" she asked her reader to consider about another sport. "What do you do *after* the horse throws you?' was the existential question a Chinese woman who grew up in an urban metropolis asked about a real-life Lakota cowboy from the Pine Ridge Reservation of South Dakota.

The Rider

In *The Rider*, directed by Chloe Zhao, Brady Jandreau stars as a fictionalized version of himself called Brady Blackburn. As one example of a scene from the film that blurs fiction and reality, the character Brady Blackburn watches harrowing footage of his fall on his cell phone. For that scene, Zhao used the real video of Brady Jandreau's rodeo accident. With its vivid attention to the setting of the Badlands and its poignant portrayal of universal emotions, *The Rider* helps us "actively reimagine" our worlds and those of others,[46] offering a vision of spiritual connection in circumstances that might otherwise tear us apart.

At least one reviewer worried some of *The Rider*'s mystical subtleties might fly under the radar, since Zhao's "restrained, unsentimental style is the opposite of preachy, which makes it all too easy to underappreciate the sublimity of her achievement. With its gorgeous frontier lyricism and its wrenchingly intimate story of a young man striving to fulfill what he considers his God-given purpose, 'The Rider' comes as close to a spiritual experience as anything I've encountered in a movie theater this year."[47]

This, though, is a movie not just enamored with "gorgeous frontier lyricism" but also respectful of the unsettling presence and spiritual potential of storms. Zhao experienced bad storms in different states, but nothing prepared her for the ominous ferocity she felt brewing in the Badlands. She explains, "When you are riding the horse, and you see the storm coming with the wind, it looks beautiful [in pictures] . . . but when you are actually there, it's uneasy because you look everywhere and there's nowhere to hide."[48] In her view, that vulnerability creates a unique relationship with nature, one not often replicated in other environments. She says, for example, that "we have a very different relationship with nature living in the city."[49] Raised as an atheist in that concrete setting, Zhao feels unfamiliar inclinations in nature's open spaces: "I almost feel religious when I'm in South Dakota—you want to bow to nature—so those scenes belong on the big screen."[50] Projecting nature in this way is part of what S. Brent Plate calls the "performative drama" of taking the real-life stuff of life and offering new angles of vision that help us to re-imagine and reconsider our place in our social worlds, and the social worlds in much broader panoramas. "Worldmaking is actively engaged with the raw materials that make up what is in the strictest sense [called] 'the earth', but importantly with the entire universe, the cosmos."[51] Accordingly, Jandreau believes distinct experiences of nature shape religious sentiment in different ways: "I've been in a lot of cities and places [that] don't feel like the hills out here. . . . I think you're much closer to God [in places like Pine Ridge] than when I was in New York or Paris—even though Paris is so beautiful."[52] This is why the analytical category "worlds" is so helpful for understanding religion in *The Rider*.

The Analytical Category of "Worlds"

William Paden explains, "The notion of world calls attention to the radical cultural and geographic diversity both among and within religious systems. . . . If life is governed by cattle herding, the religious system will naturally reflect this."[53] For the cinematic Blackburns and the real-life Jandreaus, their religious systems bare imprints of lives governed by horse-training. Indeed, Brady's relationship with horses is evidently spiritual from the earliest stages of the film. At his mother's gravesite, he prays, rubs his chest, and points to the sky, before noticing a horse figurine in the tall grass. (As he holds the figurine, we see for the first time that Brady has physical problems loosening his grip.) Brady treats his horse Gus like he knows they need each other. Brady calls him "partner" and asks him how he is doing. He pets Gus, embraces him, and leans tenderly against his muscular body, resting his head on the horse's long neck. In another scene, Brady gently applies ointment to wounds on Gus's nose. Scenes like this struck a chord with Kristen Weston, a former Lakota rodeo competitor, who has experienced the same kinds of intimacy.

> The connection the Lakota people have with horses is one of the strongest bonds one can have with the creatures of Tunkasila (God). When you look a horse in the eye, the connection is with the soul. It's almost telepathic—you feel as if you know exactly what that horse is thinking and it knows exactly who you are. One of my favorite things to do when I'm with my horses is bury my head into their necks. The scent is unlike any other: it touches your heart and brings back so many memories it makes you want to cry.[54]

Brady seems on the verge of tears for much of the film, but he reaches new depths of sorrow when his father makes a searing financial decision. Facing debt, he sells Gus.

When Brady steals a moment alone with Gus before his departure, we hear an aural reminder of the earlier visual testimony to sacred human and horse bond. Brady prays, "God, I just ask you to take care of Gus on his travels, Lord. Just be with him all the time and protect him. Keep him safe, God. In Jesus's name, I pray." The real-life Jandreau also believes in the power of prayer: "God saved my life. I definitely would not be here if it weren't for a lot of prayer—all those prayers."[55] Unlike in the film, Jandreau has a still-living Lutheran mother. His father is Roman Catholic, but Jandreau doesn't make sharp theological distinctions between the branches. "I was baptized Catholic, but . . . I'm just a Christian. Anybody that has any room to judge any other Christian isn't very Christian to begin with." He hints that his family's relationship to the land and non-human animals exceeds a typical Christian framework: "Both of my parents go to church from time to time and read the Bible from time to time. They both believe in the Lord God, our God, and his one and only Son, who died to save us from our sins, Jesus Christ. But they also understand other things, as well: nature, you know."[56]

On a theistic note, Jandreau testifies that it "makes you feel close to God just to be in [a horse's] presence" and on a possibly animistic one, he says horses are "almost like a spirit rather than an animal to me."[57] Fittingly, Weston observes, "It isn't until he gets back onto the horse when he finds out that the horse and its spirit complete him."[58] As Jandreau recalls, it was his real-life comments about a horse being divinely designed for a relationship with people that first spurred Zhao's desire to cast him in a film: "She asked what the [area] was where the horse's neck meets the saddle's back. I said, 'That's the wither, it's just a little bone that God put in there to keep the saddle on.'"[59] Zhao was dumbfounded by that statement. It might strain credulity to suggest a deity designed an animal's physical makeup to fit with the later material products of human culture, but it is in keeping with Jandreau's experience of kinship.

Being kin to an animal was one of the "centrally significant" identities growing up in his social word, similar to the distinction of "unclehood" in some societies. The late sociologist Peter Berger argued,

> The individual appropriates as reality the particular kinship arrangements of his society. *Ipso facto*, he takes on the roles assigned to him in this context and apprehends his own identity in terms of these roles. Thus, he not only plays the role of uncle, but he *is* an uncle . . . Its initial opaqueness (say to the child, who must learn the lore of unclehood) has been converted to an internal translucency. The individual may now look within himself and, in the depths of his subjective being, may *'discover himself' as an uncle*" (final emphasis mine).[60]

It is brotherhood and cowboyhood, not unclehood, that helped Jandreau discover himself, since he explains, "Gus was like a brother to me growing up." For Brady in the film, and Jandreau in real life, interacting as a "brother" to a horse restored his most profound sense of who he was after his injury. About his real life, Jandreau regained what Berger calls "internal translucency" while riding Gus. When I was laying in that hospital bed, when I woke up, I couldn't even talk right. . . . I didn't know if I would ever be able to do what I loved again. But two weeks after I was home, I rode Gus and I cried—it meant that much to me. When I first looked down those ears again, it was really powerful. I knew that there was *nothing else that I could be* (emphasis mine).[61]

Brady asked an interviewer to "imagine an animal being like a brother to someone," but his interactions with horses already bespoke kinship to one key outsider observer. Zhao recounts that pivotal moment: "I saw him training horses and he was being a father and mother and a friend and dance partner to this wild young horse and he was able to play different roles with the horse to get the horse to trust him and I thought that maybe he can do that with the audience as well." According to a *New York Times* review, she was right to trust those instincts: "Mr. Jandreau may not have much acting experience, but he has more than a touch of movie-star charisma, that mysterious, unteachable power to hold the screen and galvanize the viewer's attention."[62] There is nothing more riveting on screen than watching him train horses.

To capture that transcendence, the filmmakers sought immanence, getting down and dirty in a horse world. Paden explains how the concept of worlds can be applied to non-human animals:

> In the broadest sense there are as many worlds as there are species; all living things select and sense 'the way things are' through their own organs and modes of activity. They constellate the environment in terms of their own needs, sensory system, and values. They see—or smell or feel—what they need to, and everything else may as well not exist. A world, of whatever set of creatures, is defined by this double process of selection and exclusion.[63]

Cinematographer Joshua James Richards recounts how the crew dealt with this double process of the horse world, "The camera would come into the corral, they'd smell the camera, [and] we'd get them used to me and the boom pole. . . ."[64] Crossing human and horse-worlds required continual maintenance. "There were times when the horses were very calm. The next day, the weather might have been a little different or something might have been a different color and we'd have to do a whole desensitization process [between the horse and the crew]."[65] Once inside, the crew caught unscripted activity between man and horse that some called "artistic" and others found "astonishing."[66]

Although the final edited form of the film matches closely with the shooting script, there were portions that called for improvisation, with brief notes like, "Brady trains horses." As they were shooting an unrelated scene, a man mentioned to Brady he had a colt that no one had ridden before and that no one could "break." Jandreau asked Zhao if he could give it a shot, and she agreed. In two twenty-five-minute takes, and as the sun was setting, they captured the kind of wondrous stuff that you only get in the "magic hours" of filmmaking. Jandreau described the intricacies of the abbreviated and breathtaking process we see on the screen: "It's all through the connection. . . . You have to do the proper things to communicate with them for them to allow you to do everything because there's no way you could force a thousand-pound, 1500-pound, maybe even more, animal to do what you want to do. You have to make what you want look appealing to them. You guys have to make an agreement on the matter."[67] Brady has an uncommon ability to adapt to a horse world and mimic their movements, strengthening his sense of kinship across species; but he knows that in one painful respect horse and human journeys part ways. He hears this in the blast of a gunshot and tells it in the quiet of a living room.

After the family sells Gus, Brady's father, in a rare act of compassion, helps Brady get another horse named Apollo. Brady shows his usual skill in training Apollo. Later, though, we see Brady walking through the prairies, yelling Apollo's name with the horse nowhere in sight. Ominously, he finds fresh blood on the fence. He eventually locates Apollo standing still in the prairies, one of his legs mangled with twisted wire and ripped flesh. Brady's heart sinks. He kneels and gazes into Apollo's eyes. He takes out his gun and lifts it to Apollos's face, but when Apollo recoils, Brady can't bring himself to carry out the sad task. His father shoots Apollo instead, with Brady turned away in sorrow. Later, Brady explains to his sister, Lily, that they had to put Apollo down.

She initially protests that news. Seated on the coach together, Brady explains, in a quiet, mournful tone, "It's not fair to the horse. He can't run and play and do what he wants to do." In the opening scene of the film, Brady dreams he is a horse before waking up in the hospital. Now he has words for that ethereal connection: "You know, I got hurt like Apollo did. But I'm a person so I got to live. If any animal around here got hurt like I did, they'd have to be put down." Zhao included this line in the film because she was struck by its poignancy when Jandreau said it to her in real life. In both contexts, the implication is that people can make meaning in a way horses cannot. Human animals are expected to persevere in situations that would be considered cruel for non-humans to endure.

The Insecurity of Human Worlds and Identities

From Berger's perspective, non-human animals inhabit a more or less completed world, characterized by instincts. In this sense, a "dog-world" and a "horse-world" are mainly "closed" worlds, while humans have a much more "open" relationship with their surroundings.[68] "That is, it is a world that must be fashioned by [people's] own activity."[69] In the absence of so much of the instinctual hardwiring in non-human animals, people draw more heavily on the software of culture. "Culture, although it becomes for [people] a 'second nature,' remains something quite different from nature precisely because it is the product of [people's] own activity."[70] Culture adds a key missing ingredient to the survival instinct in humanity since it provides meaning to otherwise unendurable suffering. Geertz claims the most intense hardship can be made bearable when the pain is set within a matrix of meaning. Stuart Hall says that culture is "the way we make sense of and give meaning to the world" and Geertz points to the collective aspects of this process, calling culture "socially established structures of meaning." Without the meaning-making of culture, Geertz suggests we would be a "formless monster" and "a chaos of spasmodic impulses and vague emotions."[71] These descriptors are symbolically apt for Brady's emotional struggle with meaning after his injury. His friends compare him to the same monster Hamilton felt she resembled after losing her arm. With his partially shaved head and long, thick track of head-staples, Brady "looks like Frankenstein" to those joking buddies. As to the "chaos of spasmodic impulses," this is the most persistent of the lingering symptoms from Brady's brain injury. A physician explains, "What is going on with your hand is called a partial complex seizure. The brain is sending these signals too fast and your hand can't keep up, so it just stays clenched." Just as Brady physically struggles to unlock his grip on such occasions, it is clear that metaphorically he cannot let go of the identity-symbols from a sporting culture that clothed his life with so much meaning, but which seem increasingly ill-fitting in his new condition.

In the film, Brady doesn't just want to ride horses again, he wants to re-turn to rodeo competition, both of which the physician forbids. "No more riding. No more rodeos," she says flatly. One of his friends advises empathetically, "You just got to learn to let it go. Move on. It's gotta be tough. I understand." Brady speaks softly but adamantly to the contrary, "You don't understand." Indeed, Brady is being asked to leave the rodeo and horse-riding world where he learned who he is and who he should be. This speaks to the inherent instability of all social worlds and the concomitant precariousness of identities built within them. Berger points out that "the individual appropriates the world in conversation with others and, furthermore, that both identity and world remain real to himself only as long as he can continue the conversation."[72] It is clear from conversation with peers in the film that Brady struggles to reconcile the confident language of his rodeo socialization with the delicate reality of his new physiological condition. In promoting the film, Jandreau told one interviewer about a real-life case that shook the rodeo world's hyper-masculine confidence.

CTE and Masculinity

Ty Pozzobon became the first rodeo rider diagnosed with CTE the same way every athlete gets that definitive confirmation—posthumously. His manner of death also matched high-profile cases of CTE from other sports leagues, like the NFL. Before his suicide on January 9, 2017, the 25-year-old Canadian was one of North America's best and most tenacious bull-riders. When he broke his dominant hand, he rode with the weaker one. "He was a gritty sucker," a fellow rider named Chad Besplug says. "He would never quit."[73] More dangerously, Pozzobon continued to compete after suffering several concussions, something not unheard of at a time when the long-term effects of brain injury were less well-known on the rodeo circuit than they became after his death. Now the perils can't be ignored. Accordingly, Besplug has no tolerance for reckless persistence. "Riding a bull while you have a head injury doesn't show how tough you are, it is just plain dumb," he says. "It doesn't heal like a broken bone. The damage sticks with you forever."[74] Because of his own head injuries, Besplug decided retirement was the smartest move. Tanner Girletz, "the son of a five-time national champion," was also dismayed by his friend's death. He minces no words about the impotence of macho bravado in the face of finitude: "All I know is that I didn't feel too fucking tough when I was carrying my friend in a casket."[75] Toxic masculinity indeed.

No one seemed to know the debilitating extent of Pozzobon's pain, a psychological turmoil that eluded the comprehension of even his closest family members, like his mother, Leanne, and his wife, Jayd. "Leanne Pozzobon says she worried less about him being injured riding bulls than she did him getting hurt while driving long distances between rodeos."[76] Jayd, whose life was cruelly compressed from young bride to young widow, recognizes the singularity of her late husband's distress: "You can see signs here and there, but you don't really know how bad it is unless you are that soul living in a body that has withstood trauma."[77] The particularities of the pain may be unique, but Leanne and Jayd share a belief with many others that CTE was at the root of Pozzobon's demise. That sentiment is certainly ubiquitous among grieving loved ones of former NFL players who had the same condition. The similarities between CTE in the two sports don't stop there. Dr. Julian Bailes played a major role in the discovery of CTE, not only through his real-life working relationship with Bennet Omalu, but also in the cinematic depiction of their collaboration in *Concussion*. At a brain injury conference in Dallas, Bailes shared an emotional moment with Jayd. "He told me, 'I will do everything I can to give you the answers you are looking for,'" Jayd says. "I was bawling and had full-body chills."[78] The emotions surrounding brain injury are much more muted in *The Rider* when Brady's friends boast and he quietly squirms.

Around a campfire, Brady and his friends trade stories about their various rodeo injuries. One friend, who has taken a number of blows to the head during his rodeo career, admits, "I probably had ten-plus concussions. I mean, by NFL standards, I should probably be dead." Another friend discusses a rib injury from which he bounced back with Brady's encouragement. He challenges Brady to now show the same grit and not give up "just because your head hurts a little bit. . . ." Brady is not encouraged. He clarifies, "Your brain's a little different than your ribs." The masculine social world is not so easily toppled, though, as the friend's insistent rejoinder makes clear: "I know, but it's all the same to a cowboy. Ride through the pain." He admonishes Brady not to trade his cowboy status for that of a farmer, warning that this is the plight of those cowboys who "get scared" after an injury. Berger wrote that "the individual who strays seriously from the socially defined programs can be considered not only a fool or a knave, but a madman."[79] To his friend, it seems beyond comprehension that Brady would abandon his role as a horse-riding cowboy. He acts as frustrated as the conservative evangelical woman who refused to believe a straight man could watch *Soul Surfer* without sexual arousal. Indeed, it is religion that Berger thinks makes social roles seem "inevitable," as part and parcel of the universal 'nature of things,'"[80] and Brady cannot shake the feeling that God made him to ride. Much later in the film, after Brady tells Lily about putting Apollo down, he uses religious language to frame his social identity. He says, "You know, Lily, I believe God gives each of us a purpose: for the horse, it's to run across the prairie; for a cowboy it's to ride." Immediately after that comment, Brady prepares to enter a rodeo competition, against both his doctor's orders and his father's wishes.

His father is furious when he hears Brady's plans. Dejected with his son's stubbornness, he laments, "You never listen." Brady sees this as gaslighting. After all, Brady was always eminently attentive to his father's advice about how to be a resilient cowboy, but after Brady's injury his father radically changed the socializing conversation to one of self-care and protection. About the ways we learn who we are through conversations with others, Berger points out, "If such conversation is disrupted . . . the world begins to totter, to lose its subjective plausibility. In other words, the subjective reality of the world hangs on the thin thread of conversation."[81] Brady snaps like his cowboy world is coming undone. "I fuckin' listen to everything you say!" he yells. "What happened to 'Cowboy Up? Grit your teeth? Be a man?' What happened to all that, Dad?" As if written for this exchange, Berger affirms, "The last point is very important, for it implies that socialization can never be completed, that it must be an ongoing process throughout the lifetime of the individual."[82] Brady adapts to his changed circumstances by relying on nonverbal communication. When his sister and father unexpectedly arrive at the rodeo competition to support Brady, he decides not to go through with it. Brady reconciles with his father not through speech but through a hug. The physicality of Brady's communication keeps him in connection with others even when he feels like his world is falling apart.

Embodied Connections Across Spectrums

In a conversation with Zhao, film critic Elvis Mitchell discussed the range of people in the film with whom Brady can "really connect."[83] Mitchell asked, "I mean, be it with horses or his little sister or with his best friend and mentor, who really has no verbal communication skills whatsoever, we can see, he can make contact with people, can't he?" Zhao agreed and found Brady's communication with horses especially indicative of his unique place in our insular social conditions. She said, "We can't even communicate with someone who lives next door these days, let alone speak a different language."[84] Accordingly, Zhao wanted to make a movie that would translate easily across cultures, one that didn't rely on dense idiomatic dialogue, but would (for sighted people, at least) include more open-ended sensory experiences. She explained, "I feel like at a time like this I really love the idea of leaving a lot of space in the film for an audience to interpret, to interact with the film, to take whatever they want to take based on where they are at in their lives and how they feel about the world."[85]

Sometimes autistic people are said to be "in their own world," but Brady's sister, who is autistic in the film and in real-life, is a key conversation partner. Despite her palpable enthusiasm, though, Lily's sometimes blunted affect could make it difficult for some audiences to appreciate her deep affection for her brother. In this respect, touch and song triumph over speech. While Brady is lying in bed with a headache, she sings him a soothing Italian lullaby and gently strokes his back. Here, it is not the meaning of the lyrics that communicate sibling devotion, but the emotions Lily infuses into the song's tender notes. The movie also strikes a hopeful note about neurodivergent lives like Lily's. Brady explains to a friend (played by his real-life wife) that Lily used to throw tantrums and that the family had trouble engaging with her. Something happened, though, (and Brady is not sure what exactly) that drew Lily's attention to various objects and songs she likes. All that propelled Lily's zest for interaction.

We see the same reciprocal enjoyment in the multi-sensory communication between Brady and his best friend Lane. In real-life, Lane Scott was in an automobile accident on September 3, 2013. The South Dakotan was in Texas at the time on a college bull-riding scholarship. (The movie does not specify how Lane was injured, but without knowing the off-camera circumstances during my first viewing, I assumed he was hurt in competition.) Lane is a centripetal axis toward which the film's most salient themes unite. We hear about Lane before we meet him. Over a campfire, Brady and his friends recount fond memories of Lane's life before the injury. They beam as they laud his bull-riding skills. After hearing from Brady about his visits to Lane in the hospital, one friend suggests a prayer.

> [I] wanna say a prayer for him. I mean, it'd be best if we said a prayer every day for the guy because he sure could use it, but I just want to go ahead and say, I pray to God that he takes in all the strength from all his friends across the nation—north, south, east and west—because we all know he's got friends all over this country. [Hope he] pulls through; hope he gets to ride again, feel the wind hit his back, watch it flow through the grass. We are him and he is us. We're all one in this together. Mitakuye Oyasin.[86]

The last line is a common Lakota expression, translated "All my relations (or "all my relatives"). Brady calls Lane "brother" whenever he sees him, and he also has that word tattooed on his arm. Within the film (and in real life) Brady adds another tattoo to his back—a picture of Lane riding a bull in the backdrop of a cross. After meeting with Lane in the hospital, Brady cries in his truck. He seems sad both for his friend and himself, but the film does not perpetuate the idea that disability is worse than death. No one in the film minimizes the manifold distress of traumatic injury and accident, but neither does anyone take a depressing bow to fate. As one reviewer noted, "Zhao approaches these scenes with remarkable delicacy, never reducing her actors to their disabilities or milking them for easy pity."[87] The disabled people in the film are too complex for the supercrip mold. Brady and Lane are both impaired to widely varying degrees, but neither serves as an inspirational prop. There is sharp humor and quiet understanding between them. This is not a film about a rugged cowboy who draws on his adamantine will to "overcome" disability. The camera captures interdependence, not heroic individualism.

Indoors Brady and Lane ritualize memories from outdoors, of competition and relaxation. They watch YouTube videos of Lane's prodigious bull-riding feats, taking part in what Plate calls the "ritual retelling, reenacting and remembering of . . . stories."[88] Like Bethany and Alana, the most poignant interaction between Brady and Lane takes place in a hospital. Brady throws a saddle over a wooden bench and offers makeshift reigns to Lane. Brady narrates the ride, creating a vivid simulation for Lane by replicating the resistance of an animal. Lane smiles, but when at one point he grows tired or discouraged (or both), Brady encourages him firmly, "Keep your head up, brother." At the end of their imaginary riding, Brady hugs Lane and leans heavily against him, like he used to do with Gus. In the film's conclusion, it is Brady who needs cheering. When Lane catches Brady in a forlorn gaze, he signs, "Don't give up on your dreams." Encouraged, Brady rises to his feet and takes Lane's hands, offering his own grip as the resistance of the reins. Brady narrates a vision about Lane riding Gus again, encouraging him to imagine the wind on his face, but the viewers' closing image is Brady, not Lane, riding Gus.

Is this a hopeful ending? Zhao is cautious in her response:

> I guess it depends what you mean by hope because hope could be a word that's much more extravagant. But it could also be something that is very subtle because both films, [*The Rider* and her first film, *Songs My Brother Taught Me*], are saying that once you accept your circumstances and you make that part of who you are and you deal with it and you wake up the next morning and you just get through another day, in no time you'll be miles away and that's to me hopeful. That might be too somber for other people but it's so important that we can be okay; not necessarily happy but be okay with where we are.[89]

I turn in the next chapter to final thoughts about that subtle, even quiet, hope. A whisper that reminds us we are not forgotten.

Conclusion

"SWING AWAY"

It May be a bit disappointing initially that when we look for clear answers
to the burning questions in our lives, we are left only with titles of books,
experiences in nature, names of people, and a series of seemingly
random events . . . . But God lets himself be *suspected*!

— HENRI NOUWEN —

A strenuous pickup basketball game earlier in the week leaves me a little hobbled for a morning walk with my dog Rocky. My ankle stiffens with every step. I am just minutes away from a scheduled phone call with a woman named Hazel Thomas. She is the Chaplain Manager at a neurological rehab hospital in Houston. She also previously ministered to players on the professional women's tennis tour. She will speak to my Religion and Sports class alongside one of her former clients, Kelubia Mabatah, a Houston native who played collegiate tennis at the same institution where I teach the class. Mabatah has not played a tennis match since 2014. That is when he was attacked and left for dead in Nigeria while working in his father's business compound. He attributes his survival to both physical conditioning and God's providential care, a combination of sports and Christianity he continues to believe to be vital to his recovery. Kelubia was in a coma for six days, and it took much longer to relearn how to walk and talk. While walking Rocky, I am meditating on both Mabatah's trauma and my minor ankle pain. One is cruelly tragic, the other annoyingly trivial, but they point to a shared reality: finite lives and fragile bodies. Rocky shares the limitations. He is panting in the rising Texas heat. I need to cut this walk short.

We approach a gate in my apartment complex meant for exiting cars, but which only requires a slight bow to squeeze through on foot. I am too focused on Rocky, though, as I walk straight forward and slam my head against the corner of a jutting block of metal. I am quickly bloodied and anxious, fearful I might miss my phone appointment.

By the time I reach the apartment, my bloodied countenance shocks my wife out of her sleepy haze. She grabs paper towels, and I press them to my head. Suddenly, I bowl over with dizziness. Looking at the blur of various species gathering around me—my dog, our two cats, and my wife—I panic. I try to relax but I cannot halt the tailspin. I feel like I will vomit, though I do not. I also feel like yelling, "Oh God, somebody help me!" which I very much do.

Stories from popular culture lay behind the terror. While hustling to the apartment, I was focused on vague details I remembered hearing about some actor who had been sitting in a plane somewhere when an item of some kind fell from the overhead compartment and landed on his head. He thought he was fine. Later that day, he was dead. "Didn't the wife of the actor Liam Neeson also die in a similar fashion?" I think to myself, compounding my fears. By the time I entered the apartment, those stories had fused with mine: they were models *of* what had just happened to me and I feared they were models *for* what was about to transpire. With everything spinning out of control, I thought I was going to die. Once I manage to sit up, breathe deeply, and regain a semblance of composure, I feel a surge of empathy. In preparation for this book, I read and ruminated over stacks of stories about trauma and disability, some fictional, others from real life. At the beginning of the process, those stories moved me. But I grew disconnected when I began to dissect them with cold analytical precision, parsing them for revealing sociological patterns. Feeling for just one brief, irrational, and exaggerated moment a terrifying lack of control over the most complex organ of my body brings these harrowing accounts back to life.

Several years later, Hazel is now the skilled, compassionate, and joyful Director of Pastoral Care at the hospital where I work as a chaplain. Kelubia is a competitive bodybuilder who demonstrates and testifies to the power of God for the resilient overcomer. When I was a professor and they were guest speakers in my class, I did not imagine this future. It remains opaque in some ways. Still, all three of us are trusting the one we believe knows and holds the future. What I have seen as a chaplain has at times made me wonder whether we should be.

Chaplaincy Behind the Glass

Starting chaplaincy in the middle of a pandemic means you have no reference point from so-called "normal" times. Still, there are things I witnessed that exceed at least what I imagine as usual suffering. Steve Gleason called his online interview series "Behind the Glass" because, as a person with an underlying condition that could exacerbate the impact of COVID-19, he needed to take extra precautions. In his case, that meant quarantining from the rest of his family behind glass. At one point during the pandemic, I received a call asking that I stand outside of the glass door of a middle-aged man dying of COVID. The request came from the man's wife who wanted me to pray for her husband. Even though he was on a ventilator and could not respond, it was an urgent request that God meet him in some secret place of his heart. Earlier that day, their teenage son with "special needs" had died from the virus afflicting her husband. I walked to his hospital room from my office, prayed silently, and gestured hopefully. I am self-conscious sometimes when I make the sign of the cross over someone else. It seems ostentatious somehow and attention-grabbing, as if I am He-Man yelling, "I have the power!" But the wordless prayer was all I had in that moment, so I dropped my hand like a hammer calling heaven to earth. I then crossed the bar like an emphatic punctuation mark. I did not cry, though. Not yet.

One day, a colleague asked, "Did y'all ever have a patient say they know they are 'not supposed to ask God why'? That happens to me all the time." It had never happened to me, but later that afternoon another patient's spouse, who I will call Jan, used that exact phrase. She could not stand watching her husband, a "proud, strong, Christian man," lose his faculties and his "dignity" in the process. "I know we aren't supposed to ask God, 'why?' she says. "What makes you think that?" I ask. "I don't know. I guess it was just how we were always taught." I said what I thought about earlier in the day when my colleague had raised this issue: "In the Bible, Jesus asks God the Father, 'Why?' When he is on the cross, he cries, 'My God, my God, why have you forsaken me?' Jesus is quoting a Psalm there and the Psalms are full of emotional questions like that." I was trying to help her lament. Carrie Doehring writes, "Stories allow people to lament with each other—express anger and question all they know about life—without imposing meanings prematurely."[1] Meanings embodied in phrases like "everything happens for a reason." As Bowler persuasively argues, that framework can distort reality. Sometimes it makes murder look like it was meant to be.

Pondering Providence

Though not as religious as Oscar Pistorius's mother, Ebba adopted the theology Sheila bequeathed to Oscar, the same one he applied to his impairment. Oscar said, "I think everything happens for a reason. God had a plan when he gave me these legs. And I think, you know, at the end of the day, I'm happy.

I don't think I would have been doing athletics if I was able-bodied. I don't see myself as disabled. So, either way, you're winning from both sides."[2] Ebba was likewise convinced that Oscar's dramatic, lifechanging entrance into their life, especially her son Hadlifi's, happened for a reason. She extended that comforting belief for her own family in a much more problematic direction toward another's. When Pistorius shot and killed Reeva Steenkamp, Ebba asserted that even this unmistakable tragedy must have happened for an inscrutable purpose: "He will need a lot of courage to forgive himself and to try to have a good life in spite of it. But I think maybe in a strange way it was supposed to be. Things happen for a reason."[3]

At one stage *Signs* seems to replicate that sentiment when the character who crashed into Colleen that fateful night meets with Graham. Ray Reddy looks overwhelmed with guilt as he broaches the topic that ties them together. He says, "It went so wrong that night. I've never fallen asleep driving before. Never since. Most of the ride home there wasn't a car in sight in either direction. If I would have fallen asleep then, I would have ended up in a ditch with a headache. It had to be at that right moment, the ten, fifteen seconds when I passed her walking. It was like it was meant to be."[4]

David Wheeler knows those kinds of thoughts, the what-ifs and the if-onlys.[5] The hairline fractures between life and death, between someone else's grief and your own unbearable sorrow. He thought about that as he reflected on the movements of Adam Lanza, the 20-year-old who carried deeply disordered thinking and semi-automatic rifles into Sandy Hook Elementary school on December 14, 2012. That morning, he unloaded the anguished mix on defenseless administrators, students, and children. Not just children in some collective abstract, but on David Wheeler's 6-year-old son Ben. David explains that "if for some reason he felt you weren't paying close enough attention, he would put his hands on either side of your face and turn your head till you were looking directly at him."[6] (That gesture is repeated various times in *Signs*). David and his wife Francine wish Ben could have eluded Lanza's attention. Francine carries guilt from what she calls "signs not to send Ben to school that day." David says that Ben had a sniffle, but he thought he should go to school anyway. "I now have to own that."[7] Francine was directing a musical, and she thought about letting the kids miss classes on Friday so they could watch it. Instead, she decided to take them to the performance the night before so that they could attend school the next day. And then there are Lanza's contingent movements, turning down one hall instead of another. David speaks philosophically about that: "If you look at any catastrophic event, there are going to be places where if that person had turned left instead of right, events would not have unfolded the way they did. But that's life. That's the chaos of the universe. And I previously found a certain amount of beauty in that chaos. And now the challenge is to continue to see the beauty in that chaos. Because now the chaos has hurt me."[8] He barely gets those last words out. He cries from the fresh pain of this re-telling. Still, David's search for beauty in chaos is a reminder that the fictional Graham's vision of theism and atheism in *Signs* is faulty, blurred perhaps by his own tearful grief. Even though he has abandoned his faith by the time he has the conversation with Merrill about coincidence and happenstance, he is intolerant of ambiguity. By joining theism to meaning and comfort, and atheism to meaninglessness and fear, Graham oversimplifies a more complex reality. Happy atheists and happy theists face tsunamis of sorrow. To locate meaning-making in one camp and not the other is a false framing. Whether one believes we rejoin uprooted loved ones in heavenly rest, or that we are left to cultivate seeds of memory only in this earthly life, grief hurts like hell.

Lamenting with Popular Culture

A week ago, I gave into my wife's insistent claim that I would enjoy the ques-tion-stirring stories related in an old HBO series called *The Sopranos*. While I am thinking through the details of the patient visit with Jan, I coincidentally watch an episode that is ideally suited for processing lament over the ravages of illness. Tony Soprano's journey through lament, while watching a friend deteriorate from cancer, confirms the fruitfulness of the path I tried to lay for Jan. It also helped with someone else in dire need of lament—myself.

Tony goes to the hospital to visit a male friend named Jackie who is dying of cancer.[9] Tony is in denial, adamant that Jackie will recover. Jackie's high spirits during Tony's first couple of visits seem to confirm Tony's overcon-fident assessment. On the third occasion, though, Jackie is despondent and barely oriented to anyone but himself. Dazed in pain or depression, he does not track with any of Tony's stories. Faced with Jackie's imminent death, Tony confronts the futility of life. He tells his therapist, "I'm not afraid of death. Not if it's *for* something. You know, a war, something like that. A reason. But Jackie. To see this strong, beautiful man just wither away to nothing. And you can't do nothing about it." I'm going to cautiously interrupt Tony Soprano for a moment to explore my discomfort with the parallels between this episode and my visit.

Before the viewing, I obviously had no idea what the episode would be about. Given my mystical leanings, I am struck by serendipitous connections. If someone in ordinary time presented me the line, "To see this strong, beau-tiful man just wither away to nothing," I would have thought immediately of my conversation with Jan. Imagine how striking it is to hear it in the extraordinary time of actively and intentionally pondering that visit. This seems like the kind of synchronicity littered throughout the stories in this book. The steadfast, sometimes stubborn, belief that God enters the finest details of our lives, lighting it all up with revelation. But that is not fair once Jan is back in view.

Why doesn't she get light? Why is she, along with her deteriorating husband, left in the dark? Do not get me wrong, I do not want to trade with them. If God has chosen to use coincidence, at least on occasion, as a kind of love-light language with me, that possibility is too marvelous to take for granted. Even if I am deluded—imposing meaning and pattern on events that are only random—at the very least this meaning-making creates a kind of anesthesia. In this pain-full life, I will take it. And that is why it is so difficult for me to wholeheartedly lament. In so many ways, I know I am hanging by a thread, tethered to God by nothing but grace.

I am tempted, though, to forget tact. I want to scream about God's dereliction of duty. I want to take issue with my Sustainer: "Because I've got issues, God, why do you forsake people like this? Leaving them embedded without defenses in pointless, humiliating suffering. You, YOU! are the one who provides shitcare!" That is me. This is Tony Soprano: "And if all this shit's for nothing, why do I gotta think about it?" In *A Prayer for Owen Meany*, Owen learns through a miraculous sign the date of his death. He also has an amorphous vision of some of the details. In the Sopranos episode, Tony's therapist thinks about the more general and widespread knowledge that we will all die someday. She preserves space for lament, "without imposing meanings prematurely." She says, "That's the mystery, isn't it? The mystery of God, or whatever you want to call it, of why we're given the questionable gift of knowing that we're gonna die." Lament—finally letting the grief and anger of pandemic chaplaincy boil over in honest angry tears—turns out to be a questionable gift for me. I do not know why or how, but it gives me some peace. I am still angry, but I am an angry child of God.

Anchoring identity as children takes courage and emotional abandonment, especially for Graham and Morgan in *Signs*. When the family learns the world might be under extraterrestrial attack, Graham doubles down on his anti-ecclesiastical approach. He becomes alien to his children, monstrously cruel when they plead for prayer to allay their fears. He refuses three times, matching Peter's public denials of Jesus in the gospels. Morgan offers a stinging rebuke: "I hate you." "That's fine," Graham whispers. Morgan escalates the cruel invective, saying, "You let Mom die." Graham's face contorts with a mix of rage and grief, and he yells, "I am not wasting one more minute of my life on prayer. Not one more minute!" Bo is shaken by her father's anger and cries audibly. A single tear streams down Morgan's face. Graham spears at food on the others' plates, complaining no one will eat. His shoulders haunch, and he gasps while trying to hold back sobs.

The Message Version of Roman 8:27 might suggest Graham's angry disavowal of prayer has nonetheless morphed into a kind of groaning intercession: "If we don't know how or what to pray, it doesn't matter. He does our praying in and for us, making prayer out of our wordless sighs, our aching groans." Paul says that the groaning is like the pain of childbirth auguring something new. On the sports and pop culture website *The Ringer*, Tim Greiving metaphorically bridged pregnancy with storms: "To me, *Signs* has an atmosphere of, like, the barometric pressure before a storm. It's very pregnant. . . ."[10] In reflecting on her experience shooting *The Rider* in the U.S. Badlands, Chloé Zhao connected the universality of our painful, limited bodies to the unifying potential of storms.

> A film like this one reminds us that when there is a scar on every one of us, it will hurt. Our bodies are actually all the same, we got one heart, we are made of 90% water, that doesn't change. . . . That's why I like South Dakota in that way because when nature comes into play, when a storm comes in out there, it doesn't matter what religion you are or what politics you follow, you are going to bundle together to survive. I think by separating humans from nature so much we feel like we are complete individuals and so different from one another and we don't need each other.[11]

In these comments, Zhao subtly transitions from speaking of plural bodies to one metaphorical body of the human family, with shared scars and a single heart. The Apostle Paul makes a similar move when writing about Christian churches, which he also treats as a collective "body." The Church is the "body of Christ," sharing one another's joys and sorrows. "If one part suffers, every part suffers with it; if one part is honored, every part rejoices with it."[12] When Graham dissolves in tears, Morgan's anger melts at the sight of his father's brokenness. He rises from his chair and walks next to Graham who pulls him in for a tight embrace. Graham reaches in the same way for Bo, and finally also draws a more stoic Merrill into the group hug. The Gleasons had a similar journey of love through lament.

Less than a decade after throngs cheered his momentous punt-block, Steve could barely whisper to his father. With Steve's voice escaping him, Mike had to bend close to hear his desperate defense against Mike's religious impositions. Steve cries, "I was diagnosed with a terminal illness and I know when you get scared, you're going to jump to your camp that I need to pray like you; I need to believe all the same things that you believe." He pleads with Mike not to discount his faith, since "every time you question my faith it crushes me." Recognizing his father's terror of his terminal illness, Steve longs to convince him they are headed on the same eternal course. Steve throws feeble punches toward Mike's stomach while he gasps for every word: "My. Soul. Is. . . ." The strain of yelling through degenerating vocal cords creates a preternatural wail for the final word, "Saved!" He throws one last unsteady punch through the air.[13]

Mike pleads, "Don't be angry with me, please." He embraces Steve, erupting with his own torrent of heaving emotion: "Stephen, you're my son. You don't know what it feels like inside that I might lose you, man. You don't know what it feels like. It's killing me!" As Mike is leaving the house, Steve says, "I'm glad you came," and Mike, still sniffling, pulls him close again, declaring, "I love you, Stephen, with everything inside of me." Smiling, Steve responds, "I love you, too, Dad." Lament does not always sound or look like obvious exasperation. Neither is it always expressed in the sacred language of love. It can come out like blessed cursing. It can involve clear and steady recognition of limits and the resolute setting of boundaries. Consider Steve's partner as an example.

Just as Steve deviates from various scripts—inspiration porn, the myth of positivity, and the inordinate individual focus of the medical model—Michel also breaks molds. She refuses the part of the endlessly sacrificing female caretaker. She is long-suffering and nurturing, but she does not deny her limits or frustrations. She is unapologetic about needing a team to care for Steve. Michel recruits a tall, muscular friend whom she babysat as a youth and promises to "punch [him] in the dick" if he will not come on board to help her and Steve. Blair Casey ends up bringing levity to their lives and much needed comic relief to the film. In assessing the ways Blair collaborates with her and others in keeping Steve's spirits high and body in motion, Michel notes in satisfaction that they are a "badass team." Besides welcoming teamwork, Michel takes up a form of therapeutic art called emotional doodling to process her emotions.

Reflecting on the ways she has handled her various roles, Michel vehemently rejects scripts of saintly female devotion: "I have never wanted to be a saint. I've never been a saint before Steve. I'm never going to be a saint. I don't want to be like a devil or like a dickface, but I don't want to be a saint either. I just want to be a real person." About the gravity of her situation, she admits, "This is a motherfucker." A sly smile emerges as she points out, "I haven't lost my sense of humor." That is a hard-fought, resilient joy.

Playful Meetings

Elizabeth Newman encourages people to "participate—playfully and joy-fully—in what God is doing in our midst with these particular people whom God has gathered."[14] I think about the students gathered with me in my grief. They were sometimes intentional, other times unwitting instruments of God's grace. The next academic year after Morgan fainted, I told the story in another class. In the afternoon, I received a message from Morgan explaining she had a friend in this new class of mine who told her what I shared. Morgan wrote that by coincidence she had just last night written a paper about the strange events from nearly a year ago. I wondered what academic point she or I could make of this confusing story. If it has a lesson, it is not straight-forward. Buechner thinks educators are often expected to teach "control and competence. We say in effect that this is the world and these are the things that it is important to know in order to live controlled and competent lives in it."[15] It is competence that Mr. Fish wants to teach Owen and John through sports. It is diversely embodied connection they seek. "Fiske et al. note that people with disabilities are generally liked, but not seen as competent."[16] That I initially stood with a blank stare while a student lay immobile on the carpet calls my own competence into question. Thankfully Buechner finds a far superior pedagogical method in the writing of Walter Brueggemann.

The biblical scholar privileges "meeting" over competence.[17] Our class-room experience fits Brueggemann's description of "life-changing meetings that open one to new kinds of existence."[18] None of the most meaningful moments of that day were part of the lesson plan. They were forced detours. I was "practicing failure," in Halberstam's words, which, among other objec-tives, includes "to take a detour, to find a limit, to lose our way, to forget, to avoid mastery."[19] Bodies are limited, and knowledge is partial in all the stories I have told and analyzed in this book. No one knows exactly what is going on. Some of the bad things turn around for good, but the worst things cannot be undone, at least in this life. We are left not with answers to tragedy, but as Owen's surname suggests, meaning. This is what Bowler said we should look for in the middle of a global pandemic: "meaning without being taught a lesson."[20] Nouwen writes, "Therefore, when we pray to God or search for God in silence, we learn to recognize him in the many little ideas, meetings, happenings, signs, and wonders along the way."[21] Buechner knows the feeling:

"I think of a person I haven't seen or thought of for years, and ten minutes later I see her crossing the street. I turn on the radio to hear a voice reading the biblical story of Jael, which is the story that I have spent the morning writing about. A car passes me on the road, and its license plate consists of my wife's and my initials side by side. When you tell people stories like that, their usual reaction is to laugh. One wonders why."

I believe that people laugh at coincidence as a way of relegating it to the realm of the absurd and of therefore not having to take seriously the possibility that there is a lot more going on in our lives than we either know or care to know. Who can say what it is that's going on? But I suspect that part of it, anyway, is that every once and so often we hear a whisper from the wings that goes something like . . . "Don't ever think that you've been forgotten."[22]

Shyamalan wanted to say something like that in *Signs*. While being interviewed about why the film still resonates after all these years, and especially during the pandemic of 2020, Shyamalan pointed to its culinary genesis.

There was this weird moment where, strangely, I went to Denny's. I was sitting there and seeing a family that was silent, and they were eating. I saw a couple that was quiet, and they were eating. And I was saying to myself: I can make movies that are burdened, and that's honest for me. But I was looking at those people in the Denny's, and I knew they were coming to my movies, and I wanted to make them feel better. So I called Disney and I said, "I want to make a movie that is just joyous, and doesn't have that lens of burden on it." It can have a lot of conflict in it, but the voice, the angle, I wanted it to be inspired and childlike, almost. And so *Signs* was born that way.[23]

He could not have imagined the childlike joy that movie would give me while carrying heavy adult loads. Nouwen wrote, "In the final analysis, all we have are signs that lead us to *suspect* something unspeakably great,"[24] and the imbrication of that movie with my life leads me to a modest manifesto: I cannot prove we have divine companionship in our pain—but I believe we do, and I really hope for it. While I write this, my cat Masala has curled onto my stomach, now shaking from my emotions. I am slouched, typing through tears about all that has been lost, trembling with hope for everyone struck down in recent years before any semblance of just timing; people I never met and others so close I bear their imprint. In all these storms of the Badlands and coincidences of the Brightside, I hear something like a "whisper from the wings" that they, you, me, we are "never forgotten."

Writer Rachel Held Evans died at thirty-seven years of age after first entering the hospital for a seemingly innocuous urinary tract infection. She not only left behind a husband and two young children but a generous invitation: "This is what God's kingdom is like: a bunch of outcasts and oddballs gathered at a table, not because they are rich or worthy or good, but because they are hungry, because they said yes. And there's always room for more." The table reference makes me think of a scriptural passage I now know nearly by heart, and in two languages.

During the pandemic I proclaimed Psalm 23 at several besides and in various hallways. In fact, I said it in Spanish more times than I had read any other scripture out loud in my entire life and in my own native tongue. It starts with a metaphor of God as a shepherd who leads sheep to water where they find quiet restoration. Eventually God makes an unusual promise. God will provide God's sheep-people food in the presence of their enemies. In this book, I have enumerated obvious and subtle enemies. The overt racism that obviously kills, and the covert kind that lurks in structures of representation and political organization. I have identified the explicit denigration of people with disabilities and the deceptive marginalization that treats such people as inspirations in a world otherwise built and lived without them in mind. I wrote about the collective joy in sports, but also the kinds of sports stories that drive us past healthy limits, where, in the best-case scenarios, we crash and burn out. I have mentioned narratives that make us feel secure and loved. And others that suggest we are peculiar and abandoned. So many enemies, seen and unseen.

In the subsequent class meeting after Morgan fainted, I ended by telling students about Psalm 23. I did not mention the final line, but the closing, bold declaration was on my mind: "Surely goodness and mercy shall follow me all the days of my life, and I shall dwell in the house of the Lord my whole life long." Nouwen clarifies, "The house of love is not simply a place in the afterlife, a place in heaven beyond this world. Jesus offers us this house right now in the middle of this anxious world."[25] We talked about the enemy aliens in *Signs* and I reminded them of the antagonists of college students they identified in a previous class session: stress, anxiety, depression, perfectionism, and failure. I encouraged them to do what Merrill did despite his athletic failures: "Swing away" again. Take emotional risks to find healing connection. Resist the temptation to bear pain alone. I then removed tinfoil from homemade brownies and invited them to the table.

Afterword

Given recent events, I expect to be emotional when I use this book to teach "Religion, Health, and Meaning" at TCU in the fall. We will need to visit this section for crucial updates to my own and others' stories. There is plenty of pain and consoling hope in both.

Tim Tebow tried his hand at football again for the final(?) time. He switched to the position many experts had insisted he was most suited for in the first place: tight end. He was also reunited with his college coach, Urban Meyer, who was now at the helm of Tebow's hometown Jacksonville Jaguars. It seemed like a match made in heaven. It was a disaster. Tebow was cut after his first preseason game. An inglorious lowlight circulated online of Tebow spinning in confusion and running into one of his own teammates.

It was a far cry from the triumphant days when Tebow's highlights generated widespread searches of John 3:16. When we revisit the portions of my book that juxtapose Tebow and Bennet Omalu, I will also need to update students on a sad postscript to Tebow's "3:16 game." Less than five months after the 34-year-old Tebow was released by the Jaguars, Demaryius Thomas—Tebow's receiver on that game-winning touchdown throw with the Broncos, the man who did most of the leg work on that spectacular overtime play—died at just 33 years of age. A posthumous study of his brain revealed that Thomas had Stage 2 CTE. I will clarify that it is not clear what role the disease might have played in Thomas's death, just as it is impossible to detect whether Tebow benefited from divine intervention in that game.

If publicized cases of CTE can make football seem like a dangerous on-field battle, contact sports still do not compare to the toll of actual war. John Irving acknowledged that *Meany's* backdrop of wars in Vietnam and Nicaragua was an implicit indictment of how sports distract us from what really matters. As Irving imagined in the novel, however, sports can also create meaningful connections in the most desperate of circumstances. I talked about various pilgrimages in this book, including the fictional buddy movie *The Peanut Butter Falcon*, in which a man with Down Syndrome risks his life on a journey to meet his wrestling hero, the Salt Water Redneck. That story now has an even more harrowing parallel in real life. Misha Rohozhyn's family fled Mariupol after their home was destroyed during the Russian invasion of

Ukraine. Misha, who has Down Syndrome and is non-verbal, was initially distraught about the sudden move. His mother, Lisa Rohozhyn, conjured a ruse to comfort her son. She told him they were traveling to meet his wrestling hero, John Cena. Cena explains the coincidental timing that facilitated an unexpected visit. "Having three days off from work right at the time that I read this story, and being an hour away by air, it turned immediately into, 'We're going.'" Tears flowed and muscles flexed during the emotional meeting in Amsterdam. Lisa was overcome watching her son meet his hero, and Misha was eager to show his new hulking friend his own formidable biceps.[1]

That was also Chris Fagan's trademark with his daughter Kate. The former college and professional basketball player often called on her, and others in his vicinity, to inspect his strength. In the final stages of his life, those biceps, along with the rest of his muscles, no longer worked. I learned about that wrenching final period from *All the Colors Came Out*. That is not only the title of Kate's book, about the life lessons she learned from her father on and off the basketball court, but also lyrics from the most important song in my life.

In the foreword to this book, series editor Brian Ingrassia mused about its themes while referencing a "beautiful spring day." That was a fitting introduction, since if this book had a soundtrack, U2's "Beautiful Day" would kick things off. The band performed that song in the post-Katrina Superdome, shortly before Steve Gleason's punt block. The lyrics contain a biblical allusion to Noah's Ark, when after a 40-day flood, Noah releases a dove to find dry land. The bird bites off a leaf and returns to the ark with the encouraging sign of safe return. God then sets a rainbow in the sky, promising better days ahead. Bono proclaimed that same hope to New Orleans: "See the bird with the leaf in its mouth. After the flood all the colors came out." As leaders of a church called The Ark, Mallory and I continually revisit the song. It was also Chris Fagan's favorite.

I lost touch with Kate Fagan after she spoke virtually to my class at Miami University. She was a winsome and captivating guest. She shared about her struggles as a gay basketball player at the University of Colorado, where she was immersed in an evangelical Christian culture incompatible with her sexuality. My graduate students in "Cultural Studies of Sport" were also fascinated by her subsequent experience as a journalist and on-air personality at ESPN. When, years later, Mallory mentioned that a different woman at ESPN had liked one of her tweets, I thought of Kate and realized I had not seen her on television for some time.

I mentioned this to Mallory who did a quick Google search. She exclaimed, "No way!" She had my full attention. "What?" I asked eagerly. "You are not going to believe the name of her new book," she insisted with a smile. I was happy to hear about the connection to the song but saddened to learn why I had not seen her recently on ESPN. One of her motivations for leaving the network included caring for her ailing father after he was diagnosed with ALS.

The basketball and life lessons made me think of my own father. After the best game I ever played, my dad met me on the court with a beaming smile and a firm handshake. We are a family of huggers, and he is generous with his affection, but there was something poignant in that understated act. Like Laura holding Logan's hand, it was a transcendent moment that surpassed grand gestures. I was on memory lane with Dad teaching me his deadly half-hook-shot he employed with his dominant left hand. As an aging righthander, that shot remains one of my last effective weapons in pickup basketball, but my competitive instincts are balanced by my father's lifelong pleas for me to enjoy the process of play rather than strive for the impossibility of perfection. Dad later helped me apply that principle to my faith. Even though I was confused at times by my mixed Christian upbringing, I am now grateful for the blend I received from my parents.

In *All the Colors*, Kate acknowledges that she had initially sworn off religion after her oppressive college encounter, but that she has grown more open to the kind of eclectic spirituality embodied by her wife, Kathryn. Kathryn encouraged her to consider the auspicious significance of certain numbers, especially 108, which some call a "sacred number" of "spiritual completion." It was also the room number in the ICU where Chris spent his final hours. Though not an overtly spiritual person, Chris was encouraged by that serendipity, since he already paid attention to the coincidental appearance of numbers, especially "11:11."

Over the years, Chris habitually contacted Kate at that time. When she moved to Colorado for college, he would acknowledge their two-hour time difference with a tactile and verbal ritual. He would touch the clock at 1:11 his time and say, "Love you, Katie," in recognition that it was 11:11 her time. Kate writes that her dad "would have said, if pressed, that the number served as a reminder that life is ultimately mysterious, and we should respect the mystery and reach out to the people we love."[2] After reading her book, I decided to open an email from my dad that had been sitting in my inbox for a couple of days. I noticed that he had unintentionally sent it at 1:11 p.m. his time, 11:11 a.m. mine.

In his email, he linked to a story about Keith Smart, a basketball coach I had known since high school. Keith is famous for hitting a game-winning jumper to lift the Indiana Hoosiers over the Syracuse Orangemen in the 1987 NCAA men's basketball championship. I first met him when I volunteered as a counselor at an Athletes for Christ basketball camp in Halifax, and we met several more times when his hustle and joy made him a fan favorite for the Halifax Windjammers of the World Basketball League. At that time, he wrote me an encouraging note that I continued to read even after we lost touch. Keith had various coaching stints in the NBA, but the article my father sent focused on his return to the same competition where he first became famous. He was now an assistant coach with the University of Arkansas Razorbacks, who were in the middle of a deep run in the NCAA tournament. The article mentioned something I did not know about Keith's journey, something we now have in common. He has recovered from skin cancer and has the facial scars to prove it.

My dad had sent the article without much explanation, but he was intimately acquainted with all the reasons I would find it meaningful. Dad had talked me through my skin cancer journey, and especially the month after a major reconstructive surgery when I had daily panic attacks. I felt at the time like I was doomed to experience debilitating panic for the rest of my life. As a retired physician and loving father, he combined the expertise and care I needed to survive that psychological ordeal.

Now, in a period of less turmoil, the Spirit rustled through the pages of Kate's book, moving me to make more space and give more attention to my father. I was a little worried about what the timing of this impulse might mean. In our first phone conversation after I read his email, Dad mentioned that he had been feeling fatigued lately, and that he had an upcoming appointment with a specialist. We could only wait and pray. By that point, I had already found another sign related to Kate's work.

Given the 1:11, 11:11 connections between our two worlds, I had hunted for a 108, the sacred number which had comforted Chris in his last days. The day after reading All the Colors, Mal had a morning engagement, so I decided to go to an early movie. I went to a nearby pub beforehand and drank a Guinness in memory of Chris, since he had requested that beer the night before his tracheostomy. The movie, Infinite Storm, was a grueling and poignant depiction of perseverance and grief. There was also a more lighthearted scene in which the protagonist devours pizza. That scene made me so hungry that after the film I stopped at the closest pizza place I could find. As I parked the car and walked toward the store, I gasped when I saw the number on the door. I took a picture of the 108 and sent it to Kate.

Just a couple of weeks later, I covered the chaplain role in daily palliative care meetings with nurse practitioners, physicians, social workers, and a child life specialist. The team did not know anything about my book, but a physician asked me to provide pastoral support to a former college football player with ALS. I read a portion of *All the Colors* to the patient. I also gave Kate's book to the patient's daughter. At least one staff member purchased the book. I sent a copy of the key passage to various members of the palliative team, and one asked permission to share it with her patients and their families dealing with terminal illness.

The patient himself indicated he found the passage moving and helpful. I only know that because another staff person accompanied me who was better than I am at reading his lips. The late James Ryle, a former chaplain for the University of Colorado football team, believed this kind of teamwork is also essential for discerning spiritual meaning in our lives. He surmised that "how God speaks to one person is not always the same way that [God] speaks to another. This creates the necessity of healthy interdependence upon one another. . . . When we put our parts together the puzzle is solved, and we have the whole picture."[3]

It is difficult for me to picture all the parts of my upcoming "Religion, Health, and Meaning" class, especially now that I know my dad has multiple cancer lesions on his liver. It will probably be easier to talk about other people's stories. In addition to my book, I will draw on *All the Colors* (and a host of other supplemental material).

I know from checking the schedule online where we have been assigned to meet—Room 108. That, of course, is the same room number in which Chris died. Kate's explanation that 108 is considered a "sacred number" of "spiritual completion" provided a missing piece in my own puzzle. I realize now that 108 is the same room number I entered one morning when I was feeling faint, wondering how I would complete the semester after my friend's suicide. I didn't faint that morning, but my student Morgan did, like the Morgan in *Signs*, the film the students had watched in preparation for that uncanny class period. It was in Room 108 where I learned, in the words of Isaiah, "Even youths will faint and be weary, and the young will fall exhausted." We are only ever temporarily able-bodied. Together, we rise and complete our course.

Since change is constant, maybe we will have a different room by the beginning of the semester. Wherever we end up meeting, I hope that in some way, at some point, we all perceive a "whisper from the wings that goes something like this: 'You've turned up in the right place at the right time. You're doing fine. Don't ever think that you've been forgotten.'"[4]

Notes

Preface

1. Clifford Geertz, Interpretation of Cultures, 90.

2. Talal Asad, *Genealogies of Religion.*

3. Some people prefer identity-first language ("disabled people") over the person-first language ("people with disabilities") I use here. People who favor identity-first language do so for many reasons. Some want to stress the ways that social attitudes and structures marginalize, and thus "disable," people with physical and/or cognitive impairments. In this sense, the expression "disabled person" is meant to expose and critique that which impedes the flourishing of diverse people. Others sympathize with that activism but are focused more intently on valorizing disability as an estimable identity. Motivations for employing person-first language are equally complex and varied. Since many people labeled "disabled" have historically suffered abuse and prejudice, some people use person-first language to counter these dehumanizing patterns. I chose this style because of its popularity in the regional context, the United States, in which I am writing. Nevertheless, since identity-first language, instead of person-first language, is the overwhelming preference of the autistic community, I use identity-first language when addressing members of that specific community.

Introduction

1. *Pistorius*, Streaming, directed by Vaughan Sivell (Amazon Prime Limited Series, 2018).

2. John Carlin, *Chase Your Shadow: The Trials of Oscar Pistorius* (Harper Publishing, 2014, Kindle Edition), Chapter 14.

3. Carlin, *Chase Your Shadow.*

4. The Hebrew Bible is what many Christians refer to as the Old Testament.

5. 1 Corinthians 12:19-21, New Revised Standard Version.

6. Carlin, *Chase Your Shadow.*

7. Carrie Doehring, *The Practice of Pastoral Care: A Postmodern Approach* (Louisville, KY: Westminster John Knox Press, 2015), xvii.

8. Ibid., xviii.

9. Ibid.

10. Romans 8:22-23, NRSV.

11. Rom. 8:19.

12. Deuteronomy 23:1 states, "No one whose testicles are crushed or whose penis is cut off shall be admitted to the assembly of the Lord."

13. For example, Isaiah 56:3 states, "Do not let the foreigner joined to the Lord say, 'The Lord will surely separate me from his people'; and do not let the eunuch say, 'I am just a dry tree.'"

14. Nadia Bolz-Weber, *Pastrix: The Cranky, Beautiful Faith of a Sinner and Saint* (Jericho Books, 2014).

15. R. Murphy, "Encounters" in *Disability and Culture*, ed. Benedicte Ingstad and Susan Reynolds Whyte (Berkeley: University of California Press, 1995), 580.

16. Mariano Rivera, *The Closer* (New York, NY: Back Bay Books, 2014), 171.

17. Marie Hardin, "Disability and Sport," in *Handbook of Sports and Media*, ed. Arthur A. Raney and Jennings Bryant (New York, NY: Routledge, 2006), 580.

18. Kate Bowler, *Everything Happens for a Reason* (New York, NY: Random House, 2018), 21.

19. Jeffrey Scholes and Raphael Sassower, *Religion and Sports in American Culture* (New York, NY: Routledge, 2014), 2.

20. This story is recounted from the video short, "A Hoop Dream," found at https://www.youtube.com/watch?v=ngzyhnkT_jY.

21. Jim Johnson, *A Coach and a Miracle* (Beacon Publishing, 2011), back cover.

22. Ibid., 84.

23. Ibid., 83-84.

24. Ibid., 84.

25. Susan Eberly, "Fairies and Folklore of Disability," *Folklore* 99, no. 1 (1988): 58.

26. Ibid.

27. Ibid., 59.

28. Ibid.

29. Ibid., 30.

30. Iain F. W. K. Davidson, Gary Woodill, and Elizabeth Bredberg, "Images of Disability in 19th Century British Children's Literature," 40.

31. Paul Longmore, "'Heaven's Special Child,'" in *The Disability Studies Reader*, ed. Lennard Davis (New York, NY: Routledge, 2013), 35.

32. George Ritzer, *The McDonaldization of Society* (Thousand Oaks, CA: Pine Forge Press, 2000), 132.

33. Johnson, *Coach and a Miracle*, 78.

34. "10 Years Later, J-Mac Still Inspires," https://www.espn.com/video/clip /_/id/14783786.

35. C.S. Lewis, "The Grand Miracle," https://www.plough.com/en/topics /culture/holidays/christmas-readings/the-grand-miracle.

36. Ibid.

37. Bennett Omalu, Truth Doesn't Have a Side (Grand Rapids, MI: Zondervan, 2017), 185; Ibid.,13.

38. Ibid., 142–43; Ibid., 29.

39. 2 Samuel 9:8, The Message Version.

40. Joel Osteen, *Your Best Life Now* (New York, NY: FaithWords, 2004), 89.

41. Psalm 19:1, New International Version.

42. Ps. 19:4-5, The Message Version.

43. Scholes and Sassower, *Religion and Sports*, 5.

44. Plate, *Religion and Film*, 22.

45. Geertz, *The Interpretation of Cultures* (Basic Books, 1973), 108.

46. Patrick R. Grzanka, *Intersectionality: A Foundations and Frontiers Reader* (Boulder: Westview Press, 2014), xiii.

47. Thomas Shakespeare, "The Social Model of Disability" in *The Disability Studies Reader*, ed. Lennard Davis (New York, NY: Routledge, 2013), 214.

48. Jeremy Schipper, *Disability and Isaiah's Suffering Servant* (New York, NY: Oxford University Press, 2011), 16.

49. Ibid.

50. Ibid.

51. Schipper, *Disability and Isaiah*, 18.

52. Jay Coakley, *Sports in Society: Issues and Controversies*, 4.

53. *Gleason*, Streaming, directed by J. Clay Tweel (2016).

54. *Gleason*, DVD.

55. Geertz, *Interpretation of Cultures*, 14.

56. Stuart Hall, *Representation* (London: Sage Publications, 1997).

57. Wright Thompson, *The Cost of These Dreams*, 191.

58. Eiesland, 22.

59. "Atlanta radio program hosts fired," ESPN.com

60. Steve Gleason, "Regarding the DJ Skit in Atlanta yesterday," Facebook, June 18, 2013, https://www.facebook.com/teamgleason.org/posts/485570461518708.

61. For examples, see Scholes and Sassower, *Religion and Sports*; Eric Bain-Selbo, *Game Day and God*; Rebecca Alpert, *Religion and Sports: An Introduction and Case Studies* (New York, NY: Columbia University Press, 2015).

62. Plate, *Religion and Film*, 10.

63. Plate, *Religion and Film*, 5.

64. Marcel Danesi, *Popular Culture* (New York: Rowman and Littlefield, 2012), 58.

65. Mallory Nye, *Religion: The Basics* (New York: Routledge, 2009), 154.

66. Danesi, *Popular Culture*, 32.

67. Graham Ward, ed., *The Blackwell Companion to Postmodern Theology* (Malden, MA: Blackwell Publishers, 2001), xii.

68. Arthur Bochner and Carolyn Ellis, *Evocative Autoethnography* (New York, NY: Routledge, 2016), 50.

Chapter 1

1. Andrew Tate, *Contemporary Fiction and Christianity* (New York, NY: Continuum International Publishing Group, 2008), 90.

2. John Irving, *A Prayer for Owen Meany* (New York: William Morrow & Co., 1989), 1.

3. Ibid., 22.

4. Ibid., 23.

5. Ibid., 35.

6. Ibid., 10.

7. Buechner, 216.

8. Irving, *Meany*, 85.

9. Ibid.

10. Ibid.

11. Ibid., 87.

12. Ibid.

13. Ibid, 154.

14. Ibid., 195.

15. Ibid.

16. Ibid., 353.

17. Ibid.

18. Ibid., 178.

19. Jack Halberstam, *The Queer Art of Failure* (Durham, NC: Duke University Press, 2014).

20. Irving, *Meany*, 178.

21. Ibid.

22. Randolph Feezell, *Sport, Play, and Ethical Reflection* (Chicago: University of Illinois Press, 2006), 33.

23. Ibid.

24. Halberstam, *Queer Art of Failure*.

25. Kenneth Schmitz, "Sport and Play," *Sports and the Body*, ed. Ellen Gerber and William Morgan (Philadelphia, PA: Lea and Febiger, 1979), 31.

26. Feezell, *Sport, Play, and Ethical Reflection*, 33.

27. John Moore, "John Irving," *Denver Post*, April 2, 2009.

28. Irving, *Meany*, 303.

29. Richard Taylor, *Good and Evil* (New York: MacMillan, 1970), 260.

30. Irving, *Meany*, 612.

31. Moore "John Irving."

32. *Signs*, DVD, directed by M. Night Shyamalan (2002; Walt Disney Studios, 2003).

33. Ibid.

34. Frederick Buechner, *Secrets in the Dark* (New York, NY: HarperCollins, 2007), 215.

35. Rom. 8:28, New English Translation.

36. Rom. 8:28, The Message Version.

37. Heb. 11:34-38, The Message Version.

38. Isaiah 40:27-28, New English Translation.

39. Isaiah 40:29-31, New English Translation.

Chapter 2

1. Matthew Tabeek, "'I Feel for You, and I'm Here,'" AtlantaFalcons.com, https://sportsspectrum.com/sport/football/2020/12/04/falcons-hayden-hurst-god -gave-second-chance/.
2. 1 Samuel 17:33, English Standard Version.
3. Deuteronomy 23:1, New Revised Standard Version.
4. Acts 8:32-33, NRSV.
5. Schipper, *Disability and Isaiah*, 2.
6. Mikeal C. Parsons, *Acts*, 141.
7. Mikeal C. Parsons and Richard Walsh, *A Temple Not Made With Hands*, 154.
8. Ibid.
9. Mikeal C. Parsons, *Body and Character in Luke and Acts*, 132.
10. Ibid., 138.
11. Tabeek, "'Here for You.'"
12. Zac Al-Khateeb, "Skip Bayless has 'no sympathy' for Dak Prescott after Dallas quarterback opens up about depression," on *SportingNews.com*, September 10, 2020, https://www.sportingnews.com/us/nfl/news/skip-bayless-no-sympathy -dak-prescott-dallas-quarterback-depression/1coikxor1joro1vefvnh4msoir.
13. Hayden Hurst, "I Am Who I'm Meant to Be," https://www.theplayers tribune.com/articles/hayden-hurst-atlanta-falcons-who-im-meant-to-be.
14. Ibid.
15. Ibid.
16. Tabeek, "I Feel For You."
17. Ibid.
18. Ibid.
19. Tabeek, "I Feel For You."
20. Ibid., 21.
21. Array Creative, "Ad of the Month: Unlimited You," August 11, 2016.
22. Array Creative, "'Unlimited You.'"
23. Acts 10:34, English Revised Version.
24. Nick Vujicic, *Unstoppable* (Colorado Springs, CO: Waterbrook Press, 2012), 16.
25. Ibid., 20.
26. Ibid.
27. Ibid.
28. Ibid., 25.
29. Ibid.
30. Jeff Passan, "San Francisco Giants outfielder Drew Robinson's remarkable second act," https://www.espn.com/mlb/story/_/id/30800732/san-francisco-giants -outfielder-drew-robinson-remarkable-second-act.
31. Ibid.
32. Doehring, *Practice of Pastoral Care*, xv.

184

Chapter 3

1. Hebrews 12:1-3, The Message Version.
2. Jeffrey Scholes and Raphael Sassower, *Religion and Sports in American Culture* (New York, NY: Routledge, 2014), 79.
3. Ibid.
4. Ibid., 80.
5. Anthony Giddens, *The Consequences of Modernity* (Stanford, CA: Stanford University Press, 1990), 64.
6. Tobin Anthony Siebers, *Disability Theory* (University of Michigan Press, 2011), 48.
7. E:60, "Catching Kayla," https://www.espn.com/video/clip/_/id/11909407.
8. Scholes and Sassower, *Religion and Sports*, 86.
9. Ibid., 87.
10. E:60, "Catching Kayla."
11. Scholes and Sassower, *Religion and Sports*, 79.
12. E:60, "Catching Kayla."
13. Ibid.
14. Kayla Montgomery, personal Facebook post, July 3, 2015, https://www.facebook.com/permalink.php?story_fbid=1608117072802822&id=1502359356711928.
15. Kayla Montgomery, personal Facebook photo, October 2, 2015, https://www.facebook.com/kayla.montgomery.355/photos/slower-start-to-my-season-then-i-had-hoped-but-god-has-a-plan-romans-53-4-we-rej/1640755002872362/.
16. Scholes and Sassower, *Religion and Sports*, 85.
17. Kayla Montgomery, personal Facebook photo.
18. Lipscomb Bisons, "This is My Calling: Kayla Montgomery," https://www.facebook.com/lipscombbisons/videos/10156552280690109/.
19. Scholes and Sassower, *Religion and Sports*, 79.
20. Lipscomb Bisons, "Calling."
21. Ibid.
22. Doug Binder, "Catching Up with Kayla," https://www.runnerspace.com/gprofile.php?mgroup_id=44531&do=news&news_id=554998.
23. "Tim Tebow's Full Interview with Harry Connick Jr." Uploaded by Harry Connick, Jr., February 21, 2017, https://www.youtube.com/watch?v=cWZ4GysKSLo.
24. Ibid., 178.
25. Ibid., 202.
26. Tim Tebow, *Shaken* (New York, NY: Waterbrook, 2016), 155.
27. *Tim Tebow: Everything in Between*, DVD, directed by Chase Heavener (Summit Entertainment, 2011).
28. Sean O'Neil, "A Body Broken and Rebuilt for You," in *Identity and Myth in Sports Documentaries*, eds. Zachary Ingle and David Sutera (Toronto, ON: Scarecrow Press, 2013), 36-37.
29. Ibid., 39.

30. Scholes and Sassower, *Religion and Sports*, 81.

31. Ibid., 87.

32. Ibid.

33. As quoted in Scholes and Sassower, *Religion and Sports*, 38.

34. Tim Tebow, *Shaken*, 179.

35. Feezell, *Sport, Play, and Ethical Reflection*, 74.

36. Ibid.

37. "W15H Brings Early Christmas Gift to Former High School Quarterback," *Tim Tebow Foundation*, December 22, 2011, https://www.timtebowfoundation.org /stories/w15h-brings-early-christmas-gift-former-high-school-quarterback.

38. Rick Reilly, "I Believe in Tim Tebow," on ESPN.com, January 13, 2012, https://www.espn.com/espn/story/_/id/7455943/believing-tim-tebow.

39. Matthew 5:15-16, The Message Version.

40. Tebow, *Shaken*, 156.

41. R.A. Dickey, *Wherever I Wind Up* (New York, NY: Penguin Books, 2012), 33.

42. Ibid., 106.

43. Ibid., 108.

44. Gary L. Comstock, *Religious Autobiographies* (Toronto: Thomson Wadsworth, 2004), 219.

45. Ibid.

46. Dickey, *Wind Up*, 205.

47. Ibid., 211.

48. Ibid.

49. Ibid., 213.

50. Adam Rubin, "R.A. Dickey wins NL Cy Young," https://www.espn.com /new-york/mlb/story/_/id/8633034/ra-dickey-new-york-mets-wins-national -league-cy-young-becoming-first-knuckleballer-win-award.

51. Scholes and Sassower, *Religion and Sports*, 57.

52. Ibid., 64.

53. Ibid., 58.

54. Ibid., 57.

55. E:60, "The Kid Who Inspires Tim Tebow," https://www.youtube.com /watch?v=aHBXNsiO9pk.

56. Luke 8:46, NRSV.

57. Jason Romano, "Tim Tebow Shakes Hand of Autistic Boy, Proceeds to Hit Home Run," on SportsSpectrum.com, https://sportsspectrum.com/sport /baseball/2017/08/11/tim-tebow-shakes-hand-autistic-fan-proceeds-hit-home -run/.

58. Comstock, *Autobiographies*, 219.

59. Hebrews 4:14-16, The Message Version.

60. Maria Morava and Scottie Andrew, "For those with body dysmorphic disorder, masks do more than protect. They help them function," https://www.cnn .com/2021/02/21/us/body-dysmorphia-masks-trnd/index.html.

61. Omalu, *Truth* 34.

62. Ibid., 70.

Chapter 4

1. Jean Heller, "Syphilis Victims in U.S. Went Untreated for 40 Years," *New York Times*, July 26, 1972, https://www.nytimes.com/1972/07/26/archives/syphilis -victims-in-us-study-went-untreated-for-40-years-syphilis.html.

2. *Get Out*, DVD, directed by Jordan Peele (Universal Pictures, 2017).

3. Carrington, *Race, Sport, and Politics*, 56.

4. Ibid., 17.

5. Douglas Hartmann, *Race, Culture, and the Revolt of the Black Athlete*, xix.

6. Mohammed Ali, *Soul of a Butterfly*, 49.

7. Ibid., 59.

8. Ibid., 65.

9. Surah Al-Baqarah 2:249-255

10. Ibid., 76.

11. *Thrilla in Manila*, DVD, directed by John Dower (Time Life Records, 2009).

12. Ali, *Soul of a Butterfly*, 112.

13. Ibid., 113.

14. Ibid., 148.

15. Ibid., 147.

16. Ibid., 153.

17. Ibid., 116.

18. Ibid., 117.

19. Ibid., 111.

20. Omalu, *Truth*, 275.

21. Ibid.

22. Ibid., 34.

23. Ibid.

24. Ibid., 31.

25. Ibid., 36.

26. Ibid., 75.

27. Ibid., 91.

28. Ibid., 92.

29. Ibid.

30. Ron Lewis, "Lonnie offers strongest possible support," in *The Times*, November 21, 2005, https://www.thetimes.co.uk/article/lonnie-offers-strongest -possible-support-lrnporhm78s.

31. Omalu, *Truth*, 97.

32. Ibid., 121.

33. Ibid., 13.

34. Mark Fainaru-Wada and Steve Fainaru, *League of Denial* (New York, NY: Three Rivers Press, 2014), 29.

35. Omalu, *Truth,* 127.

36. Ibid., 121.

37. Ibid., 122.

38. Ibid., 142.

39. Ibid., 142.

40. Philip Jenkins, *The Next Christendom* (New York, NY: Oxford University Press, 2011), 9.

41. Ibid., 1.

42. David Bebbington, *Evangelicalism in Modern Britain* (New York, NY: Routledge, 1989), 2-3.

43. Philip Jenkins, "Global Schism: Is the Anglican Communion rift the first stage in a wider Christian split?" in *Pew Forum on Religion and Public Life* (May 14, 2007), https://www.pewforum.org/2007/05/14/global-schism-is-the-anglican -communion-rift-the-first-stage-in-a-wider-christian-split/.

44. Thomas Csordas, *Transnational Transcendence* (Berkeley, CA: University of California Press, 2009), 83.

45. Omalu, *Truth,* 64.

46. *Concussion,* DVD Commentary.

47. Manuel Vasquez and Marie Marquardt, *Globalizing the Sacred* (New Brunswick, NJ: Rutgers University Press, 2003), 35-36.

48. Jan Nederveen Pieterse, *Globalization and Culture* (Lanham, MD: Rowman and Littlefield Publishers, 2003), 59.

49. *Concussion,* DVD Commentary.

50. Omalu, *Truth,* 94.

51. *Concussion,* DVD Commentary.

52. *Concussion,* DVD Commentary.

53. Omalu, *Truth,* 197.

54. *Concussion,* DVD Commentary.

55. Omalu, *Truth,* 261.

56. Ibid., 202.

57. Ibid., 203.

58. Daniel Engber, "*Concussion* Lies," on Slate.com, December 21, 2015, https://slate.com/culture/2015/12/the-truth-about-will-smiths-concussion-and -bennet-omalu.html.

59. Ibid.

60. Will Hobson, "From Scientist to Salesman," on WashingtonPost.com, January 22, 2020, https://www.washingtonpost.com/graphics/2020/sports/cte -bennet-omalu/.

61. Ibid.

62. Ariel Henley, "We Don't Need Events Specifically For Disabled People,"

on Vice.com, February 28, 2018, https://www.vice.com/en/article/7x7myx/prom
-for-disabled-people-perpetuates-stigma.

63. Ibid.

64. Ibid.

65. "An Unlikely Friendship Sheds Light on Muhammed Ali's Life After Boxing," *WBUR*, June 8, 2016, https://www.wbur.org/hereandnow/2016/06/08/muhammad-ali-friendship.

66. Davis Miller, *The Tao of Muhammed Ali*, 129.

67. Ben Carrington, *Race, Sport, and Politics* (Los Angles: SAGE Publications, 2010), 129.

68. Carrington, *Race, Sport, and Politics*, 105.

69. Ibid., 112-113.

70. Ibid., 113.

71. Dave Davies, "'Get Out' Sprang from an Effort to Master Fear, Says Director Jordan Peele," *Fresh Air*, January 5, 2018, https://www.npr.org/2018/01/05/575843147/get-out-sprang-from-an-effort-to-master-fear-says-director-jordan-peele.

72. Ibid.

73. *The Peanut Butter Falcon*, DVD, directed by Tyler Nilson and Michael Schwartz (Lionsgate, 2019).

74. Eric Sullivan, "Shia LaBeouf Is Ready to Talk About It," *Esquire*, March 13, 2018, https://www.esquire.com/entertainment/movies/a19181320/shia-labeouf-interview-2018/.

75. Carrington, *Race, Sport, and Politics*, 102.

76. David Rosen, "King Kong: Race, Sex, and Rebellion," in *Jump Cut* (no. 6, 1975), 1-10.

77. Ibid.

78. Michael Cottingham, Brian Gearity, and Joshua Ray Pate, "Examining 'Inspiration'" (Canadian Journal of Disability Studies, January 2015), 64.

79. Ibid.

80. Ibid., 65.

81. Cody Benjamin, "Eagles legend Brian Dawkins says he contemplated suicide early in his Hall of Fame career," https://www.cbssports.com/nfl/news/eagles-legend-brian-dawkins-says-he-contemplated-suicide-early-in-his-hall-of-fame-career/.

82. Chris Ryan, "Saying Goodbye to Brian Dawkins and Weapon X," https://grantland.com/the-triangle/saying-goodbye-to-brian-dawkins-and-weapon-x/.

Chapter 5

1. Zack Scharf, "British Film Institute Vows Not to Fund Movies With Facial-Scarred Villains," https://sports.yahoo.com/british-film-institute-vows-not-174840737.html.

2. Ibid.

3. Ibid.

4. Ibid.

5. Ibid.

6. Ibid.

7. Ibid.

8. "Bono: The Beliefnet Interview," on *Beliefnet.com*, February 2001, https://www.beliefnet.com/entertainment/music/2001/02/bono-the-beliefnet-interview.aspx.

9. Christine Bordelon, "Ex-NFL Player, Now With ALS, Retorts: 'Relentlessly Seek Your Purpose,'" on *CatholicSun.org*, August 2, 2016, https://www.catholicsun.org/2016/08/02/ex-nfl-player-now-with-als-exhorts-relentlessly-seek-your-purpose/.

10. *Gleason*, DVD, directed by Clay Tweel (IMG Films, 2016).

11. 1 Cor. 12:26, New Revised Standard Version.

12. 1 Cor. 12:21, NRSV.

13. David Marchese, "Ignore Oscar – 'The Wrestler' is Springsteen's Best," *Spin*, January 23, 2009, https://www.spin.com/2009/01/ignore-oscar-wrestler-springsteens-best/.

14. Michael Rothman, "Hugh Jackman once told to find another job after original X-Men," https://abcnews.go.com/Entertainment/hugh-jackman-told-find-job-original-men/story?id=45862716.

15. Kevin P. Sullivan, "Hugh Jackman nearly called it quits after X-Men Origins: Wolverine," *EW.com*, March 3, 2017, https://ew.com/movies/2017/03/03/hugh-jackman-logan-xmen-origins/.

16. Ibid.

17. Omalu, *Truth*, 268.

18. Stephen Applebaum, "Interview: 'Logan' Director James Mangold," *The Jewish Chronicle*, March 3, 2017, https://www.thejc.com/culture/features/jame-smangold-wolverine-is-haunted-by-the-holocaust-1.433652.

19. "Behind the Glass: Soul to Soul with Steve Gleason with guest Hugh Jackman," May 28, 2020, https://www.youtube.com/watch?v=g4W5FgsZXHU.

20. *Logan*, DVD Commentary, Directed by James Mangold.

21. *Pistorius*.

22. 1 Cor. 2:9, New Revised Standard Version.

23. *The Life and Trials of Oscar Pistorius*, Streaming, directed by Daniel Gordon (ESPN+, 2020).

24. Carlin, *Chase Your Shadow*, Chapter 8.

25. *Life and Trials*.

26. *Life and Trials*, Part II.

27. Carlin, *Chase Your Shadow*, Chapter 11.

28. *Life and Trials*, Part IV.

29. Wright Thompson, "Beyond the Breach," in *ESPN The Magazine*, http://www.espn.com/espn/feature/story/_/id/13479768/wright-thompson-life-loss-renewal-new-orleans-10-years-hurricane-katrina.

30. Nancy Eiesland, *The Disabled God*, 93.

31. Ibid., 101.

32. Ibid., 89.

33. Ibid., 99.

34. Ibid, 101.

35. Carlin, *Chase Your Shadow*, Chapter 11.

36. *Life and Trials*.

37. *Life and Trials*, Part I.

38. Andy Crouch, "Transhumanism and the Cult of Better, Faster, Stronger," on *ChristianityToday.com*, March 15, 2019, https://www.christianitytoday.com/ct/2019/april/transhumanism-image-god-modern-technology-human-future.html.

39. Ibid.

40. Ibid.

41. Ibid.

42. "Behind the Glass."

43. Crouch, "Transhumanism."

44. Alpert, *Religion and Sports*, 50.

45. *Pistorius*, Part IV.

46. Carlin, *Chase Your Shadow*, Chapter 14.

47. Ibid.

48. Ibid.

49. *Life and Trials*, Part II.

50. *Logan*, DVD Commentary.

51. *Life and Trials*, Part II.

52. *Life and Trials*, Part IV.

53. *Logan*, DVD commentary.

54. *Life and Trials*, Part IV.

55. Isaiah 66:13, New Revised Standard Version.

56. Jody Peters, "A Look at the Past: Farmington Woman Wrote Over 5,000 Poems," April 19, 2018, https://www.hometownsource.com/sun_thisweek/a-look-at-the-past-farmington-woman-wrote-over-5-000-poems/article_56d15a92-43f4-11e8-80e9-6f90f8f297d6.html.

57. Greg Garrett, *Holy Superheroes!: Exploring Faith and Spirituality in Comic Books* (Colorado Springs, CO: Pinon Press, 2005), 31.

58. Ibid., 32.

59. Peter Berger, *The Sacred Canopy* (New York, NY: Anchor Books, 1990), 16.

60. Garrett, *Holy Superheroes*, 28.

61. Ephesians 2:8-9, New Revised Standard Version.

62. *Life and Trials*, Part II.

63. @DRRTKendall, https://twitter.com/drrtkendall/status/470943119727665152.

64. Mike Behr, "'I Have Forgiven Oscar For Killing My Daughter,'" on *DailyMail.co.uk*, April 11, 2018, https://www.dailymail.co.uk/news/article-5602689/Reeva-Steenkamps-mother-says-finished-Pistorius.html.

65. *Pistorius*, Part IV.

66. Doehring, *Practice of Pastoral Care*, xxi.

Chapter 6

1. *Unstoppable*, DVD, directed by Aaron Lieber (2018).

2. *The Rider*, DVD, directed by Chloe Zhao (2018).

3. Rosemarie Garland Thomson, *Extraordinary Bodies: Figuring Physical Disability in American Culture and Literature* (New York: Columbia University Press, 1997), 36.

4. Bethany Hamilton, *Soul Surfer* (New York: Pocket Books, 2004), xvi.

5. Ibid., 106.

6. Ibid., 121.

7. Ibid., 43.

8. David T. Mitchell and Sharon L. Snyder, *Narrative Prosthesis: Disability and the Dependencies of Discourse* (Ann Arbor: University of Michigan Press, 2000), 126.

9. Hamilton, *Soul Surfer*, 207-208.

10. Ibid., 72.

11. Ibid., 87.

12. Ibid., 78-79.

13. *Unstoppable*.

14. Hamilton, *Soul Surfer*, xiv.

15. Ibid., 141.

16. Ibid., xv.

17. Ibid., xv.

18. R.J. Berger, "Disability and the Dedicated Wheechair Athlete: Beyond the 'Supercrip' Critique, in *Journal of Contemporary Ethnography*, 37 (2008): 648.

19. Carl Kozlowski, "The Girls Behind Soul Surfer," *Relevant Magazine*, April 8, 2011, http://www.relevantmagazine.com/culture/film/features/25227-the-girls -behind-soul-surfer.

20. Thomson, *Extraordinary Bodies*, 23.

21. Hamilton, *Soul Surfer*, xv.

22. Ibid., 209-210.

23. Stacy McDonald, "Soul Surfer: Beaches, Bikinis, and… Bibles?" in *Your Sacred Calling*, April 11, 2011, http://yoursacredcalling.com/blog/2011/04/soul -surfer-beaches-bikinis-and%E2%80%A6bibles/.

24. Daniel Thompson. "Movie Reviews: Soul Surfer," https://christiananswers .net/spotlight/movies/2011/soulsurfer2011.html?zoom_highlight=soul+surfer.

25. Ibid.

26. Debra Shogan, *The Making of High-Performance Athletes* (Buffalo: University of Toronto Press, 1999), 46.

27. Arjun Appadurai, *Modernity at Large: Cultural Dimensions of Globalization* (Minneapolis: University of Minnesota Press, 1996), 179.

28. McDonald, "Soul Surfer."

29. Lesley Heywood and Shari L. Dworkin, *Built to Win* (Minneapolis: University of Minnesota Press, 2003), 77.

30. Thomson, *Extraordinary Bodies*, 34.

31. Ellen Samuels, *Fantasies of Identification: Disability, Gender, and Race* (New York: New York University Press, 2014), 79.

32. From Bethany Hamilton's Facebook account.

33. Ibid.

34. Ibid.

35. Thomson, *Extraordinary Bodies*, 25.

36. Bethany Hamilton's Facebook account.

37. Hamilton, *Soul Surfer*, 146.

38. *Heart of a Soul Surfer: The Bethany Hamilton Story*, DVD.

39. Ruth Marie Griffith, *Born Again Bodies* (Berkeley: University of California Press, 2004), 246.

40. "Shark Attack Survivor Bethany Hamilton: 'I'm Getting Married!'" in *InTouch Weekly*, July 3, 2013, http://www.intouchweekly.com/posts/shark-attack-survivor-bethany-hamilton-i-m-getting-married-26406.

41. Hamilton, *Soul Surfer*, 114.

42. Thomson, *Extraordinary Bodies*, 26.

43. "Adam Dirks and Bethany Hamilton," in *CBS.com*, accessed May 12, 2016, http://www.cbs.com/shows/amazing_race/cast/214927/.

44. *CBS.com.*

45. Hamilton, *Soul Surfer*, 123.

46. Plate, *Religion and Film*, 10.

47. Justin Chang, "Review: Chloé Zhao's cowboy drama 'The Rider' is a moving, lyrical tale of loss and recovery," *Los Angeles Times*, April 10, 2018, https://www.latimes.com/entertainment/movies/la-et-mn-the-rider-review-20180410-story.html.

48. Elvis Mitchell, "Chloe Zhao: 'The Rider,'" KCRW, April 25, 2018, https://www.kcrw.com/culture/shows/the-treatment/chloe-zhao-the-rider.

49. Ibid.

50. Ibid.

51. Plate, *Religion and Film*, 6.

52. Steven D. Greydanus, "'God Saved My Life,' Says 'The Rider' Star Brady Jandreau," National Catholic Register, June 14, 2018, https://www.ncregister.com/daily-news/god-saved-my-life-says-the-rider-star-brady-jandreau.

53. William E. Paden, *Religion Worlds* (Boston, MA: Beacon Press, 1994), 55.

54. Kristen Weston, "'The Rider' reveals the sacred relationship between a horse and rider," *America Magazine*, July 5, 2018, https://www.americamagazin.org/arts-culture/2018/07/05/rider-reveals-sacred-relationship-between-horse-and-rider.

55. Greydanus, "God Saved My Life."

56. Ibid.

57. Terry Gross, "'A Devastating Fall Couldn't Keep This Rodeo 'Rider' Off Wild Horses," *Fresh Air*, April 10, 2018, https://www.npr.org/programs/fresh-air

/2018/04/10/601122993/fresh-air-for-april-10-2018-a-devastating-fall-couldnt
-keep-this-rodeo-rider-off.

58. Weston, "'The Rider.'"

59. Meri Hilalian, "Horse Actors and a Six-Man Crew: How Chloe Zhao
Made 'The Rider,'" *Film Independent*, April 23, 2018, https://www.filmindependent
.org/blog/horse-actors-six-man-crew-chloe-zhao-made-rider/.

60. Berger, *Sacred Canopy*, 18.

61. Josh Rottenberg, "How a cowboy from South Dakota and a filmmaker
from Beijing came together on the critically acclaimed indie 'The Rider,'" *Los
Angeles Times*, April 17, 2018, http://www.latimes.com/entertainment/movies
/la-et-mn-the-rider-20180417-story.html.

62. A.O. Scott, "The Rider is an American Regional Film to Savor," https://
www.nytimes.com/2018/04/11/movies/the-rider-review.html.

63. Paden, *Religion Worlds*, 52.

64. Landmarktheaters, "The Rider - Chloé Zhao, Brady Jandreau, Joshua
James Richards, and Alex O'Flinn Q&A," *YouTube*, April 17, 2018, https://www
.youtube.com/watch?v=yYHODLpcHyE.

65. Ibid.

66. Ibid.

67. Gross, "Devastating Fall."

68. Berger, *Sacred Canopy*, 5.

69. Ibid.

70. Ibid., 6.

71. Geertz, *Interpretation of Cultures*, 99.

72. Berger, *Sacred Canopy*, 16.

73. Marty Klinkenberg, "Eight Seconds: The Life and Death of a Cowboy,"
The Globe and Mail, November 7, 2017, https://www.theglobeandmail.com/sports
/ty-pozzobon-concussion-bull-riding/article36842612/.

74. Ibid.

75. Ibid.

76. Ibid.

77. Ibid.

78. Ibid.

79. Berger, *Sacred Canopy*, 24.

80. Ibid.

81. Ibid., 17.

82. Ibid., 31.

83. Mitchell, "Chloe Zhao."

84. Ibid.

85. Ibid.

86. *The Rider.*

87. Chang, "Review."

88. Plate, *Religion and Film*, 95.

89. Mitchell, "Chloe Zhao."

Conclusion

1. Doehring, *Practice of Pastoral Care*, xv.

2. *Life and Trials*, Part II.

3. Carlin, *Chase Your Shadow*, Chapter 8.

4. *Signs*.

5. *Newtown*, Streaming, directed by Kim A. Snyder (Netflix, 2016).

6. Winfrey, Oprah. "He Has Become Our Light: Oprah Talks to the Wheelers," on *Oprah.com*, https://www.oprah.com/spirit/oprah-talks-to-francine-and-david -wheeler-sandy-hook-parents.

7. Ibid.

8. Ibid.

9. This is *Sopranos* Season 1, Episode 3, entitled "Denial, Anger, Acceptance."

10. Tim Greiving, "M. Night Shyamalan talks 'Signs,' Twists, and Crop-Circle Tattoos," in *The Ringer*, https://www.theringer.com/movies/2020/7/30/21348462 /m-night-shyamalan-signs-unbreakable-the-sixth-sense-interview.

11. E. Nina Rothe, "'I'm Constantly Not on the Right Side of History': Chloé Zhao Talks 'The Rider' in Cannes," *HuffPost*, May 25, 2017, https://www.huffpost .com/entry/im-constantly-not-on-the-right-side-of-history-chlo%C3%A9_b_5926 d3cbe4b0aa7207986b28.

12. 1 Cor. 12:26, New International Version.

13. *Gleason*.

14. Elizabeth Newman, *Untamed Hospitality* (Grand Rapids, MI: Brazos Publishing, 2007), 159.

15. Buechner, *Secrets*, 218.

16. As quoted in Cottingham.

17. Buechner, *Secrets*, 218.

18. Ibid.

19. Halberstam, *Queer Art of Failure*, 120-121.

20. Elizabeth Dias, "How to Live in the Face of Fear," on *NYTimes.com*, April 5, 2020, https://www.nytimes.com/2020/04/05/us/kate-bowler-cancer -coronavirus.html.

21. Henri Nouwen, *Discernment* (New York, NY: HarperOne, 2013), 93.

22. Buechner, *Beyond Words*, 63.

23. Greiving, *Tattoos*.

24. Nouwen, *Discernment*, 88.

25. Henri Nouwen, "House of Love," https://henrinouwen.org/meditation /the-house-of-love/.

Afterword

1. Salvador, Joseph, "Video of John Cena Surprising Young Fan Who Fled Ukraine Goes Viral," *Sports Illustrated.* https://www.si.com/wrestling/2022/06/13/video-of-john-cena-surprising-young-fan-who-fled-ukraine-goes-viral.

2. Fagan, Kate, *All the Colors Came Out* (New York, NY: Little Brown & Co., 2021), 185.

3. James Ryle, *Hippo in the Garden* (Orlando, FL: Creation House, 1993), 43.

4. Buechner, *Beyond Words*, 63.

Bibliography

"10 Years Later, J-Mac Still Inspires." https://www.espn.com/video/clip/_/id
/14783786.
"Adam Dirks and Bethany Hamilton." *CBS.com.* Accessed May 12, 2016. http://
www.cbs.com/shows/amazing_race/cast/214927/.
Ali, Muhammad, and Hana Ali. *The Soul of a Butterfly: Reflections on Life's
Journey.* New York, NY: Simon & Schuster, 2004.
Al-Khateeb, Zac. "Skip Bayless has 'no sympathy' for Dak Prescott after Dallas
quarterback opens up about depression." Sportingnews.com. September 10,
2020. https://www.sportingnews.com/us/nfl/news/skip-bayless-no-sympathy
-dak-prescott-dallas-quarterback-depression/1coikxor1joro1vefvnh4msoir.
Alpert, Rebecca. *Religion and Sports: An Introduction and Case Studies.* New York,
NY: Columbia University Press, 2015.
"An Unlikely Friendship Sheds Light on Muhammed Ali's Life After Boxing."
WBUR. June 8, 2016. https://www.wbur.org/hereandnow/2016/06/08
/muhammad-ali-friendship.
Appadurai, Arjun. *Modernity at Large: Cultural Dimensions of Globalization.*
Minneapolis, MN: University of Minnesota Press, 1996.
Applebaum, Stephen. "Interview: 'Logan' Director James Mangold." *Jewish Chroni-
cle.* March 3, 2017. https://www.thejc.com/culture/features/jame-smangold
-wolverine-is-haunted-by-the-holocaust-1.433652
Array Creative. "Ad of the Month: Unlimited You." August 11, 2016.
"Atlanta radio program hosts fired." *ESPN.com.* June 18, 2013.
Barth, Brian. "Stadiums and Other Sacred Cows." *Nautilus.* August 18, 2016.
https://nautil.us/issue/39/sport/stadiums-and-other-sacred-cows.
Bebbington, David. *Evangelicalism in Modern Britain.* Grand Rapids, MI: Baker,
1989.
"Behind the Glass: Soul to Soul with Steve Gleason with guest Hugh Jackman."
May 28, 2020. https://www.youtube.com/watch?v=g4W5FgsZXHU.
Behr, Mike. "'I Have Forgiven Oscar For Killing My Daughter.'" DailyMail.co.uk.
April 11, 2018. https://www.dailymail.co.uk/news/article-5602689/Reeva
-Steenkamps-mother-says-finished-Pistorius.html.
Berger, Peter. *The Sacred Canopy.* New York, NY: Anchor Books, 1990.
Berger, R. J. "Disability and the Dedicated Wheelchair Athlete: Beyond the
'Supercrip' Critique." *Journal of Contemporary Ethnography,* 37 (2008).
Blair, Leonardo. "Pastor Andrew Stoecklein Was Inside Church When He
Attempted Suicide, Police Reveal." ChristianPost.com. August 29, 2018.

https://www.christianpost.com/news/pastor-andrew-stoecklein-was-inside
-church-when-he-attempted-suicide-police-reveal.html.

Bochner, Arthur and Carolyn Ellis. *Evocative Autoethnography: Writing Lives and Telling Stories.* New York, NY: Routledge, 2016.

Bolz-Weber, Nadia. *Pastrix: The Cranky, Beautiful Faith of a Sinner & Saint.* New York, NY: Jericho Books, 2014.

"Bono: The Beliefnet Interview." Beliefnet.com. February 2001. https://www.belief net.com/entertainment/music/2001/02/bono-the-beliefnet-interview.aspx.

Bordelon, Christine. "Ex-NFL Player, Now With ALS, Retorts: 'Relentlessly Seek Your Purpose.'" CatholicSun.org. August 2, 2016. https://www.catholicsun .org/2016/08/02/ex-nfl-player-now-with-als-exhorts-relentlessly-seek-your -purpose/.

Bowler, Kate. *Everything Happens for a Reason.* New York: Random House, 2018.

Brown, Ian. "Jean Vanier's Comfort and Joy." *Globe and Mail.* December 18, 2015. https://www.theglobeandmail.com/news/world/jean-vaniers-comfort-and -joy-find-the-places-of-hope/article27842806/.

Buechner, Frederick. *Beyond Words: Daily Readings in the ABC's of Faith.* Grand Rapids, MI: Zondervan, 2009.

Buechner, Frederick. *Secrets in the Dark: A Life in Sermons.* New York, NY: Harpercollins Publishers Inc, 2007.

Carlin, John. *Chase Your Shadow: The Trials of Oscar Pistorius.* Harper Publishing, 2014, Kindle Edition.

Carrington, Ben. *Race, Sport, and Politics: The Sporting Black Diaspora.* United Kingdom: Sage Publications, 2010.

Chang, Justin. "Review: Chloé Zhao's cowboy drama 'The Rider' is a moving, lyrical tale of loss and recovery." *Los Angeles Times.* April 10, 2018. https:// www.latimes.com/entertainment/movies/la-et-mn-the-rider-review -20180410-story.html.

Coakley, Jay. *Sports in Society: Issues and Controversies.* New York, NY: McGraw Hill Higher Education, 2014.

Concussion. DVD. Directed by Peter Landesman. 2016.

Connick Jr., Harry. "Tim Tebow's Full Interview with Harry Connick Jr." February 21, 2017. https://www.youtube.com/watch?v=cWZ4GysKSLo.

Cottingham, Michael, Brian Gearity, and Joshua Ray Pate. "Examining 'Inspiration.'" *Canadian Journal of Disability Studies* (January 2015), 64.

Crouch, Andy. "Transhumanism and the Cult of Better, Faster, Stronger." Christi-anityToday.com, March 15, 2019. https://www.christianitytoday.com/ct/2019 /april/transhumanism-image-god-modern-technology-human-future.html.

Csordas, Thomas. *Transnational Transcendence.* Berkeley, CA: University of California Press, 2009.

Danesi, Marcel. *Popular Culture.* New York, NY: Rowman and Littlefield, 2012.

Davidson, Iain F.W.K. Davidson, Gary Woodill, and Elizabeth Bredberg. "Images of Disability in 19th Century British Children's Literature." *Disability & Society* vol. 9: 33–46.

Davies, Dave. "'Get Out' Sprang from an Effort to Master Fear, Says Director Jordan Peele." *Fresh Air.* January 5, 2018. https://www.npr.org/2018/01/05 /575843147/get-out-sprang-from-an-effort-to-master-fear-says-director -jordan-peele.

Davis, Lennard J. *Disability Studies Reader.* New York, NY: Routledge, 2013.

Dawson, Peter. "Is Dak Prescott stuck in Jerry Jones' sunken place?" *Fort Worth Star-Telegram.* August 4, 2018. https://www.star-telegram.com/sports/nfl /dallas-cowboys/article216109960.html.

Dias, Elizabeth. "How to Live in the Face of Fear." NYTimes.com. April 5, 2020. https://www.nytimes.com/2020/04/05/us/kate-bowler-cancer-coronavirus.html.

Doehring, Carrie. *The Practice of Pastoral Care.* Louisville, KY: Westminster John Knox Press, 2015.

Dravecky, Dave, Jan Dravecky, and Ken Gire. *When You Can't Come Back.* Grand Rapids, MI: Zondervan, 1992.

E:60. "The Kid Who Inspires Tim Tebow." https://www.youtube.com/watch?v =ahBXNsiO9pk.

Eberly, Susan Schoon. "Fairies and the Folklore of Disability: Changelings, Hybrids, and the Solitary Fairy." *Folklore* vol. 99, no. 1 (1998): 58–77.

Eiesland, Nancy. *The Disabled God: Toward a Liberatory Theology of Disability.* Nashville, TN: Abingdon Press, 1994.

Engber, Daniel. "Concussion Lies." Slate.com. December 21, 2015. https://slate .com/culture/2015/12/the-truth-about-will-smiths-concussion-and-bennet -omalu.html.

Engber, Daniel. "Tim Tebow 2011." Slate.com. December 5, 2011. https://slate.com /culture/2011/12/tim-tebow-2011-the-broncos-quarterback-is-making-me -question-my-atheism.html.

Fagan, Kate. *All the Colors Came Out.* New York, NY: Little Brown & Co., 2021.

Fagone, Jason. "Does God Have a Tim Tebow Complex?" *GQ.* August 10, 2009. https://www.gq.com/story/tebow-florida-heisman-nfl-photos-quarterback -injury-concussion.

Fagone, Jason. "Tim Tebow Goes for the Conversion." *Slate.com.* January 29, 2010. http://www.slate.com/articles/sports/sports_nut/2010/01/tim_tebow_goes _for_the_conversion.html.

Fainaru-Wada, Mark and Steve Fainaru. *League of Denial.* New York, NY: Three Rivers Press, 2014.

Feezell, Randolph. *Sport, Play, and Ethical Reflection.* Chicago: University of Illinois Press, 2006.

Garland-Thomson, Rosemarie. *Extraordinary Bodies: Figuring Physical Disability in American Culture and Literature.* New York, NY: Columbia University Press, 1996.

Garrett, Greg. *Holy Superheroes!: Exploring Faith and Spirituality in Comic Books.* Colorado Springs, CO: Pinon Press, 2005.

Geertz, Clifford. *The Interpretation of Cultures.* New York, NY: Basic Books, 1973.

Get Out. DVD. Directed by Jordan Peele.

Giddens, Anthony. *The Consequences of Modernity.* Stanford, CA: Stanford University Press, 1990.

Gleason. DVD. Directed by J. Clay Tweel. 2016.

Gleason, Steve. "Regarding the DJ Skit in Atlanta yesterday." Facebook. June 18, 2013. https://www.facebook.com/teamgleason.org/posts/485570461518708.

Gould, Stephen Jay. *Triumph and Tragedy in Mudville: A Lifelong Passion for Baseball.* New York, NY: W.W. Norton, 2004.

Greiving, Tim. "M. Night Shyamalan talks 'Signs,' Twists, and Crop-Circle Tattoos." The Ringer. https://www.theringer.com/movies/2020/7/30/21348462/m-night -shyamalan-signs-unbreakable-the-sixth-sense-interview.

Greydanus, Steven D. "'God Saved My Life,' Says 'The Rider' Star Brady Jandreau." National Catholic Register. June 14, 2018. https://www.ncregister.com/daily -news/god-saved-my-life-says-the-rider-star-brady-jandreau.

Griffith, Ruth Marie. *Born Again Bodies.* Berkeley, CA: University of California Press, 2004.

Gross, Terry. ""A Devastating Fall Couldn't Keep This Rodeo 'Rider' Off Wild Horses." *Fresh Air.* April 10, 2018, https://www.npr.org/programs/fresh-air /2018/04/10/601122993/fresh-air-for-april-10-2018-a-devastating-fall-couldnt -keep-this-rodeo-rider-off

Grzanka, Patrick R. *Intersectionality: A Foundations and Frontiers Reader.* Boulder: Westview Press, 2014.

Halberstam, J. *The Queer Art of Failure.* Durham, NC: Duke University Press, 2011.

Hall, Stuart. *Representation.* London: Sage Publications, 1997.

Hamilton, Bethany, Sheryl Berk and Rick Bundschuh. *Soul Surfer: A True Story of Faith, Family, and Fighting to Get Back on Board.* New York, NY: Pocket Books, 2004.

Hamilton, Ryan. "Wanted to give a shout out to this girl." Facebook. June 3, 2017. https://www.facebook.com/permalink.php?story_fbid=10109248344804739 &id=6823800.

Hardin, Marie. "Disability and Sport." In *Handbook of Sports and Media*, edited by Arthur A. Raney and Jennings Bryant. New York, NY: Routledge, 2006.

Harris, Cheryl L. and Devon W. Carbado. "Loot or Find: Fact or Frame?" In *After the Storm*, edited by David Dante Truett. New York, NY: The New Press, 2007.

Hartmann, Douglas. *Race, Culture, and the Revolt of the Black Athlete: The 1968 Olympic Protests and Their Aftermath.* Chicago, IL: University

Harvey, David. *The Condition of Postmodernity.* Malden, MA: Blackwell Publishers, 1990.

Heart of a Soul Surfer: The Bethany Hamilton Story. DVD. Directed by Bethany Baumgartner. 2007.

Held, David, Anthony Mcgrew, David Goldblatt, and Jonathan Perraton. *Global Transformations.* Stanford, CA: Stanford University Press, 1999.

Heller, Jean. "Syphilis Victims in U.S. Went Untreated for 40 Years." *New York Times.* July 26, 1972. https://www.nytimes.com/1972/07/26/archives/syphilis -victims-in-us-study-went-untreated-for-40-years-syphilis.html.

Henley, Ariel. "We Don't Need Events Specifically for Disabled People." Vice.com. February 28, 2018. https://www.vice.com/en/article/7x7myx/prom-for-disabled -people-perpetuates-stigma.

Heywood, Leslie and Shari L. Dworkin. *Built to Win.* Minneapolis, MN: University of Minnesota Press, 2003.

Hilalian, Meri. "Horse Actors and a Six-Man Crew: How Chloe Zhao Made 'The Rider.'" *Film Independent.* April 23, 2018. https://www.filmindependent.org /blog/horse-actors-six-man-crew-chloe-zhao-made-rider/.

Hobson, Will. "From Scientist to Salesman." WashingtonPost.com. January 22, 2020. https://www.washingtonpost.com/graphics/2020/sports/cte-bennet-omalu/.

Hoffman, Shirl. *Good Game.* Waco, TX: Baylor University Press, 2010.

Hoosiers. DVD. Directed by David Anspaugh. 1986.

Hurst, Hayden. "I Am Who I'm Meant to Be." *Players' Tribune.* March 30, 2020. https://www.theplayerstribune.com/articles/hayden-hurst-atlanta-falcons- who-im-meant-to-be.

Irving, John. *A Prayer for Owen Meany.* New York, NY: HarperCollins, 2012.

Jenkins, Philip. "Global Schism: Is the Anglican Communion rift the first stage in a wider Christian split?" *Pew Forum on Religion and Public Life* (May 14, 2007), https://www.pewforum.org/2007/05/14/global-schism-is-the-anglican -communion-rift-the-first-stage-in-a-wider-christian-split/.

Jenkins, Philip. *The Next Christendom.* New York, NY: Oxford University Press, 2011.

Johnson, Jim E. *A Coach and a Miracle.* Houston, TX: Wellspring, 2011.

Jones, Chris. "Tim Tebow, Overdog." *Esquire.* December 19, 2011. https://www .esquire.com/sports/a12115/tim-tebow-overdog-6619259/.

Klein, Alan. "Anti-Semitism and Anti-Somatism." *Sport in Society* 10:6 (November 2007), 1120-1137.

Klinkenberg, Marty. "Eight Seconds: The Life and Death of a Cowboy." *Globe and Mail.* November 7, 2017. https://www.theglobeandmail.com/sports/ty -pozzobon-concussion-bull-riding/article36842612/.

Kozlowski, Carl. "The Girls Behind Soul Surfer." *Relevant Magazine.* April 8, 2011. http://www.relevantmagazine.com/culture/film/features/25227-the-girls -behind-soul-surfer.

Landmarktheaters. "The Rider - Chloé Zhao, Brady Jandreau, Joshua James Richards, and Alex O'Flinn Q&A." April 17, 2018. https://www.youtube.com /watch?v=yYHODLpcHyE.

Lewis, C.S. "The Grand Miracle." https://www.plough.com/en/topics/culture /holidays/christmas-readings/the-grand-miracle.

Lewis, Ron. "Lonnie offers strongest possible support." *The Times*. November 21, 2005. https://www.thetimes.co.uk/article/lonnie-offers-strongest-possible -support-lrnporhm78s.

Life and Times of Oscar Pistorius, The. Streaming. Directed by Daniel Gordon. ESPN+, 2020.

Logan. DVD. Directed by James Mangold. 2017.

Marchese, David. "Ignore Oscar—'The Wrestler' is Springsteen's Best." *Spin*. January 23, 2009. https://www.spin.com/2009/01/ignore-oscar-wrestler -springsteens-best/.

McDonald, Stacy. "Soul Surfer: Beaches, Bikinis, and . . . Bibles?" *Your Sacred Calling*. April 11, 2011. http://yoursacredcalling.com/blog/2011/04/soul-surfer -beaches-bikinis-and%E2%80%A6bibles/.

Mikkelson, David. "Special Olympics Linked Arms Race Finish." *Snopes*. March 8, 2001. https://www.snopes.com/fact-check/special-olympics-linked-arms -race-finish/.

Mitchell, David and Susan S. Snyder. *Narrative Prosthesis: Disability and the Dependencies of Discourse*. Ann Arbor, MI: University of Michigan Press, 2000.

Mitchell, Elvis. "Chloe Zhao: 'The Rider.'" KCRW. April 25, 2018. https://www .kcrw.com/culture/shows/the-treatment/chloe-zhao-the-rider.

Moore, John. "John Irving." *Denver Post*. April 2, 2009. https://www.denverpost .com/2009/04/02/john-irving-on-religion-sports-and-owen-meany/.

Nederveen Pieterse, Jan. *Globalization and Culture*. Lanham, MD: Rowman and Littlefield Publishers, 2003.

Newman, Elizabeth. *Untamed Hospitality: Welcoming God and Other Strangers*. Grand Rapids, MI: Brazos Press, 2007.

Newtown. Streaming. Directed by Kim A. Snyder. Netflix, 2016.

NFL Films. "Steve Gleason's Blocked Punt Resurrects New Orleans." September 22, 2016. https://www.youtube.com/watch?v=rkIflqthSVw.

"NFL Super Bowl 2017 TV Commercial 'Inside These Lines.'" iSpot TV. 2017. https://www.ispot.tv/ad/A30s/nfl-super-bowl-2017-inside-these-lines.

Nye, Mallory. *Religion: The Basics*. New York: Routledge, 2009.

Omalu, Bennet I., and Mark A. Tabb. *Truth Doesn't Have a Side: My Alarming Discovery about the Danger of Contact Sports*. Grand Rapids, MI: Zondervan, 2017.

O'Neil, Sean. "A Body Broken and Rebuilt for You." In *Identity and Myth in Sports Documentaries*, edited by Zachary Ingle and David Sutera. Toronto, ON: Scarecrow Press, 2013.

Osteen, Joel. *Blessed in the Darkness*. New York, NY: FaithWords, 2017.

Osteen, Joel. *Your Best Life Now*. New York, NY: FaithWords, 2004.

Osterhammel, Jurgen and Niels Petersson. *Globalization: A Short History*. Princeton, NJ: Princeton University Press, 2005.

Paden, William E. *Religion Worlds*. Boston, MA: Beacon Press, 1994.

Parsons, Mikeal Carl. *Body and Character in Luke and Acts: the Subversion of Physiognomy in Early Christianity.* Grand Rapids, MI: Baker Academic, 2006.

Parsons, Mikeal Carl and Richard Walsh, editors. *A Temple Not Made With Hands.* Eugene, OR: Pickwick Publications, 2018.

Peanut Butter Falcon, The. DVD. Directed by Tyler Nilson and Michael Schwartz. 2019.

Peters, Jody. "A Look at the Past: Farmington Woman Wrote Over 5,000 Poems." April 19, 2018. https://www.hometownsource.com/sun_thisweek/a-look-at -the-past-farmington-woman-wrote-over-5-000-poems/article_56d15a92 -43f4-11e8-80e9-6f90f8f297d6.html.

Pistorius. Streaming. Directed by Vaughan Sivell. Amazon Prime, 2018.

Plate, S. Brent. *Religion and Film.* London: Wallflower Press, 2008.

Praying With Lior. DVD. Directed by Ilana Trachtman. 2009.

Reilly, Rick. "Believing in Tim Tebow." ESPN.com. January 13, 2012. https://www .espn.com/espn/story/_/id/7455943/believing-tim-tebow.

Rider, The. DVD. Directed by Chloe Zhao. 2017.

Ritzer, George. *The McDonaldization of Society.* Thousand Oaks, CA: Pine Forge Press, 2000.

Rivera, Mariano. *The Closer.* New York, NY: Back Bay Books, 2014.

Romano, Jason. "Tim Tebow Shakes Hand of Autistic Boy, Proceeds to Hit Home Run." SportsSpectrum.com. https://sportsspectrum.com/sport /baseball/2017/08/11/tim-tebow-shakes-hand-autistic-fan-proceeds-hit -home-run/.

Rosen, David. "King Kong: Race, Sex, and Rebellion." *Jump Cut* no. 6 (1975), 1–10.

Rothe, E. Nina. "'I'm Constantly Not on the Right Side of History': Chloé Zhao Talks 'The Rider' in Cannes." *HuffPost.* May 25, 2017. https://www.huffpost .com/entry/im-constantly-not-on-the-right-side-of-history-chlo%C3%A9 _b_5926d3cbe4b0aa7207986b28

Rottenberg, Josh. "How a cowboy from South Dakota and a filmmaker from Beijing came together on the critically acclaimed indie 'The Rider.'" *Los Angeles Times.* April 17, 2018. http://www.latimes.com/entertainment/movies /la-et-mn-the-rider-20180417-story.html.

Ryle, James. *Hippo in the Garden: A Non-Religious Approach to Having a Conversation with God.* Orlando, FL: Creation House, 1993.

Salvador, Joseph. "Video of John Cena Surprising Young Fan Who Fled Ukraine Goes Viral." *Sports Illustrated*, https://www.si.com/wrestling/2022/06/13/video -of-john-cena-surprising-young-fan-who-fled-ukraine-goes-viral.

Samuels, Ellen. *Fantasies of Identification: Disability, Gender, and Race.* New York, NY: New York University Press, 2014.

Schipper, Jeremy. *Disability and Isaiah's Suffering Servant.* New York, NY: Oxford University Press, 2011.

Schmitz, Kenneth. "Sport and Play." In *Sports and the Body*, edited by Gerber and Morgan. Philadelphia, PA: Lea and Febiger, 1979.

Scholes, Jeffrey and Raphael Sassower. *Religion and Sports in American Culture.* New York, NY: Routledge, 2014.

Shapiro, Joseph P. *No Pity: People with Disabilities Forging a New Civil Rights Movement.* New York, NY: Three Rivers Press, 1994.

"Shark Attack Survivor Bethany Hamilton: 'I'm Getting Married!'" *InTouch Weekly.* July 3, 2013. accessed May 2, 2016, http://www.intouchweekly.com /posts/shark-attack-survivor-bethany-hamilton-i-m-getting-married-26406.

Shogan, Debra. *The Making of High-Performance Athletes.* Buffalo, NY: University of Toronto Press, 1999.

Signs. DVD. Directed by M. Night Shyamalan. 2002.

Spufford, Francis. *Unapologetic: Why, despite Everything, Christianity Can Still Make Surprising Emotional Sense.* New York, NY: HarperOne, 2013.

Sullivan, Eric. "Shia LaBeouf Is Ready To Talk About It." *Esquire.* March 13, 2018. https://www.esquire.com/entertainment/movies/a19181320/shia-labeouf -interview-2018/.

Sullivan, Kevin P. "Hugh Jackman nearly called it quits after X-Men Origins: Wolverine." *EW.com.* March 3, 2017. https://ew.com/movies/2017/03/03/hugh -jackman-logan-xmen-origins/.

Tabeek, Matthew. "'I Feel for You, and I'm Here.'" AtlantaFalcons.com. https:// sportsspectrum.com/sport/football/2020/12/04/falcons-hayden-hurst-god -gave-second-chance/.

Tamburrini, Claudio and Tobjorn Tannjo. *Ethics in Sport.* Taylor & Francis, 2002.

Tate, Andrew. *Contemporary Fiction and Christianity.* New York, NY: Continuum International Publishing Group, 2008.

Taylor, Richard. *Good and Evil.* New York, NY: MacMillan, 1970.

Tebow, Tim. *This is the Day.* Colorado Springs, CO: Waterbrook, 2018.

Tebow, Tim. *Through My Eyes.* New York, NY: HarperCollins, 2012.

Tebow, Tim, and A. J. Gregory. *Shaken: Discovering Your True Identity in the Midst of Life's Storms.* New York, NY: Waterbrook, 2018.

Thompson, Wright. "Beyond the Breach." *ESPN The Magazine.* http://www.espn .com/espn/feature/story/_/id/13479768/wright-thompson-life-loss-renewal -new-orleans-10-years-hurricane-katrina.

Thompson, Wright. *The Cost of These Dreams.* New York, NY: Penguin Books, 2019.

Thrilla in Manila. DVD. Directed by John Dower. 2008.

Unstoppable. DVD. Directed by Aaron Lieber. 2018.

Vasquez, Manuel and Marie Marquardt. *Globalizing the Sacred.* New Brunswick, NJ: Rutgers University Press, 2003.

Vujicic, Nick. *Unstoppable.* Colorado Springs, CO: Waterbrook Press, 2012.

"W15H Brings Early Christmas Gift to Former High School Quarterback." Tim Tebow Foundation. December 22, 2011. https://www.timtebowfoundation.org /stories/w15h-brings-early-christmas-gift-former-high-school-quarterback.

Ward, Graham, ed. *The Blackwell Companion to Postmodern Theology.* Malden, MA: Blackwell Publishers, 2001.

Weston, Kristen. "'The Rider' reveals the sacred relationship between a horse and rider." *America Magazine.* July 5, 2018. https://www.americamagazine.org/arts -culture/2018/07/05/rider-reveals-sacred-relationship-between-horse-and-rider.

Wrestler, The. DVD. Directed by Darren Aronofsky. 2008.

Young, Stella. "I'm Not Your Inspiration, Thank You Very Much." June 9, 2014. 9:16. https://www.youtube.com/watch?v=8K9Gg164Bsw&t.

Zirin, Dave. *Welcome to the Terrordome.* Chicago, IL: Haymarket Books, 2007.

Index